BONDS OF WOMANHOOD

BONDS OF WOMANHOOD

Slavery and the Decline of a Kentucky Plantation

Susanna Delfino

UNIVERSITY PRESS OF KENTUCKY

Scholarly publisher for the Commonwealth,
serving Bellarmine University, Berea College, Centre
College of Kentucky, Eastern Kentucky University,
The Filson Historical Society, Georgetown College,
Kentucky Historical Society, Kentucky State University,
Morehead State University, Murray State University,
Northern Kentucky University, Transylvania University,
University of Kentucky, University of Louisville,
and Western Kentucky University.

Editorial and Sales Offices: The University Press of Kentucky
663 South Limestone Street, Lexington, Kentucky 40508-4008
www.kentuckypress.com

Library of Congress Cataloging-in-Publication Data

Names: Delfino, Susanna, 1949- author.
Title: Bonds of womanhood : slavery and the decline of a Kentucky plantation / Susanna Delfino.
Description: Lexington : The University Press of Kentucky, 2021. | Includes bibliographical references and index.
Identifiers: LCCN 2021049365 | ISBN 9780813154831 (hardcover ; alk. paper) | ISBN 9780813154886 (pdf) | ISBN 9780813154855 (epub)
Subjects: LCSH: Grigsby, Susan Preston Shelby, 1830-1891—Ethics. | Women, White—Kentucky—19th century—Biography. | Social change—Kentucky—19th century. | Women, White—Kentucky—Social conditions—19th century. | Women, White—Kentucky—Economic conditions—19th century. | African American women—Kentucky—Social conditions—19th century. | Slavery—Economic aspects—Kentucky—19th century. | Slavery—Social aspects—Kentucky—19th century. | LCGFT: Biographies.
Classification: LCC F445.N4 D45 2021 | DDC 976.9/03092 [B]—dc23/eng/20211027

This book is printed on acid-free paper meeting
the requirements of the American National Standard
for Permanence in Paper for Printed Library Materials.

Manufactured in the United States of America

Member of the Association of
University Presses

For Catherine, Michele, Stephanie

Noi non potemo aver perfetta vita senza amici.
(*We cannot have perfect life without friends.*)

Dante, *Convivio,* IV–XXV

Contents

Essential Genealogy of the Shelby and Hart Families ix

Introduction 1

1. Kentucky: The Promise of America's Future 11

2. Looking "Backward" to the Future 33

3. The Bittersweet Taste of Progress 58

4. Bonds of Womanhood 84

5. The World Turned Upside Down 111

Coda. Susan P. Grigsby: From Aristocratic Lady to Middle-Class Woman 136

Acknowledgments 145

Notes 149

Bibliography 181

Index 195

Essential Genealogy of the Shelby and Hart Families

Evan Shelby I (1690–1751)
m.
Catherine D. Morgan (1696–1760)

Evan Shelby II (1st of 8) (1719–1794)
m.
Letitia Cox (1727–1777)

Isaac Shelby (1750–1826)
m.
Susannah (2nd of 9) (1764–1833)

Susannah H. (5th of 11) (1791–1868) – 4th m. - James A. Fishback (1776 –1845)

Alfred (last of 11) (1803–1832) – m. - Virginia Hart (1809–1859)

Nathaniel Hart Sr. (1734–1782)
m.
Sarah Simpson (1744–1785)

Nathaniel Jr. (4th of 9) (1770–1844)
m.
Susanna Preston (1772–1833)

Sarah (1800–1883)	Letitia (1802–1866)	Louisiana (1803–1851)	William P. (1807–1868)	Virginia (1809–1859)	Mary (1814–1857)
m.	m.	m.	m.	1st m.	m.
George C. Thompson (1778–1856)	Arthur H. Wallace (1794–1878)	Tobias Gibson (1800–1872)	Rebecca Tevis (1844–1911)	Alfred Shelby (1803–1832)	William Voorhies (1800–1893)

Sarah (2nd of 10)
(1830–1907)
m.
Joseph A. Humphreys
(1826–1863)

Randall Lee (3rd)
(1832–1892)
m.
Mary Montgomery
(1845–1887)

2nd m. - Robert J. Breckinridge
(1800–1871)

Isaac
(1828–1848)

Susanna P.
(1830–1891)
m.
John W. Grigsby
(1818–1877)

Alfred
(1831–1848)

Sarah Virginia
(1832)

Alfred	Susan S.	Mary Ashley	Virginia Shelby	Hart Preston	Lilie	Letitia Wallace	Louisiana G.	Susanna P. Shelby
(1851–62)	(1852–62)	(1855–62)	(1856–1935)	(1859–1912)	(1860)	(1861–62)	(1866–1927)	(1872–1968)

Introduction

This book situates itself at the intersection of my long dedication to the study of antebellum southern manufacturing with a later-developed interest in women's history, and it owes its realization to the inspirations derived from a number of fortunate and interlocking circumstances.

It all began at the 1999 annual meeting of the Southern Historical Association in Fort Worth, Texas. There, at the conclusion of a brainstorming meeting among a few women scholars, Michele Gillespie and I agreed to undertake the joint editing of a collection of essays on free, ordinary women's work—paid and unpaid—in the Old South. This intellectually gratifying experience set in motion a virtuous circle that, in the span of a few years, would reorient my scholarship in a markedly gendered perspective.[1]

Not long after the publication of *Neither Lady nor Slave* (2002) I started thinking of a book project on the impact of economic modernization on the lives of antebellum white southern women as beneficiaries of expanded opportunities for gainful employment in an enslaving society. During my first reconnaissance, Kentucky provided a most stimulating context for my purpose, not only on account of the high rate of industrial development, low percentage of the enslaved over total population, and remarkable presence of immigrants—coming from or through the Northeast—that the state recorded in 1850. Dry statistical figures apart, upon considerations of a social and cultural nature as well, Kentucky was an ideal region for investigation. In fact, the egalitarian and antislavery attitude of its early settlers, combining over time with ever-growing influences from the Northeast via the Ohio River, gave the Bluegrass State a special character of "progressivism" that greatly contributed to placing it in the forefront of the antebellum South's difficult path to modernization.[2]

Because of the capitalistic nature of an economy based on enslaving humans, the US South was, in a sense, "modern" from the very beginning. Yet southern slavery differed from northern capitalism in important ways, and this difference impinged upon the scope and timing of the transformations simultaneously occurring in either section of the country during the first half of the nineteenth century. Genuine modernization involved, in fact, far more than economic diversification and industrial development. It entailed deep changes in mentality and sensibility toward labor and its relation to capital. These were at odds with human bondage.

Caught in a conflict between a vision of full-fledged modernization that necessarily implied the annihilation of slavery, and the immense wealth that property in enslaved persons embodied, Kentuckians were pulled between tradition and change. Anticipating the conclusion reached by the great economic historian Alexander Gerschenkron a century later—that each country or region has its own way to industrialization—even the most resolute enemies of the peculiar institution ultimately seemed to subscribe to the opinion, held by most fellow white southerners in other states, that industrial development was compatible with the continuation of bonded labor. Yet they all missed the crucial point that modernization is not simply measured by industrial wealth and industrial output. The quintessential example of the battleground between aversion to slavery and economic interest, Kentucky stood therefore as a perfect test case for the viability of modernization in a slavery-based society.[3]

Reflecting the surge in women's participation in the US labor market during the previous decade, the 1860 federal census included them for the first time in the count of the population engaged in some sort of remunerated work. The census returns did not differentiate individuals by sex, however, making it impossible to determine the precise extent of females' involvement.

Scores of white women directly contributed to the rise of the industrial order either as factory operatives or as outworkers paid by the piece in connection with the same. Others simply benefited from the expansion of businesses and continued to ply traditional trades, either as self-employed workers or as dependents at some small enterprise, signally in garment-making. Regardless of the nature of their jobs, however, all lower-class white women shared the same stringent necessity that forced them to toil long hours for trifling wages.[4]

Conversely, the many middle-class white women who, from the 1840s, increasingly engaged in income-generating occupations as directors of schools or owners of commercial undertakings like dressmaking and millinery often did so either to supplement dwindling family incomes or to seek a measure of self-affirmation through economic independence. By and large, middle-class white women were the ultimate beneficiaries, rather than the prime movers, of the cultural revolution related to modernization.[5]

In Kentucky, the participation of white women in the process of economic transformation that began around 1840 must have been impressive, but, due to the above-mentioned bias in enumeration, it was grossly undercounted. Only 11,200 women could be unequivocally identified as reporting a gainful occupation (amounting to 4.35 percent of the total). They were largely concentrated in the needle trades (4,763), domestic work (3,397), and manufacturing (1,671). In this latter field, they made up for 8.5 percent of the total industrial workforce of 19,585. The well-known preponderance of women in the textile and apparel industries all over the country suggests, however, that some of the 4,005 seamstresses counted may have been employed at the many garment factories operating in the state, and especially concentrated in the Louisville area.

Some descriptive categories adopted by the census, which were not the exclusive preserve of women, further underscore the ambiguity of the returns. How many women figured in fact among the 34,258 individuals who generally defined themselves as either "laborers," "servants," "factory hands," or "weavers"?

The field of teaching offers a most conclusive example of the unacknowledged presence of women in the Kentucky labor market. Although during the 1850s men increasingly entered what was becoming a "modern" profession, teaching largely remained women's preserve until the Civil War. In this light, we can guess that they overwhelmingly figured among the 2,617 teachers reported by the census.[6]

By focusing attention on white, lower-class, wage-earning women, I hoped to illuminate not only the complex forms of competition unleashed between natives and immigrants but also the dynamics that pitted them, collectively, against their enslaved counterparts in the fast-changing labor market of late antebellum Kentucky. Domestic service was an occupation in which white women were heavily involved, whereas the enslaved routinely were employed as hirelings—a highlight in my research plan. In this regard, I was much indebted for inspiration to Stephanie Cole's pathbreaking essay on white nurses in the Border States, which was featured in the *Neither Lady nor Slave* volume.[7]

Fascinated by contemporary philosophies in vogue in the Northeast, and eager to show their positive outlook on modernity, during the 1850s many upper-class women in the Border States, including Kentucky, engaged in the experiment of introducing white personnel, primarily as nurses and governesses, into their households, traditionally staffed by enslaved women. Northern prescriptions about domestic service, however, pushed beyond the realm of child-rearing to encompass every department of housework in the name of *scientific management.* With all the necessary adaptations to a slavery-based society, this garnered consensus among progressive-minded women of the master class. But this was also favorably looked upon by many middle-class nonenslaving whites, who envisaged the employment of a poorly paid immigrant as an alternative to an enslaved hireling, a way to share their social superiority within the quest for modernity. This tendency, which was appreciable in 1850 Kentucky, posed new challenges to enslavers but was offset in some measure by the opposite attitude of others among nonenslavers, who thought that the ability to relieve a woman from the drudgery of housework by renting an enslaved domestic conferred social status.[8]

One of the enslaving women Cole featured in her essay on white nurses was Susanna (Susan) Preston Shelby Grigsby, a plantation mistress who, despite her illustrious forebears, was largely unknown among southern historians, most likely because her name was not connected to that of a politically or economically prominent husband. I therefore approached this topic with special anticipation, eager to learn more about Grigsby's assumptions in deciding to hire white personnel, and how she related to the several women she employed during the 1850s. Because her papers were held by the Filson Historical Society in Louisville, I applied for one of their biannual fellowships and, to my great contentedness, was granted one for the spring of 2007.

As I delved deeper and deeper into Susan Grigsby's correspondence, I came to realize that the adoption of the single perspective on white domestic labor was rather reductive, vis-à-vis the amazing variety of interlocking gender, class, and race-related issues it revealed. Keeping in mind Thavolia Glymph's warning that the plantation household was not simply a private workplace but "a field of power relations and political practices," I was irresistibly drawn to the great opportunity with which I was presented to explore the dynamics of interracial cohabitation in the home of a white southern woman who united three features apparently at odds with each other. A woman who thought of herself as a fierce opponent of slavery, Grigsby in fact enslaved a large number of persons and, by Kentucky standards, was a substantial enslaver. Despite the decidedly large number of bondswomen she could draft into housework, she embraced the idea of and resolutely pursued hiring white personnel, too.[9]

When seen in the light of her liberal education and cosmopolitan experience, these characteristics definitely made Susan Grigsby deserving of much more comprehensive attention than I had initially contemplated, and I therefore recast my project in a clearly biographical way. This shift in focus, which demanded many returns to the Filson and to wherever research might bring me, did not, however, entail my forsaking of the broader picture.

Quite to the contrary, setting Grigsby's life story against the backdrop of modernizing Kentucky would better illuminate the multiple ways in which the winds of change affected not only the vision of *her own* world and its future but also those of scores of women of different class, ethnicity, and race. Hence the meaning of the title of this book. Although its content does not pretend to cover the variety and diversity of their experiences, it tries to offer at least a glimpse of the sweeping changes underway in the perception of work and its economic worth by white and Black women alike, regardless of class and status. This book provides therefore a larger body of general, background information than is usually the case with a biography. Although many students of the South may deem this abundance of detail unnecessary, nonspecialist historians, as well as general readers, might find it useful for a thorough appreciation of the transformations that occurred in the society in which Susan Grigsby's life unfolded.

Born in 1830 at Traveller's Rest, Lincoln County, right at the dawn of an epoch of impressive advancements for Kentucky, Susanna Preston Shelby Grigsby descended from two most prominent and interrelated families, the Shelbys and the Harts. Their renown stemmed from the important role that Isaac Shelby and Nathaniel Hart—her paternal grandfather and maternal great-grandfather, respectively—had played in the settlement and early structuring of the Kentucky country. Their high reputation was enhanced by an ideologically firm, yet politically moderate antislavery inclination, which earned Isaac two elections to the governorship (1792–96 and 1812–16) in a state where, despite slavery being made legal by constitutional provision, opposition to slavery remained vital among the population.[10]

Following Isaac's retirement from public life, shifting political scenarios operated to undermine the once formidable ascendancy of the name of the Shelbys of Traveller's Rest, and his death dramatically accelerated its waning. Yet Isaac's fame as an upright, humane, and progressive-minded man was forever written in the historical record, and his children clung to it as a badge of distinction in an increasingly ruthless and acquisitive world.

Having been born only four years after the death of such an illustrious grandfather, Susan Shelby was raised in the veneration of his figure, and in the pride of a prestigious family, albeit with declining status. As a result, although the idea of progress was part and parcel of the cultural and intellectual milieu in which she grew up, a special reverence for the Shelbys' glorious past nurtured in young Susan an irrepressible desire to restore Traveller's Rest, someday, to its former splendor. Introducing a note of conservatism in her outlook, this urge generated in her a constant tension between the opposing forces of modernity and tradition, which actually came to constitute the leitmotif of her approach to life. Despite her decidedly liberal education, and the innumerable initial advantages she enjoyed to seek and obtain greater empowerment than most white southern girls of her time and station might even imagine, Susan married young, enthralled like many others by the idea that romantic love was a precondition to fulfill that "companionate ideal" that was the key to achieve equal partnership in marriage.[11]

In that hope, Susan chose to take up residence at Traveller's Rest with her spouse, John Warren Grigsby, and their infant child. To her utmost disappointment, she discovered very soon that not even the strongest bonds of marital affection could override John's fundamentally patriarchal vision of male authority and female submission, especially when it came to a matter of such ideological importance as slavery. Their divergence in opinion on this delicate subject reemerged frequently, becoming a constant source of uneasiness in her marriage.

As Catherine Clinton argued in her pathbreaking 1982 book, any plantation mistress almost unavoidably developed marital stress due to the physical exertions of ordinary planter household commitments, plantation responsibilities, and bad health, largely accountable to the devastating effects of multiple childbearing. Caring for the enslaved offered an intellectual, moral, and economic challenge that weighed heavily on Grigsby's probably already fragile emotional state.[12]

Comparisons with the experience of her mother, Virginia Hart Shelby Breckinridge, who was a strong-willed and largely empowered woman, are illuminating in showing how the repressive workings of the southern patriarchal order could ultimately stymie the aspirations to autonomy by even the most advantaged and resolute women of the planters' aristocracy. Yet singleness might and did offer southern women the possibility of acquiring independent agency.[13]

Susan Grigsby's case seems to lie in the gray zone between complete self-denial and open rebellion. Although she never refrained from challenging John on matters of major family import, an uncombative nature always led her to avoid extreme clashes with him and, unlike her mother, to pursue a conciliatory course, in the undying hope that he might become more sensitive to, and considerate of, the moral travails she was undergoing as a woman who, although an enslaver by inheritance, was opposed to slavery in principle. This approach finally cornered Susan in a cul-de-sac when, following Kentucky's entry into the Civil War, John Grigsby enlisted in the Confederate army—leaving his wife torn between ideological beliefs and marital allegiance in a staunchly pro-Union area of Kentucky. If hers was true love, it was certainly self-destructive!

The imposing body of testimonies left by plantation mistresses has led modern historians to insist on the significance of the Civil War in triggering a "crisis in gender" that prepared the members of the former enslaving elite to fulfill long-repressed aspirations of personal affirmation in the economic, social, and even political domain. Single, white enslaving women decisively contributed to the reshaping of traditional ideas of southern womanhood as were articulated in the postbellum era.[14]

While also attentive to the conservative course followed by the many women who found the Lost Cause a viable dimension of public commitment, historians devoted little attention to those who, like Susan Grigsby, were devastated by the many ordeals of the war years and its aftermath. Many purposefully sought a new self—new identity—in the highly competitive society of postwar America.[15] In Grigsby's case, circumstances operated to produce that very result and transformed her, however unwittingly, into a middle-class, self-supporting woman.

Family heritage played a crucial role in the shaping of Susan Grigsby's self-identity. Chapter 1 recapitulates the saga of the Shelbys, from their Welsh origins to the building of the family fortunes in colonial British North America and, through the War of Independence, to the rise of Isaac Shelby to prominence in early Kentucky politics. His residence, Traveller's Rest, established itself as the beating heart of the state's intellectual and political life for at least three decades.

With the memory of this impressive record still vivid, Grigsby could not easily reconcile herself to her family's loss of prestige, and, as a child, she idealized its history. Chapter 2 explores the complex tangle of psychological factors and life circumstances that concurred to generate and foster an unresolved duplicity in Susan's outlook and caused her to constantly swing between a youthful, natural enthusiasm for things modern and an irrepressible desire to bolster the fading memory of the Shelbys' historical role. Traumatic changes that occurred later in the life of her nuclear family shook Susan's self-perceived identity so deeply that, disregarding the opportunities wealth offered her for retaining a large measure of personal and economic independence, she opted for an early marriage.[16]

Once resettled at Traveller's Rest under the protective wing of her husband, she thought that, from this vantage point, she could safely savor the fruits of modernity. For example, she fully anticipated enjoying the consumerist practices in which Kentuckians had long indulged and that the transportation revolution, which allowed access to a greater and more varied assortment of sophisticated goods, enhanced. She could even venture into experimentation with white domestic personnel, following the guidelines for the most modern philosophies on child-rearing and household management.[17]

A better understanding of the multiple ways in which modernization impinged upon Susan Grigsby's attitudes and choices requires an outline of the impact of economic transformation on Kentucky's labor market, with special attention to women's work. Chapter 3 argues that, despite her general understanding of the changing nature of labor relations, Susan Grigsby did not fully grasp the extent of its impact on domestic service. This failure caused her disappointments, even as she was facing new challenges as a lessor of enslaved persons, mainly young women, in that very field.

Chapter 4 explores the ideological, cultural, and social origins of the inconsistencies between thought and action Grigsby showed whenever confronted with irksome situations concerning her domestic personnel, either free or enslaved. If the insurgence of major problems with white employees simply challenged her self-perception as a woman sympathetic to the lot of the less fortunate members of her same sex and race, cases of pregnancy of some of her hirelings that were clearly the issue of their violation by a white man unsettled Grigsby in the extreme. Such instances, which were very frequent even in those parts of the enslaving states where bondage was defined as "milder," shook to the roots her self-image as a compassionate mistress and plunged her into repeated deep moral crises. Her responses invite serious reflection on the essentially violent nature of slavery, wherever it was practiced, and regardless of an individual master/mistress's negative attitude toward the institution per se.

The cases involving Susan Grigsby's bondswomen drew attention to the traumatic experience of Black girls during the time of legalized slavery. For the enhancement of this shameful aspect of the condition of enslaved women, I am indebted to Stephanie Jones-Rogers. Although her book *They Were Her Property* came out while my manuscript was already in the final stages of preparation for publication, my work benefited much from her perspective.[18]

Although a precious source of information, the rendition of facts affecting the lives of enslaved women by the enslaver herself obviously does not tell the other side of the story. Aware of this fundamental limitation, the reader should therefore consider Susan Grigsby's expressions of hatred for the institution of slavery on their own terms. They are those of an enslaver who, being a woman, was doubly trapped in the workings of an economic and political patriarchal system too pervasive and powerful for her to counteract.

The fifth, and final, chapter documents how, during the war years, Susan Grigsby navigated the ambiguities inherent in her position as a lone woman, and the wife of a Confederate soldier, in an overwhelmingly pro-Union area of Kentucky. The era of Reconstruction was, for the Grigsbys, one of great hopes and expectations, but, quite ironically, its end coincided with the vanishing of their dream to rebuild the depleted family fortunes and catapulted Susan into huge indebtedness.

Finally, the coda sets the latter part of Susan Grigsby's life against the backdrop of the post-Reconstruction South, which found many women of the former planter aristocracy eager to seek self-redemption from long economic and personal dependence through access to the new job openings within the federal government. Although Grigsby also reaped one such opportunity, she did so rather tepidly. Comparison with the life of her cousin Sarah Gibson Humphreys illustrates how differently two women of similar family background and education could respond to the reduction of wealth and status resulting from the total destruction of the Old South's world.

Susan Grigsby's tormented approach to modernity invites reflection on the possibility that she may have sensed that the idea of progress, forwarded in post–Civil War America, as a linear process of improvement and amelioration for all, was merely an ideological construction. As such, scores of people like her would never benefit from the gospel of modernity to recover from the material and moral traumas of the late war.

At this point, one might legitimately ask how typical—or atypical—Susan Grigsby's case is in the southern panorama. Although extensive comparison with the experiences of other plantation mistresses, either in Kentucky and in other states that sanctioned slavery, is beyond the scope of this book, I hope to have succeeded in showing what makes Susanna Preston Shelby Grigsby's life story worth telling.

1

Kentucky
The Promise of America's Future

The history of the Shelby family—from which Susan P. Grigsby descended—in America was closely intertwined with the exploration and early settlement of the southwestern borderlands that would later become Kentucky and Tennessee, respectively. Like multitudes of British migrants who similarly undertook the transatlantic voyage, Evan Shelby fled from the social injustice, political exclusion, and declining economic opportunities that plagued him in his homeland. Once in the New World, however, his loosely defined "progressive" social outlook was challenged by the encounter with Black slavery as a virtually unavoidable form of labor in large-scale colonial agriculture. In his quest for economic success Evan Shelby, maybe reluctantly, became an enslaver himself and bequeathed this sad legacy to his heirs and their descendants.

Although the initial parts of this first chapter mainly focus on the experiences, expectations, and aborted dreams of white settlers in the southwestern borderlands, the slavery question is omnipresent and, like a *fil rouge,* connects them to the further unfolding of the history of Kentucky, and of the Shelbys, so integral to its development. Understanding the conflicting past of Kentucky's experience with slavery is essential because it foreshadows how Susan Grigsby approached the integration of slavery into her society a century later. Intertwined with the former, it is equally important to recapitulate the spurt in modernization Kentucky underwent from 1830, the year Susan P. Shelby Grigsby was born.

The Shelbys in the Land of Opportunities

The origins of the Shelby family are traceable to Wales, where, toward the end of the 1600s, they were small farmers and sheep raisers in Cardiganshire. There, Evan II—who would later father Isaac, the patriot and hero of the

American Revolution, and Susan Grigsby's grandfather—was born to Catherine Davies Morgan and Evan Shelby in Tregaron, on October 23, 1719.[1]

In 1735, the couple immigrated to the British colonies of North America with their seven children. Although what prompted them to leave their native country is not definitively known, it might have simply been desire to enjoy greater freedom in a land that, at that time, still offered unlimited opportunities for enterprising and hardworking whites. Initially, Evan Shelby settled his family in Lancaster County, Pennsylvania, where he obtained a grant of 1,200 acres from the colony's government. Then, operating between Pennsylvania, Maryland, and Virginia, in the span of roughly a decade Shelby was able to amass considerable property—24,000 acres by deeds and patents. Among his holdings, the tract of 4,000 acres he had received from Lord Baltimore in the vicinity of Hagerstown, Prince George County, Maryland, was particularly dear to him. That's where his grandson Isaac was born to Letitia Cox and Evan Shelby II on December 11, 1750, the year before he passed away.[2]

However economically rewarding, life in the seaboard colonies apparently fell short of satisfying the younger Evan's expectations. Consequently, in 1771, when he was already in his early fifties and possessed adequate financial means, he decided to remove farther west, to a region just beginning to open to settlement. He soon identified the Holston Valley, in present-day East Tennessee, as the most suitable area to relocate his family and purchased Sapling Grove, a property of 1,946 acres, where he built a fort, Shelby's Station, and opened a store. As the operators of one of the few waystations on the westward route, Evan Shelby and his sons, who were also engaged in the fur trade, had the opportunity to become acquainted and develop friendly relations with leading men in the early exploration and settlement of the new West: James Robertson, John Sevier, and Daniel Boone, to name a few. Those encounters were crucial in shaping young Isaac's destiny as a successful man in the borderlands.[3]

The late colonial and revolutionary eras presented ambitious young men with unique prospects for self-promotion, where they could offer services to speculators in western lands—as part of companies or as private individuals. Their job, which consisted in locating, surveying, and describing the boundaries of the tracts their employers meant to preempt, was mutually profitable. In an age of land grabbing, while it allowed many members of the Virginia and North Carolina elites to secure property titles on lands within the trans-Appalachian region, surveyors were mostly given land in return for their services—usually tracts they had already located for themselves. The enormous gains accruable through the pursuit of this activity are well illustrated by the conspicuous example of George Washington, who, having undertaken the career of land surveyor at the age of sixteen, rose to become a very substantial landowner within a decade.[4]

Daniel Boone, the legendary Kentucky trailblazer, also engaged in this activity on behalf of prominent Virginian and North Carolinian families. Notable among them were the Breckinridges of Virginia, from whom Boone received an ample land allowance and, later on, a profitable position as the state land surveyor. The Breckinridges soon became one of the most prestigious and influential dynasties in the history of Kentucky, and their name is intimately intertwined with the main narrative of this book.[5]

Young Isaac Shelby pursued the career of land surveyor, too. Between 1775 and 1776 he participated in explorations of the Kentucky country under the auspices of the newly formed, North Carolina–based, Transylvania Land Company.[6] During its expeditions, he established a special rapport with Nathaniel Hart, one of the company's associates, sixteen years his senior. Despite the age difference, their friendship and mutual esteem were strengthened by companionship and camaraderie as officers in the Revolutionary War, where they both distinguished themselves for gallantry and bravery. Although Nathaniel unfortunately died in an Indian ambush at his farm near Boonesborough in July 1782, the ties between the Shelby and the Hart families were sealed officially the following year by Isaac's marriage to Hart's daughter Susannah.[7]

During the War for Independence, the American revolutionary ideal of self-government increasingly challenged the legitimacy of the colonial land speculation companies to collect rents from the settlers. Because of the vast expanse of territory on which it laid claims (20 million acres lying between the Kentucky and the Cumberland Rivers), the Transylvania Land Company became the scapegoat in a wider jurisdictional controversy over the western lands aimed at asserting the sovereignty of those states emerging from the Revolution; its defeat was therefore already in the script.[8]

Anticipating this inevitable outcome, Isaac Shelby was anxious to have his 1776 claims to Kentucky lands confirmed and validated under the laws of Virginia. Luckily, he was able to benefit from some recent legislation that accorded the right of preemption to 400 acres to all who had settled in Kentucky before January 1, 1778, and an additional allowance of 1,000 acres to any claimant who had also made land improvements by that date. Having arranged for the planting of corn since 1776, and with the building of a house the next year, Isaac Shelby was eligible for both grants. Consequently, on October 13, 1779, he filed his application, which, once certified and registered, made him the first legal landowner in a region that was still largely wilderness.[9]

The winning of independence accelerated the race for land acquisition by US—and southern—speculators through the trafficking in military and treasury warrants that were given to veterans in compensation for service in the Revolutionary War. George Washington himself solicitously engaged in the business but—as he would often advise his friends—did so in a low-key manner, always showing apparent indifference for, and scant interest in, such matters.[10]

Both Evan Shelby and his son Isaac, by trafficking in military warrants between 1783 and 1788, were able to secure for themselves at least 15,000 acres of prime land, even while aware that a considerable part of them fell under the jurisdiction of North Carolina. Following the 1779 definition of the transmountain extension of the Virginia/North Carolina line, Sapling Grove also turned out to lie within the territories claimed by the latter state. But Evan Shelby was reluctant to contemplate leaving his home, and the region where most of his landed properties lay. So he remained, while his son Isaac decided to remove to Kentucky, where he fixed his residence on the 1,400-acre property he had already elected as the ideal place for him to settle. As a result, father and son found themselves subjected to two different jurisdictions, that of North Carolina and Virginia, respectively, in the transmountain region.[11]

An established landowner, Evan Shelby soon became involved in North Carolina politics and, in 1781, was elected a state senator from the Washington District—as the three easternmost transmountain counties of North Carolina were by then collectively designated. As a public officer, he could not avoid entanglement with the strong separatist movement of a radical-democratic bent developing there, and finally coming to maturity in 1784 with the aim of creating a new commonwealth, the state of Frankland—meaning the land of the free.[12]

An enslaver by inheritance, Evan Shelby's "progressive" social outlook possibly included the hope that the plague of human bondage be swept away from the Southwest before it could become too deeply rooted in its socioeconomic soil. With this perspective, he may have sympathized with the radicals in the separatist movement, but, as a public servant of North Carolina, he could not condone their design to void all land titles held by nonresidents, even if the measure was essentially meant to curb wild speculation at the expense of the common settler's ability to purchase land at a fair price.[13]

However, the circumstances that surrounded the defeat of the Frankland provisional constitution by conservative forces in mid-1785, and their naming the new state Franklin—in honor of the great Pennsylvanian—made Shelby realize that it was only a farce, an exercise of Realpolitik concocted, with the tacit complicity of some local leaders, to appease the radicals with the ultimate aim of bringing the seceded counties back in the fold of the parent state.[14] So, when he was asked to become the new state's governor, Shelby prudently declined the offer. And his suspicions were well grounded, for the very first act passed by the Franklin Assembly was in fact to guarantee the validity of land titles held by North Carolina citizens, regardless of their place of residence.[15]

Despite his desire to keep a distance from the looming internecine strife, Evan Shelby could not avoid involvement. Having been appointed brigadier general of the militia of Washington County in the previous year, in 1787 he was in fact ordered to crush the separatists' last resistance militarily. Whether because of the impossibility of obtaining additional troops from North Carolina or out of reluctance to engage in what actually amounted to a fratricidal war, in late October 1787 Evan Shelby resigned his post and retired to private life at Sapling Grove, where he died six years later, at age seventy-five.[16]

Traveller's Rest

At the time of his father's demise, Isaac Shelby had long fixed his residence on the 1,400-acre tract of Kentucky land that had been granted him by the Virginia legislature in 1779; he called his estate Traveller's Rest.

Shelby's chosen name for his estate was intended to convey that, after a long warfare among whites, and between them and the Natives, his residential property might become a living symbol of reconciliation and peaceful coexistence for any passerby. The residence was intended to be not only a resting place for ordinary pioneers heading farther west and a gathering point for members of the intellectual and political elites of both regional and national stature who happened to be in the area, but also a camping ground for friendly Indians. As a matter of fact, Shelby had inaugurated the latter policy even before his house was completed, hosting them on his land and providing them with food and other assistance. For his generosity, he earned from the Natives the appreciative appellation of "Old King Shelby."[17]

While his house was being built, under the supervision of a stonemason named Campbell, Shelby and his bride, Susannah Hart, lived in tents, and their first two children, James and Sarah, were apparently born in one of them. Despite Shelby's friendly attitude toward the Indians, in the early 1780s threats of belligerence had not yet subsided, prompting him "to keep a guard of armed men stationed around the house" while the roof was being put on.[18] The persistent state of alarm among the settlers explains why the house was conceived with a defensive design, the outer walls being made of rough stone almost three feet thick; a feature that gave the building the aspect of a little fortress. In stark contrast with the aerial elegance of contemporary colonial mansions in the seaboard states, with their white-columned, graceful design, on the Kentucky frontier, where settlers were constantly exposed to Indian attacks, houses were, by necessity, conceived on the "safety-first" principle, with narrow windows and solid, if only wooden, walls. Only the wealthiest could afford to use stone, which was found in inexhaustible quantities in the beds of the Ohio, the Kentucky, and other nearby rivers. Testifying to Isaac Shelby's largeness of means, Traveller's Rest boasted a magnificent stone mansion—the first erected with that material in the trans-Appalachian South.[19]

Some decades later, Pennsylvania-born physician Henry McMurtrie, who was one of the earliest historians of Kentucky, explained that the use of stone and marble for house building became common in the state only in the late 1790s. Thanks to its proximity to sources of supply, Louisville was the precursor in this development, acquiring soon after its founding (1780) the solid look of an old northeastern city. Visitors from both the eastern states and abroad marveled at its style.[20]

The Shelbys' completed residence looked very handsome, with a main body two stories high and single-story wings extending from either end—one accommodating the master bedroom, the other the kitchen. Initially, it was composed of seven rooms, but an additional, large one was built later at the end of the long back gallery. Commonly referred to as the "weaving room," it was the place where the enslaved manufactured linen and woollen cloths for household and plantation use alike, under the expert supervision of their mistress, Susannah Hart Shelby.[21]

A similarly solid-looking stone-and-brick building stood on the right side of the mansion, to house the bondspeople Shelby had inherited from his father. Amazingly well-preserved to this day, with its original doors and window frames, the sight of that structure invites comparison with the more typical quarters for the enslaved, usually amounting to shabby wooden barracks, that can still be seen near a good many plantation houses built in the Southwest from the 1820s (Andrew Jackson's "Hermitage" home near Nashville, for example). The contrast makes the observer wonder about the extent of wealth the leaders in the early settlement of the trans-Appalachian South could command. In all probability, the solidity of Shelby's quarters for the enslaved was motivated by the same concern that had inspired the erection of the master house, that is, defense, mostly from the Indians. While protection of his valuable human property must have been paramount among Isaac's priorities, his well-known sympathies may have also played a role in prompting him to provide his own bondspeople with a comfortable shelter, which, by the way, far outstripped the average dwelling of a common white settler of the time.[22]

Thanks to its location in Lincoln, one of the three counties established by the Virginia legislature in 1780, and to its proximity to Danville, which was by then the most important town in the Kentucky country, Traveller's Rest affirmed itself as the vital center of its social, political, and cultural life several years before statehood. This was achieved not only by virtue of Shelby's military and personal prestige but also thanks to the exquisite manners and sociability of his wife, who was praised for her remarkable beauty as much as for her sharp intellect and "industrious management" of the estate.[23]

Having become the seat of the first courthouse established in the Kentucky country, during the 1780s Danville was the beating heart of the political and economic ferment that was so crucial in forging the identity of Kentucky as a candidate for statehood. In the second half of the decade, the small town was the arena of hot political debates between two distinct groups of the elites whose respective members entertained a different vision of the future of Kentucky. As Patricia Watlington argued, the "old elites" were large landowners who, like Isaac Shelby, had participated in the early phases of the region's settlement. The "new elites" were instead mostly professionals, judges, and lawyers who had arrived during the 1780s. While the former supported the aspirations of petty farmers and landless people for an equitable land distribution and the exclusion of slavery, the latter envisioned the economic future of the state of Kentucky in an entrepreneurial, commerce-and-manufacturing-oriented vein. As a result, this group thought that enslaved labor might constitute an asset toward that end. To advance their vision, in 1786 the leaders of the "new elites" founded the Danville Political Club for the purpose of discussing the most urgent problems inhibiting economic development. Three years later they created the Kentucky Society for the Promotion of Manufactures, which coincided with the launching of what is believed to have been the first cotton mill in the West.[24]

The nearly even strength of the two parties confronting each other was unequivocally revealed by the fact that it took the calling of no fewer than *nine* conventions to reach an agreement on the terms of Kentucky's adhesion to the federal Union. Finally, the "new elites" got the upper hand, and, in 1792, Kentucky became the fifteenth state in the Union with a constitution that made slavery legal within its borders. Although this was a scorching defeat for the antislavery forces, they continued to entertain fair hopes that the slavery clause might be expunged from the constitution at the convention scheduled to meet in 1799 to either confirm or revise its text. Irreversible changes were at play, however, that promised to leave those hopes unfulfilled. From the early 1790s, enslavers like John Breckinridge of Virginia flocked to Kentucky in growing numbers. By mid-decade, their ability to influence the state's institutions in the protection of their lucrative economic interests rooted in slavery had become formidable.[25]

The wealth generated by slavery-related activities—from both the Atlantic and the domestic trade, and from the exploitation of enslaved labor in agriculture, mining, and manufacturing—caused a major shift in consensus among the population for an economically modernizing yet socially conservative vision of the state's future. The trend was signaled by a process of marginalization that Danville, the core of old agrarian wealth, underwent. For a while, the town continued to retain its primacy, but the relocation of Transylvania University to Lexington in 1789 heralded its inexorable decline, which was finally decreed by the selection of Frankfort as the state capital.[26]

The choice of Isaac Shelby for the governorship appeared to everyone to be the best bet to secure compromise between the contending forces within a still-heated political climate. His military prestige, which had earned him the appellation of "Old King's Mountain" among whites, combined with his unblemished reputation as an honest, "plain and forthright" man made him an ideal candidate. His moderation offered sufficient guarantees that he would pursue a fair policy toward property holders and the propertyless, the enslavers and the nonenslavers alike. Aware of the critical role he was called to play, Shelby agreed to serve as the state's first governor.[27]

With his election in 1792, the prestige of Traveller's Rest was further enhanced, and it continued unabated through Shelby's second gubernatorial term (1812–16). In the words of his granddaughter Susan P. Grigsby, during those decades "no home in Kentucky ever entertained as many distinguished guests—president Madison, General Jackson, Aaron Burr, Clay, Benton, and others equally as great." After 1817, however, the heyday of Traveller's Rest drew rapidly to a close. It was the end of an era three years later, when Isaac Shelby was partially paralyzed by a stroke. Impaired in his body but not in his mind, he survived six more years, and finally died of a second stroke in July 1826, at the age of seventy-six.[28]

It was indeed mere coincidence that two outstanding men in the building of the nation—John Adams and Thomas Jefferson—also passed away in the same month of the same year as Isaac Shelby. Their simultaneous demise sadly announced to the world the disappearance of the whole revolutionary generation from the American political scene. However sincere the statesmen and politicians who would replace them might be in their determination to consolidate the nation built by their fathers, things would never be the same again—for the good and for the bad—either in the country at large or the microcosm of Traveller's Rest.

An Enslaving State, Distinctive in Its Own Right

"Self-conscious children of Virginia," as one author defined them, Kentuckians always honored the bonds of brotherhood and the sense of belonging to the same cultural heritage that tied them to their parent state. Yet, from the very beginning of settlement, they developed certain expectations that qualified their social, political, and economic aspirations as "an egalitarian-based nationalism," if for whites only. Although theirs certainly was a more progressive outlook than that prevailing in the Old Dominion—their quest for more democratic practices having been enshrined in the state constitution through the lifting of property qualifications either for voting and for office-holding—the legality of slavery in Kentucky remained untouched.[29]

Sensitive to the condition of the enslaved population, only two days after his inauguration, which took place in Frankfort on June 4, 1792, forty-one-year-old Isaac Shelby immediately called for laws compelling the proper treatment of bondspeople and, throughout his tenure, never hid his wish to see the slavery clause expunged from the constitution. Alarmed at the governor's unconcealed views on emancipation, John Breckinridge, a most influential politician in the state with major interests in slavery, unsuccessfully tried to sensitize him to the dangerous implications that a general liberation of the enslaved would have on property titles of all descriptions. However, the conservative backlash produced by the spreading of large-scale, slavery-based agriculture in those years lent Breckinridge a powerful argument to hammer down his point with Shelby. In effect, the drastic weakening of the antislavery thrust in Kentucky was signaled by the increasingly ambiguous position that most churches, and especially the Baptists, were taking on the subject of emancipation. Deprived of the fundamental source of inspiration and guidance provided by ministers of the Gospel, the antislavery forces suffered a crushing defeat at the second constitutional convention, in 1799. To Shelby's great disappointment, that was the end for a vision of Kentucky as a land for yeoman farmers. Instead, it would become a region for capital-intensive speculation in land and enslaved Blacks.[30]

This failure triggered a massive out-migration to Ohio, Indiana, Illinois, and Missouri by landless people and petty farmers, who had deluded themselves that the newborn state might conjugate the principles of white democracy with the rejection of human bondage. Such a remarkable loss in population was offset by an inflow of immigrants from enslaving and free states alike. Those crisscross migrations advanced networks of familial and friendship ties that ran east and west, north and south. All combined, they brought Kentucky to increasingly act as an economic bridge and cultural broker between the two sections' expanding business and trade relations, and to finally affirm itself as the exemplar of a hybrid state between North and South, slavery and freedom.[31]

Although economically stimulating, such developments had a negative counterpart in complicating the Kentuckians' already ambivalent approach to slavery, further blurring the line between antislavery feelings and entitlement to own humans in the economic realm. In preindustrial Kentucky, enslaved labor was generally deemed compatible with the quest for industrial development, but the two were bound to become at odds in the long run. The diverging paths followed by Lexington and Louisville, respectively, anticipated the veracity of this prediction.

By the time of statehood, the two towns had already been vying for economic primacy. Founded in 1779 at the heart of the Bluegrass region, an area blessed with an extremely rich soil fit for tobacco, hemp, flax, wheat, and corn cultivation, as well as for cattle and horse raising, Lexington was endowed with all the requisites to become an important commercial hub for those staples in the Upper South. Easy access to raw materials also constituted a comparative advantage for the development of a manufacturing basis, an opportunity that did not escape the attention of its elites.[32]

Louisville, laid out by William Pope in 1780, was not gifted with as rich and agriculturally productive a hinterland as Lexington's. Yet its enviable geographic location at the falls of the Ohio River made it a candidate to become a major entrepôt and distributing center in the Ohio Valley for goods coming in from every quarter of the nation. Through mercantilist pursuits, Louisvilleans were soon able to invest spin-off funds in manufacturing ventures that began to impress on Jefferson and neighboring counties the character of an economically modernizing area.[33]

Such promising beginnings drew the attention of outside observers, both American and foreign, who, in their accounts, tended to express equally flattering opinions of both towns. In 1800, H. Denison of Natchez reported: "In Lexington there are seven cotton, cloth, etc. manufactories on a large scale." Four years later, British visitor F. Cumming wrote of Louisville: "I had thought Cincinnati one of the most beautiful towns I had seen in America, but Louisville, which is almost as large, equals it in beauty, and in the opinion of many, exceeds it."[34]

In 1806, with the volume of trade constantly growing, the construction of a canal to bypass the falls of the Ohio was proposed. Yet the project was set aside due to the strong opposition of local merchants of a conservative mind. The idea was resurrected in 1811, when the advent of steamboat navigation suddenly presented the business community of Louisville with unprecedented trade prospects. The steamboat revolution dramatically accelerated the rise of the town as the leading commercial, business, and manufacturing center of Kentucky. Testifying to these remarkable developments, in 1812 a branch of the Bank of Kentucky was opened in Louisville, and the first iron foundry established there by A. Skidmore. Between 1817 and 1818 two more banks were opened, the first being a branch of the Bank of the United States, and the second the Commercial Bank of Louisville.[35]

Writing in 1819, historian Henry McMurtrie, who had settled in Louisville three years earlier and become an ardent advocate for the canal, noted that some of its brick buildings were very handsome, comparing well "with any of the most elegant private edifices of Philadelphia or New York." McMurtrie's prediction that the town was destined for a brilliant future was not disavowed.

Louisville's urban growth was in fact so rapid that it soon outstripped Lexington's and, in 1827, finally qualified it to be classified as a "city" by national census standards.[36]

In the eyes of contemporaries, Kentucky's formidable achievements were not immediately correlated to slavery, the least so by Europeans, who, in the early phases of immigration, were largely propertied people. A case in point is that of Frenchman Nicholas Gautier. Sometime after landing in the United States in the early 1810s, he finally settled down in Logan County, Kentucky, where he owned 400 acres and an undetermined number of enslaved hands who tilled his land. From his new place of residence, in 1812 he wrote his brother Etienne back in Brest: "The people of this state are a polished well informed body of Citizens; schools & every establishment calculated to civilize man. . . . This country is made up of all sorts of people—French—Germans—Dutch—Danes—Turks—Spaniards—Scotch—Welsh—Irish—English & Negroes. Yet we all harmonize like brothers."[37]

Although somewhat premature, Monsieur Gautier's evaluation of Kentucky society contained a grain of truth. What he saw as the absence of extreme interethnic and interracial frictions were in fact the echoes of an egalitarian thrust that, despite failure to ban slavery by constitutional provision, continued to manifest itself in an open attitude toward peoples of diverse origin and, most of all, in what appeared to be a marked sensitivity to the plight of the enslaved. This man coming from Europe, where the poor were doomed to a life of suffering and privation in the midst of the general indifference of the affluent, sensed this camaraderie. In reality, the lot of the lower orders in the United States was only apparently lighter than that befalling their European counterparts, and the treatment of bondspeople in many instances harsh and cruel.[38]

This apparently liberal climate seemed to reign in the state, leading a number of foreign observers to predict the final demise of slavery in Kentucky in the not-too-distant future. Others, however, saw it differently. With its highly diverse economic and social landscape that combined so well with the distinctive traits of both northern and southern societies, Kentucky might become an ideal benchmark to prove the compatibility of slavery with economic modernization.

Holding the Wolf by the Ears

In the 1820s, some northeastern political economists viewed Kentucky's experiment as the promise of America's future, the workshop where regional differences could be smoothed over and reconciled, to stave off the unleashing of a sectional conflict of major proportions of which the 1819–20 Missouri Crisis had been the harbinger. Prominent among them was Pennsylvanian political economist Mathew Carey. An admirer of Henry Clay, he enthusiastically supported Clay's idea that America ought to create a vast domestic market through the adoption of a protective tariff and the launching of a massive program of industrialization. Along this line, Carey maintained that no real conflict of interests existed between the manufacturer, the merchant, and the farmer and thus, by extension, between northerners and southerners. Hence, he argued for the compatibility of slavery with industrialization.[39]

No other state presented a more suitable ground for Carey to carry home his point than Henry Clay's Kentucky, and, within its fold, no town better served his purpose than Lexington. Writing under the pseudonym of "Hamilton" in 1828, he published a broadside in Philadelphia, titled *Some Notices of Kentucky, Particularly of Its Chief Town, Lexington,* in which he extolled the city as the quintessential expression of the state's economic achievements and promising prospects. Building upon its enviable location at the heart of the Bluegrass region, Lexington had rapidly become the center of a thriving export trade. With time, some of the accumulated money began to be invested in those "unfailing sources of wealth and prosperity" that manufactures represented. In Carey's estimate, in 1828 the town boasted ten manufactories of cotton bagging and bale rope, in which three thousand people were employed "of whom *not more than two per cent are white* [italics mine]," along with "ten cotton manufactories, some of them on a large and respectable scale," and "three woollen manufactories." A vast array of establishments "embracing all the varieties of employment that conduce to human comfort and security," from gristmills to foundries, to paper mills, and so forth, completed Lexington's industrial park.[40]

In Carey's opinion, the remarkable economic diversification achieved by a town lying in a county (Fayette) that recorded the highest proportion of enslaved population in the state—above 40 percent—did not reflect the stereotypical image of a drowsy slavery-based society so widespread among northerners. Castigating "the prejudices of the generality of the citizens of other states," Carey described instead Lexington's society as a polite, refined, and respectable one, and the character of its people "on the whole estimable," and not dissimilar from what was found in the Northeast.[41]

With its cultural and educational institutions, including a library containing almost six thousand volumes, Transylvania University, a theater, and various literary associations, in 1828 Lexington was proclaiming itself the "Athens" of Kentucky. Yet, as Carey failed to record, the town was about to surrender to the Falls City—as Louisville came to be called—the sceptre in trade and manufacturing.[42] Described in 1826 by Pennsylvania-born writer and journalist Anne Royall as the handsomest settlement she had seen on her tour out west, once the canal to bypass the falls of the Ohio was completed in 1830, Louisville rapidly consolidated its position as the largest and most economically dynamic urban center in the state—on which Lexington itself came to depend for large-scale commercialization of its products—and also began to seriously challenge the latter's primacy on the cultural plane.[43]

The different relationships the two urban centers bore to their respective hinterlands in terms of extent and composition of the population intimated the divergence of their paces of growth. In 1830, the counties of Fayette (Lexington) and Jefferson (Louisville) reported equivalent numbers of inhabitants (25,098 and 24,000, respectively). Yet the Falls City counted many more urbanites (10,341) than Lexington (6,026). The latter's ability to catch up with Louisville's rate of growth was thwarted by the eminently agrarian character of Fayette County's economy, with its enslaved population of 10,933, while Jefferson counted only 6,934. The gap between the two urban centers would dramatically widen over the next couple of decades, and, by 1850, the population of the Falls City was more than five times larger than Lexington's.[44]

Little by little, exposure to the challenges of economic development unavoidably impinged upon the emancipationist views of Kentuckians; but, alas, did so in a conservative way. In 1808, less than a decade past the confirmation of the slavery clause by constitutional provision, the antislavery movement was revitalized by the founding of the Kentucky Abolition Society (KAS), the mission of which was to formulate schemes for gradual emancipation. Henry Clay, who was by then the rising star in western—and American—politics, was one of its most ardent paladins. Early on, the growing entrenchment of slavery in the state's economic fabric combined with widespread concern that the soaring number of free Blacks—a phenomenon that actually involved the whole South—might destabilize race relations, convinceed KAS's members of the advisability of embracing a more prudent course. The "repatriation to Africa" project championed by the American Colonization Society (ACS), to which Clay himself enthusiastically adhered, offered a viable answer to their moral qualms.[45]

Founded in 1816 at the national level, the ACS had its Kentucky affiliate established in 1828. Although a latecomer, in 1830 it already boasted twenty-one branch societies, a number that, according to one source, reached thirty-one by 1832. At that time, only Virginia (with thirty-four) and Ohio (with thirty-three) had more. The further proliferation of branch societies in the state has been explained by one student as the exigency felt by Kentuckians of an antislavery inclination, who were nevertheless uncomfortable with the idea of a general liberation of the enslaved population, to congregate with people of like feelings, as in a club, where they could vent their anxieties without necessarily committing themselves to immediate action. Be that as it may, from the early 1830s growing numbers of Kentuckians included the "removal to Africa" clause with their testaments, as a sine qua non for the emancipation of part or all of their bondspeople.[46]

By offering enslavers the opportunity to relieve their consciences of the moral burden of enslaving humans without openly challenging the prevailing social attitudes on the subject, the "repatriation" plan forwarded by the ACS became popular in every part of the Upper South. In the bordering state of Tennessee, where the once-vital antislavery movement had rapidly withered during the first decade of the 1800s, a notable proponent was iron manufacturer Montgomery Bell. The owner of more than two hundred bondsmen whom he mostly employed at his renowned ironworks, in his senior years Bell provided for the emancipation of nearly ninety of them by testament, subject to their willingness to remove to Liberia, the territory the ACS had secured for the freedpeople to organize an independent state of their own.[47]

In Kentucky, the significant support for the colonization alternative quickly dwarfed the already faltering influence of the antislavery movement. As a result, some of its staunchest activists decided to leave the state, as Danville-born James G. Birney did in 1835, when he moved to Cincinnati, Ohio, and joined the ranks of militant abolitionism.[48]

As the nineteenth century progressed, the two souls of Kentucky's cultural/social heritage found a ground of convergence in a shared economic interest in bonded labor among members of the business community—whether merchants, industrialists, or agriculturalists—regardless of personal opinions on slavery as an institution. Although Kentucky recorded one of the highest ratios of enslaved to free population, bondspeople constituted nonetheless a sizeable proportion of its workforce. Paradoxically, as the state's economy was becoming more and more manufacturing-oriented, and immigrants coming from or through the Northeast were increasingly voicing their hopes that Kentucky might soon become a free labor society, slavery seemed to be all the more embedded in its fold. Furthermore, and much to the dismay of its opponents, steamboat navigation made the lucrative trafficking in human beings, in which the state participated with the Deep South down the Mississippi River, easier and faster. Reportedly, about 77,000 enslaved persons were sold to the Lower South from Kentucky during the entire antebellum era and, on the average, 3,400 per year during the 1850s.[49]

Allegedly, the majority of Kentuckians thought of themselves as very sympathetic to the plight of the enslaved. In a sense, as one author put it, they held "the benevolent aspects of slavery as one way of ameliorating their complicity in perpetuating the peculiar institution," and tried to relieve their consciences by treating their bondspeople humanely. In the public realm, the mainstays of their benevolence consisted in the lifting of legal restrictions on teaching the enslaved to read and write, and in the far greater freedom of movement the Kentucky bondspeople were allowed compared with the enslaved in the Lower South. In the private sphere, Kentucky enslavers who considered themselves sensitive to the plight of the enslaved took pride in showing concern for their well-being, and closely monitored the situations of those they hired out. In this latter regard, one author made the important point that, while preserving their financial investment in human beings was paramount among the concerns of considerate enslavers, by the late antebellum era the practice had become so crucial to their economies as to make them particularly attentive to their hirelings' satisfaction, aware that "slaves knew masters needed their acquiescence."[50]

Indulging himself in the belief that he was a compassionate enslaver, however, did not stop a master from selling his property in human beings, although he usually did so only if compelled by financial distress. In such an unfortunate predicament, the Kentuckian usually sought, in the first instance, placement opportunities with some trustworthy family. With the necessity to turn to a trader for fiscal assistance, the owner often included a contract clause to the effect that the enslaved person in question should not be forwarded to the Lower South—where living conditions were inhumane. Instead, he or she might be resold, preferably within the state or at least somewhere in the Upper South. Traders in the enslaved could be unscrupulous in contravening the pledge, however, as in a case involving Susan Grigsby.[51]

The above sketches of the ferment, division, and contradiction that marked Kentucky life in its formative decades provide a backdrop for the unfolding of the early history of the Shelbys and its most closely allied family, the Harts. A scion of both, Susan inherited from her forebears all the unresolved inner conflicts that went along with being a substantial enslaver who, this notwithstanding, thought of herself as a person of firm antislavery persuasion. As a woman, she responded to the challenges of modernization according to her personal experience and special needs.

Thomas Jefferson admirably synthesized in a famous phrase—"holding the wolf by the ears"—the concept that enslavers—who, despite all evidence to the contrary, insisted on considering themselves people with antislavery feelings—could hope to steer their vessel loaded with its inherited cargo of human beings amid the rough waters of change only by constantly balancing economic interest in the institution with awareness of its fundamental injustice; and prepare for "letting it [the wolf] loose," someday.[52]

Even if Jefferson did not say so explicitly, those enslavers were bound by moral imperative to render the plight of their bondspeople as bearable as possible. Susan Grigsby unreservedly subscribed to this philosophy. She believed it was a creed proudly embraced by her ancestors, and it was adhered to by the vast majority of her kin and close relatives. Yet, along the way, she sadly found her ability to keep faith with those ideas severely curtailed by her gender in a patriarchal society. The antebellum South, by denying women full legal rights to their properties, deprived them of independent agency not only in the public but in the private sphere as well. Yet, like Susan and her mother, Virginia Hart Shelby, scores of women across the South were intelligent and adept enough to carve measures of independence and agency for themselves by wisely maneuvering within the fixed boundaries of legal and social prescriptions.[53]

End of an Era

In his will, Governor Isaac Shelby amply provided for his spouse and eight surviving children in the most equitable manner. To his "beloved wife," Susannah Hart, he willed all the things (furniture, utensils, etc.) relating to the house, as well as the livestock. To his youngest son, Alfred, who was twenty-two at the time of his father's death, he bequeathed twenty-three of his bondspeople and Traveller's Rest, to share with his mother during her lifetime, or until she remarried. Although his liberality in providing for Alfred may have been so that he could take care of his mother, Isaac Shelby's willing to him his "Library of Books," consisting of 312 volumes, hints at the intellectual affinity that may have made the relationship between father and son a special one. It also adds further evidence to the already established opinion that frontier life was not incompatible with learned culture.[54]

On June 14, 1827, barely one year after his father's passing, Alfred Shelby married Virginia, the fifth child of Susanna Preston and Nathaniel Hart Jr. The bride was turning eighteen the very day of the wedding, which was celebrated at Spring Hill, the historic home of the Harts in Woodford County. Like most of the Hart women, including Governor Shelby's wife, Virginia was very good-looking, but her beauty was further enhanced by a special graciousness, and sweetness in deportment and manners that would make her persona more and more attractive with the passing of time. Decades later, when she was in her forties, longtime friend Angelina Henry would remark with half-concealed envy that, while Virginia "still retained [her] beautiful appearance," she herself was not endowed by nature with the same blessing.[55]

The marriage between Alfred Shelby and Virginia Hart, who were first cousins, was thought to be by members of both families not only an auspice of a healthy continuity, both in lineage and association, between them, but also a pledge that the legacy of Traveller's Rest as a shrine for their joint role in the building of the state be proudly preserved and transmitted to future generations. The newlywed couple wholeheartedly shared in the vows.[56]

For a few years, Alfred and Virginia led a serene life, spent in the enjoyment of their successful efforts to consolidate and even expand their holdings. Satisfaction for their remarkable achievements was only outstripped by the joy they derived from the rapid increase of the family. The birth of Isaac in 1828 was followed two years later by that of Susanna (whom everyone called Susan from the very beginning) and, not long after, of Alfred (1831). All seemed to be going well at Traveller's Rest, with Virginia tending to her little ones while at the same time being tutored by her mother-in-law and aunt, with whom she reportedly entertained a relationship of mutual esteem and affection. All the skills a plantation mistress ought to possess for a competent management of her estate were imparted, but weaving held a special place. Susannah Hart Shelby had developed remarkable abilities in this craft, to the point that her linens and fine cloths were regularly displayed at local and state fairs, where they were much praised and even won prizes.[57]

In 1832, Virginia was expecting her fourth child, whose arrival would have further increased the couple's happiness. However, their dreams to build a solid future for their offspring as the heirs of a prestigious dynasty tragically shipwrecked on December 1, when Alfred Shelby accidentally died at age twenty-nine in a hunting party. His twenty-three-year-old wife became a widow with three small children and a fourth on the way. Born in April 1833 and named Sarah Virginia, the baby unfortunately survived only twenty-five days. A few months later Alfred's mother, Susannah Hart Shelby, also passed away.[58]

The loss of her husband, youngest child, and mother-in-law in the span of only seven months must have thrown Virginia into a state of total bereavement. Despite her young age, however, she was possessed with the fortitude to work out the grieving and mourning through positive action. Although still largely inexperienced in business matters, Virginia Hart Shelby resolutely took over the management of the estate, to preserve its integrity for the benefit of her offspring.

As scores of biographies of plantation mistresses reconstructed by historians illustrate, Shelby's was not an uncommon resolve. The laws regulating woman's property rights in the southern states attributed to widows a degree of agency in their quest for an economic stability. Yet only a few managed to achieve true economic independence. Widows who found themselves in greatly reduced circumstances sought support in a new marriage, but this option was rarely advisable for those belonging to affluent families, for it would have meant the loss of control of nearly every property, including their original dowers. Moreover, wealthy widows could not freely dispose of the money left by their deceased husbands, its administration being normally entrusted to testamentary executors. In cases of conflicting interpretations of a will, or in the presence of relevant circumstances arising after its registration that made its implementation problematic, women entered lawsuits in the hope of obtaining what they thought their offspring and they themselves were entitled to be adjudicated. Falling within this latter category, Virginia Hart Shelby chose to avoid remarrying, at least until her inheritance and that of her children were clearly determined and secured.[59]

In his testament, Alfred had bequeathed to his wife "everything except [his] mules on hand and [his] money." While the latter was to be "loaned out for the benefit of his wife and children" by his testamentary executors (his brothers Evan and Thomas Shelby), the mules were to be sold when his eldest child, Isaac, reached the age of twenty-one. By that time, he was also to inherit Traveller's Rest with all the lands appertaining to it, "six of the choice of [his] negroes," plus an equal half of those under fifty and over fifty years of age, and

1,000 dollars "to purchase stock for his farm." As was customary for daughters, Susan did not inherit any land but, rather, a half of her father's bondspeople (after deducting those given to Isaac and those over fifty) and 10,000 dollars, that she would receive upon her "marrying with the approbation of her mother."[60]

Alfred Shelby also devised for Isaac—the only son in his will—a section of his real estate known as "Arcadia." Completed in 1836, the handsome, Greek Revival–style brick residence, surrounded by more than 600 acres of bluegrass land, was very different from Traveller's Rest both outside and inside. With its very finely decorated and handsomely furnished fourteen rooms, Arcadia testified to the consolidation of the Shelbys' fortunes over time. Just like at Traveller's Rest, a two-story brick bondspersons' house stood near the masters' mansion. Its worse state of preservation, probably due to the use of poorer materials or to less attention in its construction, may suggest a diminished concern for the physical safety of the enslaved at a time when the Indian threat in that part of the region was but a distant memory.[61]

Sudden death had prevented Alfred Shelby from including either of his younger children, Alfred Jr., and Sarah, in his testamentary dispositions. This circumstance, compounded by Sarah's premature demise, necessitated a reapportionment of shares of inheritance among his heirs. Furthermore, having chosen to be the statutory guardian of her youngest child, Alfred, Virginia claimed access to part of the money held in trust by executors to provide for his support and education. She therefore initiated a lawsuit that, after many conflicting decisions by the several levels of the judiciary, in 1842 resulted in the definitive ruling by the Court of Appeals of Kentucky in favor of her claims, allowing for the final settlement of the accounts.[62]

For almost a decade previous, Virginia Shelby had worked indefatigably toward the consolidation of the estate. In her new managerial role, she had closely supervised the many activities being conducted there, from the raising and monitoring of the quality of crops and livestock, to their sale. In this latter regard, she had from time to time turned to her father for advice on the marketing strategies to adopt, especially in connection with hemp, the most valuable of her cash crops. Besides that, she had assiduously controlled every aspect of household life, including the rearing of three small children and the coordination of the work of several enslaved Black domestic servants. Among other things, she had proudly carried on the tradition, begun by her mother-in-law, of having fine linens manufactured at Traveller's Rest.[63]

Virginia Hart Shelby's experience as a widowed plantation mistress was not much dissimilar from that of Keziah Brevard of Richland County, South Carolina. They both chafed at the limitations imposed on their sex by social conventions in the interest of the "master's authority." This, they knew, was a political question of the highest importance, especially in the management of the enslaved. Brevard probably felt this problem more acutely than her Kentuckian counterpart, due to the extremely protective prescriptions regulating white women's movement in those parts of South Carolina where Blacks easily outnumbered whites. Yet both women wielded full master's power in every respect pertaining to legal ownership of their property in human beings.[64]

Relative advantages did not exempt Virginia Shelby from strict social scrutiny. Looking after all the aspects connected with the running of her estate involved extensive traveling. Society neither encouraged nor approved of an upper-class woman—and a mother of three—undertaking frequent and even extended absences from home. She would be charged with maternal negligence and publicly shamed. Aware of the disapprobation to which she was exposed, Virginia Shelby was required to redouble efforts to reconcile business imperatives with an impeccable running of her household. Apparently, she successfully met both challenges, bringing up her children in a serene, loving atmosphere, and at the same time attending to her several business commitments so competently as to finally earn community appreciation.[65]

While evidence of Isaac, Susan, and Alfred Shelby's strong attachment to their mother is apparent in correspondence they began during adolescence, Virginia's success as a businesswoman is confirmed by private and public sources. In 1833, soon after the death of her husband, her taxable property amounted to $20,597, but in 1842 it was valued at $28,300 and included thirty-two bondspeople. The same year, her son Alfred appeared for the first time in the tax records as the owner of a separate estate valued at $16,180.[66]

To achieve her goals, Virginia Hart Shelby paid a heavy toll, both in physical and mental strain. In 1843, when their property titles were finally confirmed, her children were already in their teens. Isaac, the oldest, was almost fifteen, Susan turned thirteen in February, and Alfred was eleven. Relieved from the all-absorbing duties involved with their early rearing, Virginia Shelby could finally concentrate on business. Contradicting the older assumption that plantation mistresses were mostly unprepared to take over the management of their estates, her example adds weight to the case made by Kristen Wood that planters' widows largely excelled in entrepreneurial abilities.[67]

When she finally remarried, in 1847, Virginia Hart Shelby turned over to her children an estate that, although located in an economically declining area of Kentucky, had more than doubled its original worth. Further, she brought to her new husband, Robert J. Breckinridge, a handsome fortune that she had accumulated for herself. However, as wealthy widows frequently did, she retained some of her properties in sole and separate ownership and, signally, a town lot, with a house, in Danville.[68]

The irony of destiny often trumps humans' perspective on momentous events touching their own lives. So it happened with the children of the late Governor Shelby, who, although aware of the loss of position his demise caused them among the Kentucky gentry—and the national political establishment—took for granted that the prestige attached to the family name combined with extensive wealth would be sufficient guarantees of their undiminished social status. Such expectations vanished for the inheritors of Traveller's Rest with the untimely death of Alfred Shelby in 1832. In her efforts to consolidate the family estate and raise her children with pride for their ancestry, Virginia drew strength from veneration of a bygone past and faith in her ability to build a new future. She built on ashes, adopting a positive, forward-looking attitude.

The subtle equilibrium between sentimental attachment to the past and liberation from its psychological moorings seems to have been achieved, even if this was too difficult for her young children to understand. Having been prematurely orphaned of the important figure of the father, and brought up at a place rife with mementoes of a glorious family past, Isaac, Susan, and Alfred Shelby clung to memory in their youthful search for identity.

Susan came to feel the legacy of Traveller's Rest so intensely as to find it impossible to imagine her own future away from a place so suffused with memories of both loss and joy.

2

Looking "Backward" to the Future

In 1830 Susanna Preston Shelby was born in a Kentucky on the precipice of economic and social expansion. However, those expectations were short-lived both for the dwellers of Traveller's Rest and Kentuckians at large. Much as the former's were broken by Alfred Shelby's sudden death in 1832, the latter were checked by the economic depression that came on the heels of the financial panic of 1837.

From that major setback Kentuckians emerged stronger, and more confident in their capability to cope with the challenges of the new age of progress just opening up for them. From her perch at Traveller's Rest, Virginia Hart Shelby wholly shared in the general optimistic outlook on the future. It is hard to tell, however, to what extent her still-young children responded to or shared their mother's forward-looking attitude. Susan, in particular, seemed to entertain a particularly strong attachment to—almost a veneration of—the family's glorious past.

The early social and cultural effects of modernization manifested themselves at a very critical time, a true watershed in the lives of Virginia Hart Shelby and her daughter. This chapter explores how they first responded to the challenges of the new times.

Born at the Dawn of New Times

The second child and, at the time, only daughter of Virginia Hart and Alfred Shelby, Susanna (Susan) Preston Shelby first opened her eyes to this world at Traveller's Rest on February 13, 1830.[1]

That year—a veritable landmark in Kentucky history—marked the opening of the canal on the Ohio River near Louisville, and inaugurated an epoch of increasing expansion for the Falls City and the state at large. The quickening of river traffic triggered a virtuous circle of urban and economic expansion. A corresponding rise in immigrants' arrivals dramatically enhanced the city's cosmopolitan character. Testifying to its growing role as an economic springboard for enterprising whites coming in from every quarter of the nation, in 1832 a recent immigrant from Pennsylvania reported to his family back home, "The city of Louisville is said to do a larger business than any on the Western waters except New Orleans."[2]

Other signs of Louisville's vitality abound. In 1830, the Lexington, Frankfort & Louisville Railroad was incorporated, and George D. Prentice began the publication of the *Louisville Journal.* For Kentucky, the 1830s were indeed a decade of portentous advancements on the road to modernization. Between 1833 and 1835 three new banks were chartered, and the Galt House, which was then reputed to be the finest hotel in the United States, was built. In 1838, the railroad tracks linking, respectively, Frankfort to Lexington and Louisville to Portland, downriver, were completed. Facilitating the movement of people and merchandise across the state, the new infrastructure allowed for a greater integration between strategically relevant areas.[3]

The depression stemming from the panic of 1837 hit Kentucky harder and longer than expected, causing "all classes to groan under it." Although in 1842 a number of counties still remained in a terrible condition because of the scarcity of money, prompting the legislature to adopt relief measures, Kentucky's march to progress had slowly picked up again from 1839, a year that brought to Louisville another undisputable blessing of modernity: gas street lighting.[4]

Last, but not least, the 1830s saw the takeoff of the iron industry in an area of southwest Kentucky comprising the counties of Trigg, Caldwell, and Lyon, where rich ore deposits had been discovered sometime earlier and first exploited by enterprising Middle Tennessee manufacturers—the Hillmans, the Stackers, and the Vanleers. Thanks to this development, in the late antebellum era Kentucky became one of the main producers of iron in the United States.[5]

The importance of the 1830s for the history of Kentucky was not confined to the economic domain, however; the social/cultural sphere was also involved, with the creation of the Office of Superintendent of Public Education (1838), which laid the bases for major developments in the field in the following decade.[6]

Without railroad connections, during the 1830s, Danville continued its downward spiral by remaining a small country town. However, it retained relevance as the nearest urban location of any importance for the affluent planter society of Lincoln and nearby counties: the core of old agrarian wealth where the fortunes of the Shelby and Hart families were rooted.[7]

Having been born and raised at a place rich with an only recently withered prestige, Susan P. Shelby had the privilege of learning Kentucky history firsthand. As a child, she listened to stories told within the family circle about frontier times, the role played by her paternal grandfather (Isaac Shelby) and maternal great-grandfather (Nathaniel Hart Sr.) in the Revolutionary War; Kentucky's quest for independence from Virginia; and the many difficulties overcome to finally win statehood. From the same sources, she also heard descriptions of landmark events in the early life of her family in the wilderness, such as the wedding of her paternal grandparents, Isaac Shelby and Susannah Hart, and the building of the mansion at Traveller's Rest.

Childhood memories remained vivid in Susan's mind as she was growing up, constantly rekindled by mementoes religiously preserved in the house: the saddle her grandmother mounted on her bridal day; the "French embroidered muslin over white satin pettycoat [*sic*]" dress she wore at the inauguration of her husband's first governorship in Frankfort; "several pieces of silver . . . and a blue English stone china . . . captured from the English . . . which were carried to Kentucky in knafesacks [*sic*] on mules backs" during the Revolution. In Susan's later recollections, in 1833 at the death of Grandmother Shelby, objects of both affective and intrinsic value were distributed among her several children. But a fair number of them, including the blue English stone china and very fine table linens and bed sheeting that had been manufactured by the enslaved, remained at Traveller's Rest, where she continued to reside with her mother and two brothers until 1847.[8]

Despite the untimely loss of their father, Isaac, Susan, and Alfred Shelby apparently enjoyed a relatively normal childhood, well attended to by household bondswomen—either under the direct supervision of their mother or that of some kin—whenever she left for business reasons. No measure of loving care ministered by even the most affectionate relative could quench the three children's thirst for their mother, to which they spontaneously responded by closely knitting together. In particular, Susan established a privileged relationship with Isaac, her older brother. By the same token, although she felt affection for every member of her extended family, Susan's "Uncle Will" (William Preston Hart, one of her mother's brothers) occupied a special place in her heart, and soon became her main male mainstay, the trustworthy counsellor and adviser sought by an adolescent orphan. On the Shelby side of the family, Susan developed a similarly strong tie with Susannah Hart Shelby Fishback, who was a sister to grandfather Isaac Shelby. Reportedly a woman of extreme beauty, three times widowed and remarried a fourth time, "Aunt Fishback" constituted for Susan the second-most-important feminine support and guidance, after her own mother, during adulthood.[9]

Most significantly, Susan and her two siblings were raised in a cultural milieu carrying on the Shelby and Hart families' traditional despisal of human bondage. This was considered a badge of honor in a society increasingly committed to enslaving humans not merely as a matter of economic interest. Amid growing hostility to emancipation, they struggled to maintain a moderate stance on the subject and, like scores of Kentuckians of similar mind, pretended that compassionate attitudes and behaviors toward the enslaved might assist the eradication of the evil plant of slavery from the southern—and the national—soil.

Women of the Shelby and Hart families usually married men with antislavery inclinations and, in a number of instances, men outspoken in their opposition to human bondage. Tobias Gibson, the husband of Virginia Shelby's sister Louisiana, was the owner of four plantations and several hundred bondspeople. Yet his daughter Sarah maintained that he "was at hart opposed to slavery," and suggested that this attitude was part of a larger mind-set that made of him a man "far in advance of his time" on matters of rights and equality. Gibson, in fact, taught her that "taxation without representation" was as unjust to women as to men. Hatred of any form of total submission, whether defined by race or gender, was so deeply ingrained in Sarah's education that, after the Civil War, she became a champion in the struggle for women's rights and, from that vantage point, acknowledged her father's influence on her intellectual formation by defining him an *ante litteram* women suffragist.[10]

As a large enslaver in an area that recorded one of the highest concentrations of enslaved persons in the entire South, Tobias Gibson found the hypothesis of emancipating his own bondspeople utterly impracticable. An intelligent but also realistic man, he considered that a few hundred freedpeople would stand very scant chances of survival in an extremely hostile environment. Personal reservations did not stop him from publicly expressing his opinions on matters of equality, however, thus exposing himself to near-ostracism from Louisiana planter aristocracy.[11]

While Gibson was highly skeptical of the efficacy of the "colonization" project in providing a satisfactory answer to the slavery question in the United States, Dr. James Fishback, the fourth husband of Susannah H. Shelby, was a convinced member of the American Colonization Society (ACS). A medical professor at Transylvania University, lawyer, legislator, and pastor of the Baptist Church, at his death in 1845 he granted emancipation and fifty dollars to any of his bondspeople "who desire[d] to go to Liberia."[12]

The most well-known among Susan's relatives with antislavery feelings, however, is her mother's second husband, the Presbyterian divine Robert J. Breckinridge. Yet, despite distinguishing himself as the champion par excellence of the antislavery cause in late antebellum Kentucky, and later supporting Lincoln's emancipationist policy, Breckinridge remained an enslaver until the institution was legally dissolved.[13]

With such conspicuous examples in her family that enslaving humans could coexist with the entertaining of theoretical antislavery feelings, Susan's cultural and intellectual formation was interwoven with contradiction, and her adolescence was shaped by the interlocking elements in the complicated web of southern social relations.

A Woman's Life at a Crossroads: Education versus Family

As was customary among the southern upper classes, the early instruction of the Shelby children was conducted at home. The first notice we have of Susan's prospective school attendance dates to January 1842, when Letitia P. Wallace, in a letter to sister Virginia, remarked: "We are all poor instructors, so occupied with sick negroes, we do but little else," and suggested that the time had come for both her own son William and niece Susan to be offered a course of formal education.[14]

Virginia responded to her appeal positively, and the decision was quickly made to enroll both William Wallace and Susan Shelby in a Lexington school. By the end of June 1842, twelve-year-old Susan sounded quite contented with the new experience and wrote her mother that she was studying every subject with proficiency, but especially liked philosophy. Yet the frequent correspondence she entertained with her parent was not enough to mitigate the girl's homesickness, and she eagerly looked forward to a long summer vacation at Traveller's Rest, where she would be reunited with her dear mother and two brothers.[15]

Following Alfred Shelby's death in 1832, Louisiana and Tobias Gibson had taken the fate of his young widow and offspring especially to heart, becoming more assiduous in visits and often inviting them to spend time at their plantation home in Louisiana. During those sojourns, Susan developed special ties of affection with cousin Sarah, who was her same age, and the feelings of sisterhood then established would evolve into more mature bonds of gender solidarity and mutual support during adulthood. The Gibsons also owned a magnificent house in Lexington, where they used to spend the summertime visiting with family and friends, and it was precisely from that location that, in mid-July 1842, Tobias informed his sister-in-law that he had been able to employ one Mr. Meriaux "to give lessons in French" to his own daughter Sarah and Susan as well, and urged Virginia to "let her come at once." The two girls would receive, in addition, instruction in English, music, and dancing.[16]

Although reluctant, Susan had to leave. Once in Lexington again, she wrote her mother several times, asking insistently when she would come visit, while Mr. Burns—her tutor—kept repeating to her that mother had "a god [*sic*] deal of business to attend to," and would certainly come see her whenever possible. Susan immensely enjoyed the study of French under Mr. Meriaux, so much so that, when in October she was enrolled in Mrs. Mentelle's school—the same as Mary Todd Lincoln attended—she remarked to her mother that, although the other disciplines were taught to her satisfaction, she was not happy with the teaching of French, which she deemed inferior to that imparted by Mr. Meriaux. We don't know whether dissatisfaction about the instruction she was receiving at Mrs. Mentelle's school or Virginia's realizing that her daughter needed to see her more often caused the girl's withdrawal from the Lexington school and her enrollment in the Danville Female Institute (DFI)—which was much closer to home. Be that as it may, Susan Shelby graduated from DFI on March 20, 1845, at age fifteen.[17]

The year Susan completed the first cycle of her studies was a transition toward the affirmation of the principle that girls were entitled to equal education with boys. This idea, which had been circulating for at least a decade previous, became explicit only in 1847, with the vast reform program launched by Dr. Robert J. Breckinridge as superintendent of public education.[18]

Although women were still barred from attending university, from the late 1840s increasing numbers of young women began to question not only the haphazard and largely incomplete instruction that the members of their sex received compared with boys, but also its quality. The curricula of the vast majority of female academies, in fact, featured only subjects of study that were considered "appropriate" for young ladies. They usually included English, French, poetry, music, dancing, drawing, plus elements of history and geography, supplemented by a sprinkle of elementary arithmetic. In an era in which the role of the mother as the first educator was increasingly insisted upon as crucial in molding the character of her offspring, the above disciplines were deemed sufficient to prepare a girl to perform at best the role of a housewife and a mother, under the prevalent philosophy that postulated domesticity as the true dimension through which women could fulfill their feminine nature.[19]

We have been reminded, time and again, that the affirmation of the "cult of domesticity," with its assumption of the existence of a "natural" vocation for women and men to operate within the bounds of their respective "separate spheres," was a consequence of the emergence of a modern middle class. The tenets of this philosophy, however, were rooted in a long-standing belief that females' intellect was inferior to that of males. With few exceptions, until the 1820s the majority of southern upper- and upper-middle-class mothers subscribed to the view that their own sex was not possessed of the attributes of determination and steady concentration that were indispensable to successfully complete a long and challenging curriculum of studies. Frances Respess, a member of the Corlis-Respess family of merchants/entrepreneurs of Providence, Rhode Island, who had migrated to Kentucky in the early 1810s and settled in Bourbon County, was one of them. In an 1816 letter to her daughter Evelina, who was attending school in Lexington, Frances dispensed every possible kind of advice to make sure that she fully understood the nature and extent of her commitment. While admitting that the neglect of female education was to be regretted by the "thinking part of society," she could not conceal her opinion that "females in general lack that perseverance which is all important in obtaining a useful education."[20]

Elizabeth Gamble Wirt, the wife of Virginia lawyer, judge, and sometime US attorney general William Wirt, took for granted that their daughters should receive only the formal education traditionally contemplated for elite girls. In 1820 she encouraged her oldest child, seventeen-year-old Laura, to abandon her studies for "finery and housewifery" to prepare for "courtship and marriage" but, apparently, with poor results. On the same assumption, in 1827 Elizabeth Wirt withdrew her three younger girls from school and, her priority being to secure good matches for each and all of them, "acted as the girls' social director," occasionally hosting sumptuous receptions either in the capital and, later, in Baltimore, to offer them the best opportunities to find a suitable husband.[21]

Despite the emotional difficulties involved by separation from her mother, three years in school away from home not only afforded Susan Shelby a whole world of learning, the importance of which she came to value, but it also made her more independent from her mother. As a result, in the summer of 1845 she wished to join cousin Sarah Gibson in going to Philadelphia to attend a very exclusive French school run by Mr. Charles Picot, who was, by the way, a staunch believer in equal rights for Blacks and women alike. Virginia gladly yielded to her daughter's desideratum, and, in October, Susan was in the City of Brotherly Love. As Anya Jabour convincingly contended, southern girls were aware of the many trials soon awaiting them as housewives and mothers and therefore relished every bit of the carefree time they enjoyed during the school years. They made the most of it by developing a "counterculture of resistance" to early marriage, which they perceived as a sort of "civil death." So did Susan Shelby and her cousin Sarah Gibson, who were not, however, haunted by such an impending fate. In fact, both Virginia and the Gibsons placed a premium on female education over early marriage and left the two girls free to decide whether, where, and for how long to continue their formal instruction.[22]

During her sojourn in Philadelphia, Susan entertained what became a voluminous correspondence with several relatives, and an especially significant one with her beloved brother Isaac. His letters contained not only general information on family, friends, and life in Lincoln and Boyle Counties but often pushed into a more intimate realm. In one letter Isaac limited himself to ironically reporting that "The good people of Danville continue at their old trades that is some getting married and some dying," but in another missive, written at a time when their mother was away in Louisiana, he disclosed to Susan his innermost feelings: "You cant [*sic*] tell how lonesome I am when I am here [at Traveller's Rest] from college. . . . I wish you were here to keep me in good spirits."[23]

It was precisely from one of Isaac's letters that, in March 1846, Susan was appraised of "that change which is a little whispered of about but which has kept the mind of all both black and white in a very uneasy state for some time past." The change in question was the likelihood that, after fifteen years of widowhood, their mother might remarry, her suitor being none other than cousin Robert J. Breckinridge![24]

A son of US senator John Breckinridge and of Mary Hopkins Cabell, Robert had in 1823 married Ann Sophonisba (Sophy) Preston, daughter of Francis Preston of Abingdon, Virginia. She was therefore a cousin to Susan Grigsby. The couple had eleven children, the last of whom had been born in September 1844, but, only three months later, forty-one-year-old Sophy had died in Baltimore after a short but painful illness, possibly of a postpartum nature, leaving Robert a widower with a remarkably large family. Although he had been offered the pastorate of the Second Presbyterian Church of Lexington—which would have enabled him to remain close to his children—Robert preferred to take the presidency of Jefferson College in Canonsburg, Pennsylvania. In view of his moving, he entrusted the care of his offspring to several different relatives, and cousin Virginia H. Shelby took with her sixteen-year-old Mary. Such an arrangement necessarily put Virginia and Robert in a closer epistolary contact than had been the case previously, thus providing them with the opportunity to get to know each other better. At that time, Virginia was only thirty-seven, and her children were all entering young adulthood. After so many years of self-sacrifice, she probably felt the desire to have a new companion who might relieve her of the cares that had preoccupied her in the days of her youth. Robert, too, was ready to start a new, important emotional relationship, and, almost inevitably, the two fell in love with each other.[25]

Susan, who had attached no particular meaning either to her mother's engaging way of speaking of cousin Breckinridge in her correspondence or to both Robert and his daughter Mary's frequent letters, was aghast. Although Isaac enthused that "Mr. Breckinridge is a man whom I like very much," that theirs "would be a very equal match," and that he did not consider the acquisition of new brothers and sisters "a complication or a problem," Susan's uneasiness was increased by Isaac's candid conclusion. "I don't think," he wrote, "that I could respect him as a *father*."[26] Why so? Was Isaac's statement the emotional reaction of an eighteen-year-old who revolted at the idea of his mother forming a new matrimonial alliance that would have unavoidably distracted her attention from himself and his two siblings? Did it stem from his feeling that, at his age, the authority represented by the natural father was irreplaceable? Or, did Isaac's reservations spring from knowledge of Breckinridge's ill-tempered personality? A man of refined culture and an inspired social reformer, he was indeed one of the most brilliant minds of his time. These qualities were offset, however, by a strong-willed and at times irascible temperament that often made him intractable. In sum, Robert, at times generous and tender, could suddenly turn inflexible, and even vindictive. These traits probably led Isaac to think that Breckinridge was not a good choice for a woman who, frankly, was in the position to pick the finest apple from the basket.

Although remote, the possibility that Isaac's concerns may have included financial considerations cannot be completely discarded. With the new wedding, Virginia would have brought her own substances in dower to her husband, and the eventual birth of children of their own would have further reduced the inheritance accruing to those from her first marriage.

Be that as it may, the prospect of their striking a matrimonial alliance was looked upon with deep suspicion by Virginia's kin. Her sisters wondered why in the world a well-to-do lady who enjoyed social prestige, economic independence, and freedom of movement wanted to immolate the remainder of her youth in the upbringing of many stepchildren and expose herself again to the physical dangers and psychological strains connected with childbearing. Sister Letitia Wallace, in particular, warned her: "if you don't come soon, you will be so tied down with that troup [*sic*] of children, you will be constrained to take leave of every thing like liberty, and *I am* sure of happiness too. You had better think well before you act. It is easier to keep your head out of the water, than to get it out once in."[27]

Alarmed by the unfavorable reports she was receiving from every quarter, Susan could not resist the impulse to personally ascertain her mother's feelings and firmness of purpose as well. Toward the end of 1846 she therefore made the difficult resolve to interrupt her studies in Philadelphia and hastily made her way back to Danville. There, she found Virginia in a state of emotional confusion, prey to dark thoughts about Robert's ability to meet her expectations of happiness vis-à-vis the warnings of her siblings. Yet Susan was able to determine that her mother was really in love with Robert, to whom she would address passionate words like: "Oh my Cousin, my Cousin . . . what have I promised you that you *not* promised me. . . . My heart is happy this morning and full of love for my dear, dear Cousin." Robert fully reciprocated her feelings, and, against all advice to the contrary, the two were finally wed in Danville on April 1, 1847.[28]

While Sarah Gibson continued in attendance at Mr. Picot's school until the spring of 1852 (although on and off due to her mother's illness and final demise in February 1851), Susan never returned to Philadelphia to complete her studies. Concern for Virginia's emotional frailty prompted her to remain close to her mother and be of support to her in the challenges that marriage might have in store for her. With both of her brothers out at college, Susan was elated at the idea of living again under the same roof with her mother, and, following the wedding, she removed to her stepfather's house in Lexington, confidently looking for a fresh chapter in life.[29]

Yet Susan did not feel completely comfortable with her new situation and soon began to develop lingering feelings of being a misfit in the Breckinridges' household. So she seized opportunities to travel and visit with relatives and friends across the country. In early February 1848, while she was spending time with some old friends in Memphis, Susan was hastily recalled home by news of her brother Alfred's illness. By mere chance, she got there just in time for the premature birth of her half sister, Virginia Hart Breckinridge, the first of three children her mother would bear to Robert. In light of her emotional vulnerability, Virginia's early parturition may have been provoked by extreme distress about her son Alfred's infirmity, the precise nature of which is not revealed by the sources. In announcing to Tobias Gibson the happy event of his daughter's birth, Robert Breckinridge only cursorily mentioned: "Alfred continues without any perceptable [*sic*] change and I am not without anxiety still, concerning the issue of the case; though . . . the chances are in his favor." Intimations that Alfred's health would have greatly benefited from a sojourn somewhere in the Caribbean, a choice destination for wealthy southerners affected by lung diseases, suggest, however, that his condition may have been of that character. This inference is also supported by knowledge that pulmonary illnesses exacted a heavy toll among the Harts. Louisiana Hart Gibson would die of consumption in Havana in 1851, and Claude, one of her children, succumbed to the same disease in 1863. A younger one, McKinley, also battled consumption in the Civil War years.[30]

Largely on account of uncle William Voorhies's family business connections, Cuba was soon selected as the safest place for seventeen-year-old Alfred. In the hope that "the trip may be of great service to [his] health," Voorhies immediately alerted his brother in New Orleans of Alfred's imminent arrival, asking him to provide his nephew with all the necessary information and to "procure letters from merchants who have [correspondents] in the area." Whether Alfred's health benefited or not from sojourn in Cuba will never be known, for he perished in the shipwreck of the steamer *Crescent City* in the Gulf of Mexico on December 2, 1848, probably on his way back to the United States for the holiday season. His untimely passing in such a tragic circumstance threw Virginia and Susan into a state of unspeakable prostration. Yet that was not the end of their ordeal for, only twenty-two days later, on Christmas Eve, Isaac also died suddenly.[31] December was not a lucky month indeed for the Shelbys of Traveller's Rest. Just like their father in 1832, sixteen years later both of his sons, Isaac and Alfred, passed away that same month.[32]

The loss of both of her dear brothers was devastating for eighteen-year-old Susan. Although their demise left her the sole heiress of the fortunes of the Shelbys of Traveller's Rest, it also meant that the branch of the family to which she belonged, and of which she was so proud, had been reduced and would not bring direct descendants. With her mother remarried, Susan may have experienced a sense of loss of family identity and been led to reflect on the role she was called to perform as the only surviving custodian of the family heritage embodied by Traveller's Rest. Because of her minority age, however, Susan had to content herself with her present situation, and she found consolation in helping her mother with the care of baby Virginia and her several half siblings. Although on occasion she would attend one of the many events that a culturally and socially refined town like Lexington had to offer—from theater to concerts, to balls, and to receptions—Susan often preferred the company of a good book over that of pampered girls about her own age, whose main occupation was to fish for a wealthy, good-looking husband. A liberal education had in fact made her overly aware that, for a woman, marriage was a source of never-ending trouble and physical suffering. Like scores of young ladies her age across the South, she was therefore inclined to postpone matrimony as long as possible and was therefore reluctant to commit herself to any of her suitors. So she graciously but firmly checked their exuberance, as she did with W. C. Anderson of Danville, whose courtship she politely declined in July 1849, intimating that they were too young "to form a matrimonial alliance." Despite Anderson's rejoining that the seriousness of his intentions and the depth of his feelings constituted a solid premise to start a liaison, Susan had already made up her mind not to accept any further attentions from Mr. Anderson. Most assuredly, her rejection of Anderson's proposition was not determined by a firm attitude of opposition to early marriage, such as she may have developed during the school years in Philadelphia but, rather, by her not being emotionally involved with him. In fact, when she finally fell in love, Susan Shelby did not hesitate to set aside dreams of personal independence; complying with traditional expectations, she married when she was only twenty.[33]

Love at First Sight

During 1849 Susan Shelby was probably beginning to feel the desire to form a family of her own, but she honestly thought that the nature of her feelings toward Mr. Anderson was not conducive to the realization of a happy matrimonial union. In other words, she believed that romantic love was indispensable to establish an equal partnership purported by the ideal of companionate marriage, which, from the early 1800s, had increasingly supplanted the patriarchal model of male hegemony and female submission.[34]

Perhaps unwittingly, her animus was fertile ground, and, to her surprise, destiny presented her with the right opportunity sooner than she may have wanted. In early 1850, while she was spending vacation time with the Gibsons in Louisiana, Susan met John Warren Grigsby, a handsome and fascinating Virginian twelve years her senior. The son of Joseph Grigsby and Mary Ashley Warren Scott—a niece of Gen. Winfield Scott—in 1837 Grigsby had secured a law degree from the prestigious William and Mary College. Shortly after, he had been admitted to the Virginia bar and had practiced law until 1839, when he had obtained an appointment as US consul in Bordeaux, France, and had resided there for the following ten years. Upon his return to the United States, in 1849, Grigsby had formed a law partnership with one Colonel Davis of South Carolina, and, in the winter of 1850, he happened to be in New Orleans on a business trip. When he and Susan met, it was "love at first sight." Their parting, in Louisiana, was replete with pledges of mutual dedication and promises to stay in close epistolary touch, in the expectation that they would soon be reunited. During her journey back home, Susan could not contain her excitement, and as she landed in Portland, she wrote her mother that she had "a *great* deal to tell her," for she had had "the most *indescribably* [happy] visit" she had ever enjoyed there.[35]

Early on, Susan and John began to exchange romantic letters. In May, from White Sulphur Springs, where he was spending a period of treatment for his chronic respiratory problems, John reiterated his passionate love to his belle: "Be careful for your own and for my sake for, dearest, you are all to me, I love you with my whole being, Susan. . . . How I wish to live for you to love you . . . and cherish you and to endeavour to render you happy. . . . I will try always to be worthy of your love and shall love you always."[36]

News of Susan being so desperately in love with John Grigsby, and of her intention to marry him, raised a big fuss among relatives. Not a small number of them looked at the match with suspicion, fearing that, despite his brilliant diplomatic career, Grigsby might be a dowry-hunter. In fact, nothing was known about either his financial circumstances or his family in Virginia. Although the most sincerely devoted among her kin endeavored to sound optimistic, they all secretly prayed that Susan might wake up from her dream-like state and see the folly of her proposition. As the date appointed for the wedding drew closer and closer, cousin Letitia H. Vance wrote her: "I have heard that Mr. Grigsby was in Lexington and have been expecting the fulfilment of your promise to bring him down to see us. I have heard all sorts of stories about your being so desperately in love, it would be a curiosity to me, to see you in that state, come and let me see how you look."[37]

In the beginning, the possibility of Susan marrying Grigsby was not welcomed by her mother either, but she finally agreed to the wedding, having become persuaded of the sincerity and depth of their mutual love, and considering the importance of her consent as far as her daughter's dowry was concerned. Because Susan was still "an infant" before the law, she also had to obtain the permission of her guardian, Evan Shelby, who granted it and, on November 5, 1850, underwrote an agreement with John Grigsby to that effect. The following day the nuptials were officially celebrated in Lexington.[38]

Whether real impediments or disapprobation prevented John H. Todd, Mary C. Shelby—two of Susan's closest cousins—and other relatives from attending the ceremony, the tone of their apologies betrayed their discomfort with the idea of participating. Protesting the "near approach of the circuit court," John Todd expressed his regret not to have "the pleasure of an acquaintance with Mr. Grigsby." His attempt to dispel doubts of personal reservations, in light of the rumors circulating about Grigsby, was rather awkward. "He is doubtless the man . . . you think he is," Todd wrote, "for I have so much confidence in your taste and judgement, that I know he cannot be otherwise." Lamenting protracted infirmity, Mary Shelby apologized for her inability to attend the wedding and sent excuses also on behalf of a couple of other kin. She betrayed her true feelings, however, by sardonically adding: "when I see you again you will be married, and I expect so much interested in *another* you cannot take the same interest in your old friend."[39]

Virginia's ill-concealed uneasiness about her daughter's marriage exposed her flank to unmerciful comments on the part of family members. Writing from Steubenville, Kentucky, where she was in school, a mere fortnight after the wedding, cousin Susan Wallace conveyed to the bride the belief that hers "must be a case of love at first sight," for she could not see "how it could be otherwise." Then, rather maliciously, she went on, asking, "Has Virginia's love for Mr. G. increased, or does she still love him a pound of cream candy?"[40]

In spite of all criticism, over the years John Grigsby won the regard of his mother-in-law and of many of his wife's kin as well. Yet he remained surrounded by an aura of mystery, for none of his relatives had attended the wedding, and, except for his brother James, who finally paid a visit sometime toward the end of the 1850s, no one else ever showed up. Nor did John ever take his wife to Virginia to meet the rest of his family. Susan, therefore, had to always content herself with sparse correspondence with some of her in-laws.[41]

Back to Traveller's Rest

A few months after their wedding, the Grigsbys were off to Europe, John having been appointed attaché to the American legation in Paris. During their fourteen months on the Continent, they traveled extensively, and their first son, Alfred, was born in Florence, Italy, in October 1851. For Susan, the European period was like an extended honeymoon, only saddened by awareness that such a status could not continue forever. Although cousin Susan Wallace encouraged her to think that the happiness she was enjoying might "be increased ten fold in time to come," Susan was fundamentally correct in anticipating that her *real* life as a married woman would be much different.[42]

Yet, if not completely ready, she was eager to go back to her home country, and when the Grigsbys finally returned in mid-June 1852, Susan wanted her newly formed family to take residence at the Shelbys' ancestral home she had inherited. John consented. Having been neglected for the previous five years or so, the house was in a terrible state of decay, but Susan gladly undertook the imposing feat of refurbishing and embellishing its interior. Her dream to reinstitute Traveller's Rest in its past splendor clashed, however, with a number of objective circumstances she had not contemplated and did not seem to acknowledge. Unlike her mother, who, once widowed, had courageously adopted a proactive, forward-looking approach to life, Susan remained enthralled with an idealized vision of the family past, which she thought she could resurrect. Such a backward-looking attitude both cost her severe disappointment and led to errors of judgment. For example, she refused to take notice of the further decline in importance that Traveller's Rest had undergone in the community with its long desertion following her mother's remarriage, her two siblings' demise, and, lastly, her own absence in Europe.

While Susan had expected that her resettling at Traveller's Rest would have been warmly welcomed by the best society of Boyle and Lincoln Counties, the Grigsbys' arrival received only a frigid response, and, much to her dismay, two years later they were still largely excluded from local social life. Embittered and at the same time angered, Susan commented to her mother, "as far as I am concerned, my preference would be to decline every invitation given us on account of other persons for I think some little hospitality has been due to Mr. Grigsby as a stranger and I, the daughter [granddaughter?] of an old and admired citizen." Her chagrin escalated whenever she discovered that some relatives or friends who happened to be in the area had not paid a visit, or even taken the pains to send a note of apology. Maybe the sort of quarantine to which she and her husband were subjected was connected with the still-strong prejudice attached to her mate. Regardless, the snubbing incensed Susan enough to bring her to conclude, "we cannot expect much better behavior of persons who are innately vulgar and low-bred."[43]

Susan Grigsby also had to confront the reality that, over the years, Danville had largely remained that "dull, uninteresting little place" her late brother Isaac had described back in 1846. It could not, therefore, offer the variety of fashionable articles and supplies she had been used to accessing in the capitals of Europe and the expert craftsmanship she needed to renovate her house. Yet the advent of the railroad era made a big difference, allowing her to procure whatever she wanted either directly from Lexington or from Louisville in a reasonably short time.[44]

With the Grigsbys settling at Traveller's Rest, the intimate relationship between Susan and her mother was further strengthened. Although they visited when they could, pregnancy and motherhood often intervened. While Virginia was busy with the care of her children, health problems connected with pregnancy and the nursing of her own babies often impeded Susan from traveling even the little distance to Lexington.[45]

Shortly after her return to the United States with her husband and son, Alfred, Susan gave birth to Susan Shelby (1852) and, during the 1850s, to three more children: Mary Ashley Shelby (1855), Virginia Shelby (1856), and Hart Preston (1859). She was therefore almost uninterruptedly encumbered with pregnancies, confinements, and nursing. As was common in the South, Susan and her mother satisfied themselves in an almost daily exchange of notes, which were delivered back and forth by trustworthy enslaved Black servants along with goods and gifts of different descriptions.[46]

Given their frequency, these messages didn't even carry the indication of the year, rarely that of the month, most of the times reporting only the day of the week or, at best, the day of the month. It is therefore extremely difficult to organize them chronologically, but reference to a specific situation or event—such as a pregnancy or the birth of a new baby—allows us to formulate reasonable guesses in a good number of instances. Nevertheless, this correspondence is an inestimable source of information on the ordinary lives of both Susan and her mother, and extremely valuable in providing insights on their personalities, feelings, and attitudes on a variety of subjects, from the more frivolous to the most serious.

They illuminate, for example, Susan's sense of extreme loneliness, often bordering on despair, and how her mood was aggravated by illness, which made her perceive the always looming danger of death as all the more impending. This fear was amplified manifold in the presence of any real threat. When a major epidemic of cholera ravaged the Danville area in the mid-1850s, making "good many deaths," Susan wrote her mother, "we are kept anxious & uneasy regarding the cholera, for there are so many deaths recurring in the neighborhood that we feel our time is yet to come."[47]

While cholera spared the Grigsby household, not so erysipelas. Being itself of an epidemic nature, this infectious disease was not lethal but aggressive, for it progressively spread a rash across the affected body, becoming chronic. Both Susan and one of her little daughters became infected with erysipelas. No specific remedy existed for that affliction, though patients were administered calomel and epicea, two medicines that, in those times, were multipurpose and therefore of uncertain efficacy. Seeing their poor results on her own body, Susan was distressed and, sometime between 1855 and 1856, lamented to her mother: "I am tired of trying medicines. . . . [E]rysipelas which is in my arms & feet very badly at present . . . is so deeply rooted in my whole system that no medicinal treatment can eradicate it."[48]

Susan Grigsby's health was also undermined by circulatory problems—which made her legs sore and swollen—asthma, and dyspepsia. Compounded by the occasional insurgence of a cough, backache, or ear pain, these ailments made her miserable much of the time, her mood melancholic, and her personality depressed at the idea that infirmity was preventing her from dispatching her many household obligations in the proper manner. Poor health often confined Susan to her bedroom for long periods, enhancing her sense of inadequacy, especially when John was away, during which times she was supposed to manage their large estate as well as the household.[49]

Childbearing was a physically debilitating, often devastating, and at times even fatal experience in antebellum America, and southern women were more frequently exposed to the attendant risks, if for no other reason than that they usually bore more children than their northern counterparts. According to the 1850 census, one southern white woman in twenty-five died in childbirth, which represented twice the maternal mortality rate in the North. And even if a woman survived, she often had to battle with the long-term consequences of childbirth. Depending on the circumstances, a woman might remain in bed for weeks and even months, afflicted by fevers, chills, headaches, and severe pains of many descriptions. Many southern women thought of confinement as a dreadful experience, and, given the high incidence of infant mortality, their anxieties were exacerbated by fear of losing their newborn. No wonder that increasing numbers of them tended to postpone marriage as long as possible with the aim of limiting the risks of pregnancies.[50]

Louisa S. McCord, daughter of the South Carolina judge and politician Langdon Cheves, and a prestigious writer of essays and books on southern political economy and the position of women in its context, was one of them. Having witnessed her mother's health decline with each new pregnancy, the total number of which amounted to fourteen, she delayed marrying until the age of thirty, reportedly from concern about the consequences of childbearing. Other women who married in their early twenties, however, were able to limit the number of their pregnancies to only a few, as Susan's cousin Sarah Gibson did.[51]

Despite her "modern" education, Susan was not perhaps possessed of the same feminist spirit animating her cousin Sarah. But even if she had been, that aspiration was powerfully overridden by her strong emotional attachment to an idealized marriage and the procreation of many children—to fulfill dynastic duty. While she trusted that romantic love could provide her with a way to make married life bearable, Susan was aware of the disagreeable aspects that the life of a plantation mistress entailed, such as loneliness.

On Christmas Day of 1853, perhaps heartened by the momentary break she was enjoying from the physical inconveniences that had marred her second pregnancy, she wrote her mother a very accommodating, yet fundamentally sad letter. Despite "the wretched day so cold & windy," urgent business matters had forced John to leave home, and, because of his susceptibility to respiratory diseases, she was much worried about his health. Cousin Adaline had left for her Tennessee home a few days earlier, leaving Susan to tend her two children alone so that she could not go to church even on such an important religious holiday. Nevertheless, she reassured her mother that she felt "quite contented," finding in "reading, writing & the babies . . . inexhaustible sources of enjoyment."[52]

As the years went by, however, Susan resented her husband's absences more and more acutely. Sometime in the mid-1850s, when she was probably pregnant with either her third or fourth child, she lamented, "I look for my dear husband tomorrow and I will feel lost if he doesn't come for I am not only lonely but so much more timid than I need to be that I have scarcely slept since he left."[53]

The two close pregnancies of the mid-1850s put such a strain on Susan's body as to significantly undermine her already scarce self-reliance. Too weak almost to leave her bedroom, she felt completely powerless, and she would write her mother desperate lines such as, "I wish you were with me for I am truly lonely when Mr. Grigsby is absent," and, "I am lonely and very unhappy. . . . I will be closely confined at home all summer and doubt whether I will be farther from home than Danville for a year or more," and, "This is one of the lonesomest [*sic*] places on earth and except for being within a day's ride of you [Lexington] I would as soon be in Africa."[54]

Apparently, John Grigsby's absences were not only extremely frequent but could also be of considerable length. On a Monday, sometime between 1856 and 1857, he had set out for Lexington, where he was supposed to remain several days and then proceed to New York to join the 110 heads of cattle he had forwarded there the previous week. Furthermore, he intended to take the opportunity of his being in the East to stop over in Virginia on his way back home to see his kin and old friends. This planned extension of his trip added to Susan's uneasiness, for it exacerbated her chagrin and embarrassment about John's continued failure to have her meet his family. So, in communicating the news to her mother, she only laconically stated, "I fear that Mr. Grigsby will be absent several months as he contemplates spending some time amongst his relations and friends in Virginia."[55]

Although he never declared himself opposed to such an encounter in principle, John procrastinated, from time to time blaming business commitments for his inability to arrange a meeting. This inexplicable attitude on matters concerning his family constantly puzzled Susan, but she never dared address the subject in less than respectful terms, thus showing both trust in him and a fundamentally hierarchical vision of partners within marriage. Maybe his strange behavior was caused by altercations or disagreements within his family of which she was not aware, but Susan did not seem to care, and perhaps did not even want to know. All she sought was the establishment of "normal" family relations.

Over the years, Susan entertained a sparse correspondence with some of John's kin, namely with his sister, unmarried brother, and uncle. Although their letters to her were always very tender and affectionate, at some point she started to develop the suspicion that they might think that she herself was the source of the failure to meet. Her forbearance reached a limit in 1857, when, at the news of his mother's death, John left for Virginia without taking her along. Deeming this a real affront, Susan finally summoned the courage to fully disclose her inner feelings to him, although in writing. Thus far, she argued, "his little disposition to see or visit them" had often stopped her from broaching the subject, but she wondered whether her children "will grow up under the impression that their father never had a relation." Unable to find answers for her husband's quite strange behavior, Susan gushed: "whether your kinspeople are *rich* or *poor* or *fashionable* or *ostentatious is not a concern,*" her only wish being "to be allied to a *respectable* family." She then implored John to take her with him on his next visit. "*I do not wish,*" she wrote, "your family to think harshly of me—but on the contrary would like to prove to them, even at the eleventh hour, that I am not a proud, heartless creature."[56]

Finally, sometime toward the end of the 1850s, John's brother James paid them a visit. Afterward, he and Susan corresponded, but John persisted in never taking his wife to Virginia to meet the rest of his family. Susan's inability to ever obtain from her husband a frank, openhearted explanation for his odd behavior signaled indeed the shipwrecking of the dream of companionate marriage she had passionately pursued for years. Perhaps to compensate for this failure, she sought refuge in the gratifications she could draw from the material comforts of life that defined her social status.

Trying to Lead the Good Life

Wealth afforded Susan Grigsby the possibility of purchasing even very expensive items, following the lifestyle she had become accustomed to in Europe.

Although not more pronounced, her buying habits were, however, probably more varied and sophisticated than those of her many of well-to-do neighbors in the Danville area.

Early upon her resettling at Traveller's Rest, Susan's intense enthusiasm for the refurbishing of the mansion was evident: she immediately asked her mother to send from Lexington some pieces of furniture belonging to her, among which was her "day chair," along with some personal items—a "Leghorn" hat and a "blue silk" bonnet she had left behind. Her expectations of a busy social life included the hosting of dinners and receptions, and, in this connection, she completely relied on her mother's advice on how best to make her dining room reflect her social standing. "How many pieces of silver," she once inquired, "you think I ought to have to my service? . . . My pitchers I admire exceedingly and like all my silver alike, but if you think differently, that it would be handsomer and more durable perfectly plain I will act accordingly." Early on, she manifested the wish to have "a pair of curtains for the dining room of handsome muslin." Creating the perfect atmosphere in an elegant dining room also required the use of scents like "vanilla, lemon, orange, rose & c.," which she requested "in large quantities," and of spices such as "nutmeg and cinnamon," to accompany the serving of sophisticated foods.[57]

Between 1853 and 1854, when Susan's hopes of entertaining were still high, she begged her mother to send her enslaved servant Becky to "Long's" and get her six pounds of macaroni. Between 1854 and 1855 her orders included more olive oil from the usual merchant, "6 or 8 lbs. of good cheese for macaroni," and "the nicest pickles," for she was expecting company at her table. On a different occasion, she asked for lemons, fresh oysters, oranges, and celery to be sent over from Lexington. On still another instance, she requested "1 doz. champagne glasses (rounded glasses) and 5 lbs. of parmesan cheese." All of the above were definitely upper-class supplies during the 1850s. Quite surprisingly, celery also was considered a special delicacy on the tables of wealthy Americans and, even in the Northeast, continued to be deemed so until the end of the nineteenth century. This fact further confirms how sophisticated the demand for goods could be even in a remote corner of mid-1850s Kentucky. Wrongly thought to be far behind in cultural and social refinement by northeastern standards, the Danville area could in fact access all of them through Lexington, thanks to the new railroad. Susan did not deny herself any little caprice, either, such as that of owning a French-style "coffee dripper" like the one she had seen at aunt Mary Voorhies's and, in that regard, was very positive in directing her mother: "If Bassitt [Bassett?] has not one perhaps he could order one from Louisville."[58]

After the birth of daughter Virginia, in 1856, Susan Grigsby slowly entered a period of respite from the physical discomforts of pregnancy and confinement. Eager to enjoy the pleasures of social life, she therefore enthusiastically resumed the refurbishing of her mansion in view of future receptions. Major cleaning, and the fixing of the parlor were paramount among her priorities, but she also engaged painters and plasterers to work at the back gallery. At least cousin-and-stepfather Robert Breckinridge and Aunt and Uncle Voorhies paid visits.[59]

From the mid-1850s, reduced family finances forced Susan to scale down her purchases and become judicious in her spending. This unpleasant circumstance was the consequence of an initially promising, but in the long run unsuccessful, investment in Chicago real estate that John had underwritten in 1853 as a partner in the Lexington banking firm Taylor, Shelby & Co. Initial expectations of high profits, however, had given way, little by little, to skepticism about it ever yielding any returns whatsoever. Seeing her husband increasingly worried and harassed about the unfortunate eventuality, Susan begged her mother to help persuade him "to sell his interest in the Chicago venture." John, however, was inflexible in refusing to do so, thus asserting once more his full autonomy in making important decisions affecting the family.[60]

Such a critical situation prompted Susan to be very selective in her buys according to cost/destination considerations, and even careful in everyday purchases. She therefore began to scrupulously compare local prices with those commanded on the Lexington market, which, as a larger one, might offer goods at competitive prices. Sometime between 1855 and 1856, being "in much need of sugar and coffee and finding the prices so high in Danville," she asked her mother to send them over from Lexington, along with information about prices for ham, lard, soap, and butter there. These latter requests seem to suggest that provisions that were normally manufactured in rural households were not produced on the Grigsbys' farm or, if they were, not in quantities sufficient to satisfy their needs.[61]

Ordinary apparel for her children and husband, and some for herself, for which Susan secured the fabrics from Lexington through her mother, was normally sewn at home or given out to some local seamstress. Sewing was a major and time-consuming chore in every rural household, and the making of garments for family and the enslaved persons as well was indeed a big production at the Grigsbys', requiring the collaboration of some expert seamstress, which Susan sought pretty soon after resettling at Traveller's Rest. This sort of help, however, was not easy to find in rural areas, and, if found, was often at exorbitant fees, so that, when she was finally able to secure the services of one Mrs. Dolbins, Susan complained to her mother that the woman, aware of the crucial importance of her services, definitely knew "how to charge." As an alternative, she also employed one Miss Peckham, who was more reasonably priced, but the woman soon left for Springfield, where she had gotten a good job, leaving Susan with Mrs. Dolbins as her only resource.[62]

As for formal clothing, Mrs. Grigsby usually had her best dresses and cloaks made or renovated in Cincinnati, under the supervision of Mrs. White, her agent's wife. Only at times of greater financial largess did she patronize one of the most fashionable dressmakers in the Northeast. This happened, for example, in early 1859, when both Susan and her mother each had a dress made in Philadelphia by one Miss A. W. Clement.[63]

Susan's resumption of a high-maintenance lifestyle between 1858 and 1859 was probably encouraged by news that the Chicago speculation was finally approaching a happy ending. In late May 1858, she confidently wrote her mother, "My dear husband has had good news from Chicago . . . the sale of 115 acres of ground" for a good price, though most of the money was to be due in instalments during the following two or three years. "I trust from the bottom of my heart," she concluded, "that there may be no mistake about it—as his interest to be received would enable him to pay the most pressing of his private liabilities."[64]

Although the Chicago venture never yielded the returns hoped for, forcing John Grigsby to borrow money to honor his debts, in the second half of 1859 Susan ordered wallpaper from Cincinnati through Mr. White; made purchases in Lexington at "Campbell & Krauss," dealers in carpets, wallpaper, curtains, and cornices; and planned on buying new furniture. All of these expenses seemed excessive and, frankly, unnecessary to Aunt Fishback, who, remarking to her niece that her house already looked quite all right, wondered why she wanted to also purchase furniture at that "particular time." Susan, however, persisted in her buying craze, even after the first effects of the economic crisis triggered by the outbreak of the Civil War began to be felt also in neutral Kentucky. In September 1861, she paid the sum of $7.80 to the Lexington firm "K. Long's" for the purchase of fancy foods such as canned green salmon, ginger preserve, pineapple cheese, and parmesan cheese.[65]

Whether out of incompetence or sheer bad luck, John Grigsby never was a successful businessman, and, at the outbreak of the Civil War, he owed several thousand dollars to a number of people, including Susan's beloved Uncle Will. Despite his continued efforts, he could not steadily guarantee that his wife would enjoy the same comfortable standard of living with which she had grown up, making us wonder how Susan Grigsby could live so expensively vis-à-vis her husband's chronic indebtedness.

Following the death of her two brothers in 1848, Susan had become the only heiress of a vast estate in land and enslaved people. Evan Shelby, her guardian, held them in trust until she reached majority age, by which time, since his niece had already married, he turned her properties over to John Grigsby, her husband. Whether to definitively dispel doubts of his economic interestedness in marrying Susan or to shield her patrimony from any possible, future seizure by creditors, in April 1851 Grigsby reverted to his wife full ownership of her properties, present and future, as well as of their yields, retaining by law only their management and administration. Susan's empowerment was unusual enough that, until 1857, the tax office continued to show John Grigsby's name as the owner of her properties. It took the filing of an additional statement, reiterating his previous deed of conveyance, to have Susan P. Grigsby's name finally appear in the 1858 tax records as the owner of her estate. This notwithstanding, from the early 1850s Susan Grigsby was in a position to dispose of the proceeds derived from her agricultural, stock-raising, and related activities, as well as from the hiring of her bondspeople, according to her own judgment.[66]

Historians' effort to look for explanations of human behavior by venturing into the psychological terrain is often baffling. Even more so is their attempt to understand the inner dynamics of a couple's relationship. Yet the evidence provides some important clues on the unfolding of the Grigsbys' marital rapport. All in all, it illustrates how divergent their respective perceptions of a happy marriage proved to be over the years.

Wholeheartedly devoted to his wife, John Grigsby probably thought that his endeavors to procure her a comfortable lifestyle, even at the cost of indebtedness, amply demonstrated the sincerity of his dedication. Yet deep-seated cultural legacies of male dominance surfaced in him from time to time, causing John to reassert his patriarchal, decision-making prerogatives, thus reproducing the hierarchical pattern of submission/domination that Susan had sought to avoid. This became very evident in the two cases concerning, respectively, relations with John's family in Virginia, and the Chicago real estate speculation. In all probability, Susan considered her husband's independent behaviors as patent illustrations of the failure of the "companionate ideal" in her marriage. Cheated by the cult of romantic love like scores of southern girls of her generation, Susan Grigsby tried to counterbalance the disagreeable aspects of a plantation mistress's life—loneliness, physical discomfort connected with childbearing, hard work, and heavy responsibilities—with the self-gratification accruable from the display of her wealth.[67] The glittering prizes of status were intended to substitute for the unattainable reward of an egalitarian partnership.

3

The Bittersweet Taste of Progress

Susan Grigsby's encounter with modernization was a Janus-faced experience. As suggested by northern scientific household management, she confidently looked to employ white personnel to meet her specific problems. Yet, she was doing so at the moment when Kentucky was modernizing with both new industry and an influx of immigrant workers, which resulted in reshaping the labor market in a more markedly capitalistic way than before.

The entry of larger and larger numbers of white women into the world of labor was accompanied by growing competition between native-born and immigrant white workers. In the field of domestic service, the former responded to the challenge by pushing the idea of professionalism, which implied demands for higher wages than those commanded by the largely unskilled, in contrast to the cheap labor of immigrant counterparts. Precisely because of these characteristics, the latter, and especially the Irish, were simultaneously exerting an impact on the hiring market for the enslaved.

These concomitant developments doubly affected Susan Grigsby. On the one hand, her misunderstanding the expectations emerging among native white domestics was the source of major problems she had with several employees during the 1850s. On the other hand, Susan's quest for an efficiently run household was constantly challenged by her need to compensate for her husband's failing finances. Increasing the income generated by hiring out her enslaved women appeared to Susan as the most immediate answer to her problems, but this happened at a time when the market for enslaved hirelings was becoming more and more depressed by competition from cheap immigrant labor.

To provide a framework for Susan Grigsby's ambivalent, and often contradictory, attitudes as she faced the new reality, this chapter opens with an overview of the economic, social, and cultural transformations that stirred Kentucky in the last decade of the antebellum era.

The Economic and Social Transformations of the 1850s

Slavery posed special problems to southerners in their quest for economic emancipation from the Northeast. Yet, during the last two decades of the antebellum era, Kentuckians tenaciously pursued this goal, multiplying efforts to develop a manufacturing base.[1]

The Bluegrass State successfully responded to the challenge, more than trebling the value of capital invested in manufacturing between 1840 and 1860. Most remarkably, during the 1850s the state reported a decennial increase of 1.7 percent in industrial investment and output as well. Such an impressive record in the southern panorama owed much to the expansion of the iron industry, which, in 1852, earned the state fifth-place ranking in the production of pig iron, and seventh in the manufacture of castings, nationwide.[2]

The 1850s were also "the period of greatest development in river trade and travel." Louisville reaped its advantages fully, winning from one contemporary the appellative of "mistress of commerce of the South."[3] The quickening of trade combined with high rates of population growth and rising per capita incomes to give further impetus to the already thriving manufacturing economy of Jefferson County, which became the core of mechanical industry in the state. According to Richard Deering, the author of an early commercial and manufacturing history of Louisville, in 1859 the city's industrial park boasted seven large foundries and machine shops. Together with a number of factories of regional prominence specializing, respectively, in the production of agricultural machinery and implements, railroad cars, furniture, and paper products, the former group constituted the stepping-stone for the development of a strong manufacturing sector. In 1860, the number of establishments operating in the Falls City, including small enterprises and artisan shops, was estimated at 436.[4]

Although on a much more modest scale than Louisville, the economies of the other two major population centers of Kentucky, Lexington and Frankfort, followed similar trends. Between 1840 and 1860, the latter more than doubled its population to reach 4,000 inhabitants. Merchant firms proliferated in town so that, by the mid-1850s, "the range of goods and services available [there] was considerable." In the same span of time, the number of manufacturing concerns also doubled, not only owing to the expansion of traditional industries such as bagging, flour milling, and distilling, but also to the more recently established cotton and wool manufactures. Most conspicuously, the pork and beef slaughtering and packing business was Franklin County's largest enterprise.[5]

Described in 1831 as a town "in a state of rapid improvement," twenty years later Lexington boasted a wide array of manufacturing establishments. Besides several factories turning out wool cloth, agricultural implements, plows, bagging, ropes, and cigars, they included a furnace, two foundries, three machine shops, an equal number of producers of hardware, nails, stoves, and one boilermaker. Three more factories specialized in the manufacture of sewing machines, among which Grover & Baker enjoyed a regional reputation and tapped even distant markets in the Middle West and Lower South as well. Reportedly, South Carolinian Charles Colcock Jones's daughter, who owned a Grover & Backer sewing machine, extolled this blessing of modernity, which simplified dramatically the laborious and time-consuming task of making clothes, from season to season, for white and Black people alike. Such an innovation produced a true and proper revolution in household work for plantation mistresses. This and other achievements notwithstanding, in the 1850s Lexington surrendered the sceptre of economic primacy to Louisville, retaining for itself the role of the most socially and culturally refined urban center in the state.[6]

Economic prosperity was signaled by a general raising in per capita incomes, which averaged 2.7 percent over the entire period 1840–60, and by a parallel surge in the rate of urbanization, which jumped from 4.5 in 1840 to 11.1 percent in 1860. As suggested by a number of scholars, the impact of the plantation economy fostered the growth of select urban centers in the South rather than the proliferation of smaller ones, as was true in the North. In proportion, southern urbanites lived in cities that were not only bigger than their northern counterparts but, thanks to a larger presence of foreign-born people, also more cosmopolitan. This favored the formation of a modern urban class structure in southern cities, and Louisville was the epitome of this distinctive pattern.[7]

During the 1850s, growing numbers of immigrants flocked to the city from every direction. A good many of them, however, were only "transients," that is, people who either immediately proceeded to their intended, farther destinations or stopped over for various lengths of time before resuming their journey westward. In 1852, Superintendent of the Federal Census James D. B. De Bow estimated those coming in from downriver, only, to be no fewer than fifty thousand per year. Combined with even more sizable arrivals from the Northeast, the phenomenon became so impressive that, in 1857, twenty-four-year-old John Jefferson, son of a wealthy merchant in groceries and dry goods, noted in his diary, "Large masses are constantly passing the city—boatmen, merchants, laborers, mechanics & c. are all in high spirits in expectation of immediate employment."[8]

Allured by prospects of considerable business and job opportunities, many migrants from the Northeast and Europe reached Louisville with the intention to fix their residence, if not in the city proper, at least in its vicinity. Those possessed of some capital engaged in commerce or manufacturing, whereas the propertyless added to the pool of residential workers or, when unable to find employment in the city, fanned out across the state in search of a job, thus contributing to Kentucky's labor markets becoming highly fluid and competitive. In 1850, foreigners figured conspicuously among the 27,000 manual laborers reported by the federal census for the state as a whole. In Louisville, where they constituted almost one-third of the white population of upward of 36,000 persons, the foreign-born were overwhelmingly represented in manual jobs. Thanks to the decisive contribution of immigrants, ten years later the Falls City was the twelfth-largest urban center in the nation, with a total population approaching 70,000 inhabitants.[9]

At the beginning of the 1850s, the Bluegrass State was on the path to a modern economy, and, although the majority of its citizens did not question the compatibility of slavery with economic progress, a few did. One of the most resolute paladins of this idea was Cassius Marcellus Clay—a cousin to the famed statesman Henry Clay. As early as the mid-1840s, Cassius Clay had in fact begun the publication of a journal in Lexington, the *True American,* for the purpose of sensitizing fellow-Kentuckians to the irreconcilability of enslaved labor and modernization. In a similar vein, the *Louisville Examiner* also advocated emancipation but, like the *True American,* did not call for equality for the freedpeople.[10]

Immigrant entrepreneurs usually joined theorists in questioning the possibility of true economic progress for workers alongside slavery. Among the many examples on record, John Irwin Jr.'s is particularly worth detailing, also because of its loose connection with the Hart/Shelby families. A Pennsylvania-born Quaker with a family background in iron-making, young Irwin had migrated to Louisville in 1832 to start an independent iron-manufacturing business. Four years later, having secured the necessary financial backing from William and Mordecai Miller, he founded Nelson Furnace—in the homonymous Kentucky county—in partnership with the Millers, and because of his knowledge of the technicalities of iron making, he also became its manager.[11]

A man of firm antislavery persuasion by religious credo, Irwin intended to recruit highly skilled workers from Pennsylvania and hire local whites for a common workforce. Although aware of the comparative advantage of inexpensive bonded labor, conversations with local people led him to think that the termination of slavery in Kentucky was imminent, thus reinforcing his original determination to use only white labor. His expectations of a profitable iron-making business were stymied not long after, however, by the financial panic of 1837. In that predicament, finding that "labouring [white] men will not move without being paid for it, and then you cant [*sic*] put confidence in them," John Irwin made the momentous decision to hire "negroes to depend on by getting them for a year at a time."[12]

Perhaps reluctant to betray his moral convictions altogether, for the next couple of years Irwin employed a mixed labor force composed of hired bondsmen for two-thirds, and of whites for the remainder. Yet this arrangement failed. Although most of his Black employees were "good boys to labor," Irwin sadly had to admit that the waste of time involved in having a new set of workers to train every year did not make hiring enslaved persons the panacea for which he had hoped. Because the disaffection of his workers—both white and Black—ultimately derived from his inability to pay their wages, Irwin could not help but to conclude that "no iron-manufacturing business could thrive in a slave state that did not own its work force."[13]

Amid the recurrent financial crises of the late 1830s, John Irwin held on until, between late 1840 and 1841, he finally sold his interest in the concern. After what may have been a number of changes in ownership, Nelson Furnace was finally taken over by Richard Alexander, scion of a prestigious family of Scotch ancestry in Kentucky, with a solid background in iron manufacturing in their homeland and an equally strong antipathy for slavery. In partnership with J. B. Patterson, who was also the furnace manager, Richard successfully ran the concern well beyond the Civil War. Richard Alexander was the husband of Susan (Sue) Wallace, a first cousin and dearest friend of Susan Grigsby. Apparently the couple lived at the furnace, for all of Sue's letters to Susan during the period 1859–60 were postmarked "Nelson Furnace." There, Sue had only one enslaved domestic at her service—whether owned or hired—supplemented by a free Black servant. This particular suggests that the Alexanders may have either owned only a few family bondspersons or had none at all. It is not unlikely, however, that, given its continued success, their iron-manufacturing business may have thrived thanks to the use of enslaved labor, either company-owned or the property of one or both of the two partners in the enterprise. If so, Alexander's experience corroborates John Irwin's conclusion that even the staunchest enemies of the peculiar institution among immigrant entrepreneurs finally had to bow before evidence that times were still unprepared for the elimination of enslaved labor from Kentucky's economy, and in particular from the iron industry, the alternative being to give in, as Irwin actually did.[14]

Economic growth benefited not only merchants and manufacturers but also the farmers. The great transformation brought a wave of prosperity to farming counties such as the ones where the Shelbys and the Harts resided and carried on their plantation activities. Access to better and faster transportation allowed planters and stock raisers to widen the markets for their staples and, thanks to the concomitant rise in demand, to increase production. The mercantile classes shared in the bonanza and joined in the farmers' enhanced economic investment in slavery. Six years of recurrent financial downturns (1837–43) had shown Kentuckians that, as iron manufacturer John Irwin sadly concluded, only the ownership of the labor force could shield a business from default in times of financial crisis. The recovered prosperity therefore found fewer and fewer of them inclined to sacrifice their property in human beings on the altar of economic progressivism.[15]

White Women in an Amazingly Diverse World of Labor

In 1850, the wage-earning population of Kentucky was not only extremely diverse in racial, ethnic, and gender composition but also far more numerous than local and national statistics collected at the time suggest. The discrepancy largely stemmed from the inadequate guidelines provided to census takers to reflect the new social and economic realities in all their complexities. On the one hand, short-term hiring practices, high rates of geographic mobility, and patterns of seasonal work migration consigned scores of whites—either native or immigrant—to the "underworld" of the state's laboring population. On the other hand, cultural biases on social self-perceptions contributed to shroud the real occupation of many Kentuckians in a veil of historical invisibility. This was especially true of white women, to whom the unprecedented opportunities for economic emancipation did not come without a good measure of travails and setbacks, making the fruits of progress taste to them sweet and bitter at the same time.[16]

Regardless of their immediate cause, the difficulties white women encountered stemmed invariably from a longtime cultural legacy of female submission and dependence, which the Victorian cult of domesticity had formalized into a full-fledged doctrine of "separate spheres" for males and females. Its discourse was more theoretical than real, however, aiming at delegitimating women's work and undervaluing the pecuniary worth of their labor. As a result, the myriad lower-class women who of course did not stop working could rest assured that they would continue to do so for trifling wages compared to men's. Likewise, women of the middle class seeking personal affirmation through the pursuit of a profession would sadly find their exertions undervalued by low remuneration.

The limitations American society imposed on women's agency in the public realm were stricter in the South, where any attempts to seek agency or autonomy were resisted even more stubbornly. Whatever peak of excellence a southern white woman—whether single, married, or widowed—might achieve in her field of pursuit, she would not receive any public encouragement unless backed by a male relative. Only widows stood fair chances of success as entrepreneurs without incurring social disapprobation, especially if their late husbands' concerns were of major importance, in which case their engagement in business was viewed as a form of self-sacrifice for the benefit of the offspring.[17]

Susan Grigsby might well have known of several successful female entrepreneurs in Kentucky like, for example, Margaret Cawthon in Louisville. After the death of her husband, sometime in the 1830s, she took over the management of his thriving furniture-manufacturing business and expanded it to win state and regional renown. In the mid-1850s, when she retired to private life, Cawthon left to her children an empire in furniture manufacturing. Besides a large chair factory employing fifty hands—the Broadway Mills—which an article in the *Louisville Weekly Courier* described as "not inferior to the Eastern manufactories," and "far better than any . . . in the West," it included a furniture factory located between Ninth and Jefferson Streets.[18]

In her pioneering book on the free women of Petersburg, Virginia, Suzanne Lebsock pointed out that less affluent widows who wanted to continue in their late husbands' business activities, or start a new one altogether (for example as dressmakers or milliners), often sought a second marriage to procure the necessary financial warrant. Middle-class women needing an income faced social disapprobation, especially if married—their engagement in paid work being understood, and tolerated, only as "temporary" and ancillary to their primary role as housewives and housekeepers. It is little wonder, then, if, psychologically oppressed by social conventions, many such women were unwilling to admit to their condition of being wage earners. As Faye Dudden remarked in her critical discussion of census records, when women's occupations began to be listed in 1860, enumerators mostly relied on self-identification, "resulting in large amounts of unrecorded but remunerative women's work." Those who took in work of several descriptions, from sewing to washing to ironing, or boarded people at their premises were not inclined to expose the precariousness of their financial circumstances. By the same token, women who lent their services in the field of housekeeping clung to the qualification of near-peer coadjutors suggested by their traditional, tactful designation as "domestic helps," and refused to be categorized as "servants" altogether. As Dudden concluded, "the census takers didn't ask and women didn't say."[19]

From the 1830s, the ever-growing inflow of immigrants willing to work for trifling wages eroded the bargaining power of native workers, thus upsetting labor markets across the nation. Its disruptive effects were felt most acutely in the South, where whites had derived a measure of steadiness in employment from the tacit affirmation, over time, of separate fields of engagement—or tasks within a single trade—between themselves and the Black people, either free or enslaved. The arrival of Irish immigrants, who were recruited in large pools to work on internal improvements and building construction under short-term contracts, introduced a new dimension of competition in the southern labor market.[20]

By virtue of its geographic location on the Ohio River, Louisville was perhaps, after New Orleans, the second-most-important port of entry in the South for foreign immigrants, among whom the Irish figured significantly. Yet, while Louisiana retained only a small percentage of them within its borders, the high demand for labor generated by Kentucky's ever-expanding economy offered immediate employment opportunities to those who reached Louisville by way of the Ohio River. The number of Irishmen working at Kentucky's internal improvements during the last two decades of the antebellum era must have been impressive considering that, in the fall of 1838, "one thousand Irishmen" were reported to be working at turnpikes and bridges in Nelson County alone.[21]

The Irish were also conspicuously represented in the state's iron industry, where only free status—if quasi-servile—spared them from being lumped in with the enslaved—either hired or company owned—in the hierarchy of labor. The racial composition of the manpower of many ironworks, however, did transcend the mere Black/white dichotomy, featuring, from the 1820s, the growing presence of Chinese. By the early 1850s, the phenomenon could no longer be ignored by the press, and the *Louisville Courier* devoted an article to William Kelly's successful experimentation with Chinese, "who sold themselves for a number of years [as contract laborers]," at his Suwanee Furnace and Union Forge in Lyon County. Reportedly, their docility and diligent work ethic pleased Kelly so much that he contemplated importing more of them. However, this intention on the master's part triggered a strong reaction by Blacks within his workforce, unleashing both interracial tensions among the workers and friction with factory management. This finally led Kelly to put an end to his experiment with Chinese labor.[22]

The abundance of cheap, immigrant labor depressed the wages of native whites in every field of employment. In the mid-1840s, in Paducah and its vicinity, "labouring white men, Irish, Dutch & natives [could] be had in any number at 75 cents to 1 dollar per day and board themselves. Mechanics at 1 dollar & board themselves." These were indeed reduced wages, especially for the South, where they had traditionally been higher than in the North.[23]

Intense competition exacerbated friction among whites, who, in vying for jobs, were pitted against each other by divisions along ethnic lines. Occasional fights, like one in 1840 at the Louisville Galt House between several Irishmen and three native whites—among whom was a tailor—gave way to increasing mobs and riots. By the early 1850s, the city was a powder keg ready to blow. No wonder that, in such an explosive atmosphere, many native whites embraced the nativist credo, paving the way for the electoral successes reported by the American Party. Interethnic clashes among whites climaxed in August 1857, when, on what became sadly known as Bloody Monday, twenty people were killed in a riot between foreigners and the nativist Know-Nothings.[24]

The labor force in Kentucky had more than white and native immigrant workers, of course. Free African American workers also vied for jobs. Because they occupied a gray zone in the hierarchy of labor in a modernizing yet enslaving society, the free people of color were increasingly targeted by mob fury. A tragic incident to this effect occurred in Louisville in May 1857, when an angry crowd of whites dragged out of the jail and summarily "hanged to lampposts about the courthouse" three Blacks who had been acquitted by jury from the charge of murdering a white family—a fourth convict having meantime committed suicide for fear of falling prey to the assailants.[25]

Racial solidarity among whites, however, was undercut by class divisions. Because of its sizable manufacturing and commercial economy, Kentucky constituted the ideal milieu for the development of labor activism in an enslaving state, not only by white and skilled workers but also among some African Americans. For example, in March 1859, 129 white draymen, and a like number of Black draymen paraded together in Louisville to represent their joint demands for higher wages and better living conditions. Although their marching together did not imply the overcoming of racial barriers, the event itself was suggestive of the white draymen's acknowledgment that their Black fellow-workers were entitled to the same improvements they were seeking.[26]

Apparently, some select white women also enjoyed their new empowerment and sought to organize and push back against the conditions of their work. In fact, women figured among the representatives of twenty-two trades who, in August 1853, traveled from all over the South to convene in Frankfort—Kentucky's capital—for the purpose of agreeing upon a common set of requests to present to employers in their respective states. Besides voting unanimously for an up to 25 percent increase in wages, and for the general adoption of the ten-hour workday, they also resolved that the wages of women ought to be raised in the same proportion as men's. Although of little or no immediate consequence, this was an important step forward in the century-long struggle for equal remuneration regardless of gender.[27]

However sporadic, events such as the trade union meeting and the draymen's strike suggest that workers in Kentucky were oppressed by employers as well as empowered to act in their own interests. Hiring and keeping any workers in such a context could prove difficult, but men clearly had more options, and thus more room to protest. Of all free women workers, the unskilled faced enormous difficulties in mounting effective collective action. Despite growing competition by European immigrant labor, native whites had a clear advantage over the native-born women of color. In the needle trades, white women were challenged by free African Americans but also by Asian women. Scottish immigrant D. McNaughton reported in a letter to John Brunton, a merchant tailor back in Edinburgh, that the latter were particularly well represented in the field of men's apparel. "Pantaloons, vests &

summer articles," he wrote his friend, "I believe are here [in Louisville] made entirely by Lady Tailors . . . the female part of human creation, white, black & yellow being all 'Ladies' and 'Ladies of colour [*sic*].'"[28]

Fierce competition dramatically hit native-born white women engaged in the already undervalued and underremunerated sewing trades. This caused many to yield to the allure of a steady, if very modest, income offered by several new garment factories operating in Louisville—of which there were nineteen in 1857. Yet native white seamstresses definitely had an advantage over fellow-workers of color, as they were better able to draw public attention to their appalling poverty. Despite long hours of toil, their wages were well below subsistence level. Encouraged by the protest mounted by their New York sisters, in 1850 the white seamstresses of Louisville collectively denounced their pitiful work and living conditions. Supported by the press, and especially by the *Louisville Weekly Courier,* they were able to obtain a raise, which, although minimal, marked a great victory for them. Joint action could and did offer even the humblest members of the white female laboring class a chance to obtain some measure of positive response from the master classes.[29]

Domestic Work in a Quasi-Modernizing Enslaving Society

Susan Grigsby must have been aware of the labor conflicts stirring Kentucky society, and of white working women's growing empowerment, as she was looking for a white employee to staff her household. The widespread perception that domestic service was "house help" may have induced her to think that this category of work belonged to a field apart. Moreover, its traditional association with enslaved women in the South may also have led her to surmise that only needy white women would apply for a job at the house of an enslaver, women who would therefore not advance any pretenses. These assumptions proved utterly wrong.

The mistress of Traveller's Rest probably missed the critical point that the kind of qualified personnel she sought could be found only among native whites, who, to differentiate themselves from the largely inexperienced immigrants, were pushing the concept of professionalism in their field of employment. Unfortunately, as Susan soon discovered, their demands in terms of remuneration and personal treatment were seldom matched by correspondingly high standards of performance. Considering the mixed feelings that even northerners showed in adjusting to a modern understanding of the employer/employee relationship in the field of domestic service, failure to grasp the change underway in its very nature was complicated for Susan, as for every other Kentucky woman who engaged in the experiment. Difficulties notwithstanding, the demand for all white, including non-native born, domestics soared during the latter part of the antebellum era, with clear effects on the traditional source of domestic labor: the market in hired bondswomen. Commenting on this fact, in early January 1850, the *Louisville Weekly Courier* noted: "White labor is coming quite in vogue here. Numbers of families have made the experiment of hiring German and Irish girls to perform the labor of their households, with . . . most satisfactory results," and anticipated that "it will not be many years before white labor will almost entirely supersede slave labor in Louisville, and the influx of white labouring population is already beginning to be felt on the price of negro hire."[30]

In spite of the increasing encroachment by immigrants, the market for enslaved hirelings in the field of domestic service held on, largely due to the ambivalent attitude of prospective employers. As was often the case, a white domestic might quit her job anytime at her pleasure rather than her mistress's. Conversely, a hired bondswoman guaranteed continuity in service for a full year, unless major complaints were raised either by the lessor or the lessee.[31]

Furthermore, the ability to hire a nonwhite domestic conferred social status for nonenslaving but comfortably well-off families, a privilege that women in that class were not ready to renounce easily. As argued by John Zaborney, this was a powerful factor in sustaining the market for enslaved hirelings in late antebellum Virginia, and the analysis of the *Louisville Weekly Courier* may have held true for Kentucky as a whole. Yet Keith Barton's general contention that access to bonded labor allowed southern women to achieve a domestic ideal does not seem to apply to many upper-class enslaving women, who, at least in the Upper South, were in fact seeking social esteem through the employment of *white* personnel.[32]

The ideal of "domestic refinement" to be achieved through a careful distribution of tasks according to skills, so popular in the cities, was also pursued by plantation mistresses, whose daily lives were far from matching the romantic image of leisure and pleasure that is part of the legend of the Old South. Unlike the wives and daughters of yeoman farmers, access to the labor of the enslaved spared plantation mistresses from performing the most physically exacting chores. Yet they could not avoid physical exertion in quite challenging operations, when necessary, including in the making of butter, which was a traditional activity carried out on farms and plantations.[33] Its churning, a task requiring considerable physical energy, could be performed by an expert Black servant under the close supervision of the house mistress. Sometimes, however, she had to take over the process to ensure its correct completion. Although in the 1850s faster transportation allowed rural, upper-class Kentuckians to procure butter from even relatively distant locations, some of it continued to be manufactured on plantations for household consumption. Susan Grigsby followed in the trend, wisely balancing household production with the purchase of butter on the Lexington market depending on price. The butter manufactured at Traveller's Rest had its fans, among them G. P. Lowitt, a riverboat captain for the Louisville and New Orleans Line of Steamers. In an 1859 letter to Susan, he flattered her: "I should like of all things to have some of your Butter. . . . To get *good* butter is almost impossible, and without it no table is complete."[34]

In an age when the first cookstoves and hand-cranked wringers were still at a very rudimentary stage of technical development—having appeared in American cities only in the 1820s—laundering and cooking were the most onerous daily activities for every plantation household. Cooking on the open fire was not only a dirty and dangerous job, because of the difficulty of handling and moving around heavy iron pots and skillets, but also one requiring a good deal of mastery to avoid foods being either too raw or accidentally burnt. Keeping the kitchen clean, hauling fuel in, removing the ashes, and scraping the fireplace were additionally laborious but indispensable operations. Checking the state of preservation of meats and produce, which, before the advent of the refrigerator were—in the rosiest instances—stored in ice cellars, was of crucial importance. The decay of foods was a major source of gastrointestinal disturbances. The sanitary condition of a kitchen was therefore of special concern to house mistresses, who did not—or refused to—acknowledge that the enslaved servants' failure to maintain standards of cleanliness may not have been due to poor understanding of its importance but, rather, was likely a form of resistance.[35]

The lack of any effective systems of refrigeration necessitated the timely processing of meat and fowl to preserve them for several months. Although pork salting and ham smoking were performed by bondspeople under the watchful supervision of the house mistress, other preparations were most often carried out by the mistress herself, albeit with the aid of some servants. Most of these activities took place between late spring and midsummer, when the plentiful garden and orchard produce needed to be processed quickly for later consumption. Such physically taxing incumbencies did not spare Susan Grigsby, who, on a summer evening of 1855, reported to her mother of being exhausted from having "just gotten through a long, tedious day, preserving, drying & c.," which would have been even more depleting had not been for the precious help of the enslaved servant Rachel in "working with tomatoes & c."[36]

Certain to find a sympathetic ear among female relatives, plantation mistresses would often mention in correspondence the difficulties they encountered in handling major aspects of household production. Lucinda Helm (the mother of Benjamin Hardin Helm, later a brigadier general in the Confederate army and a cousin to Susan Grigsby) in an 1857 letter not only conveyed to her daughter the sense of the psychological strain produced by day-to-day and season-to-season careful planning and subsequent coordination of activities, but she also mentioned the renunciations that these priorities entailed for a "country housekeeper"—as she liked to call herself—such as participation at social events.[37]

April was the month when, in anticipation of the hot season, light garments were to be made up "for white & black" alike. Depending on the number of people to clothe, this undertaking might be enormous, requiring the collaboration of additional hands, usually elderly bondspersons and children, and often the hiring of one or two white women to help, especially with cutting operations. Unfortunately, however, they were not always competent enough to avoid the mistress's direct intervention. Having engaged one Miss Polly for that purpose, Lucinda Helm sadly had to acknowledge that, although she "would do the best she knew how . . . she [could] cut nothing out not even make the waist of a little dress by herself."[38]

Such an imposing seasonal production—added to the routine requirements of a large family—made sewing and mending real nightmares for a plantation mistress. The owner of upward of thirty bondspersons, Susan Grigsby constantly faced worries that she could not complete this very exacting task. On this account, sometime in the mid-1850s she preferred not to go out with one Mrs. Green, in order to have "any winter work all finished before Mr. Grigsby gets back and the servants as well as myself can do much more when alone."[39]

Susan's anxieties grew exponentially with every new pregnancy, as she anticipated long periods of confinement and physical debilitation. In the fall of 1854, when she was expecting her third child, she wrote her mother, "I am making a . . . [illegible] effort to have the principal part of my sewing finished before my confinement." The following year, she reported: "Sarah, Jennie [two enslaved women], Mrs. Dolbins [a white seamstress], Mary [a cousin] and I are all hard at work."[40]

In the attempt to steer herself in the *mare magnum* of household incumbencies, and eager to live up to the expectations usually placed on an accomplished house mistress, the intellectually open-minded and cosmopolitan Susan Grigsby consulted modern theories of housekeeping and child-rearing for inspiration in the solving of her specific problems. Probably like many of her peers in the Upper South, her approach to the issue of hiring white personnel principally revolved around the candidate's background—whether native or immigrant—and her requirements as an employer, without much concern for the impact that the introduction of a white woman might exert on the enslaved Black house servants. This was something she would discover only through direct experience.

Enthusiastic at the prospect, Susan Grigsby had not considered, either, that her ability to hire white domestics did not so much depend on wealth per se as on the disposal of cash for their remuneration. Despite her remarkable holdings in land and enslaved people, budget limitations largely connected with her husband's almost chronic indebtedness forced her to scale back her initial ambitions to have more than one white woman at her service, and, as it turned out, all she could afford in terms of her cash on hand was a maid-of-all-tasks. This was not a job white women took on readily in the rural South. Confronting such limitations, and aware of the near-impossibility of having high standards of performance in several departments of housework united in a single person, Susan had a hard time determining her priorities—whether she mostly needed a nurse, a general housekeeper, or a cook—vis-à-vis her multiple and equally pressing demands.

Within the Grigsby Household: The Political and Moral Economy of Domestic Service

Susan Grigsby's hiring decisions were connected to the complications of how she would pay regular wages. Doing so was wrapped up in a problem many southern enslavers encountered: that of hiring out those enslaved persons whose work skills did not match those needed by their enslavers, nor, perhaps, the expectations of prospective lessees. For Susan, the problem was compounded by the fact that her bondspeople overwhelmingly included children and young adolescents—largely females—who needed training.

When Susan P. Grigsby turned twenty-one, in February 1851, she had already been married for several months. Her guardians—uncles Evan and Thomas Shelby—therefore transferred the legal property of her estate, which also included about forty enslaved persons, to her husband. As we have seen in the previous chapter, probably from desire to dissipate still-lingering suspicions of his financial motivation in marrying Susan, in early April 1851 John Grigsby filed an instrument in writing with the Lincoln County Clerk Office, by which he waived any right to his wife's properties, both personal and real, present and future, and conveyed them in trust to Thomas Shelby for her "sole and separate use and benefit."[41]

Regardless of any knowledge of John's intention, in January Susan had anticipated that, as was customary with plantation mistresses, she would enjoy a good leeway in decisions concerning the hiring out of the family's enslaved persons for domestic or light manual work, and was determined to make good profits from the practice. From France, where she temporarily resided with her husband, who was a member of the American legation in Paris, she had therefore written in this connection J. P. Mitchell, her mother's and her own trustworthy agent. To her questioning whether the annual rates set for the hire of Vicy and Judy (who were aged twenty-six and forty-one, respectively) were not perhaps too low, Mitchell replied in respectful yet firm accents. As he calmly explained to Mrs. Grigsby, in forming his decisions on the subject he had long followed the philosophy of her mother, whose way of managing "her business & her servants" he deeply admired. From Virginia Hart Shelby (now Breckinridge) he had learned that, although putting "the servants on the block in some cases they would hire for higher prices . . . the interest of the Estate would be better preserved & humanity better served by fixing upon the servants full & fair prices & hiring them privately to *reliable persons* who would take good care of them [italics mine]."[42]

Such policy—Mitchell contended—did not, however, conflict with the enslaver's legitimate expectation of good profits, the forty-five dollars per year that either Vicy or Judy yielded being, in fact, above the regional average. Susan ought therefore to be contented with the present arrangements and rest assured that the well-being and "happiness" of the two enslaved persons in question were under his constant monitoring. In this connection, he solicitously informed Mrs. Grigsby of the satisfactory outcome of an investigation he had recently conducted on a controversial case involving Vicy, who was hired out to one Mr. Batterton. Having collected the woman's direct testimony that "her service is not hard" and ascertained that "she looks well is well clad & in every respect well provided for," Mitchell had deemed it safe to renew the contract with Batterton for another year at the rate of forty-five dollars. As for forty-one-year-old Judy, he had thought prudent to hire her to his son-in-law, Dr. Lasley, in the belief that "her service would be light & . . . she would be kindly treated." Once apprised of her mother's philosophy, Susan never departed from the new "golden rule" that it was better to hire out the enslaved to considerate families, if for a little cheaper, than to make more money by leaving them in the hands of harsh people.[43]

John Grigsby's deed of conveyance to Susan, filed from Europe, was either flawed by procedural faults that prevented its application or, more simply, contradicted tradition, which led the tax office to disregard. Be that as it may, for several years afterward, Grigsby continued to appear in the records as the owner of his wife's estate and, consequently, any transaction or contract concerning Susan's properties, including the hiring of bondspersons, had to carry his signature. Given Susan's self-proclaimed sensitivity to the plight of her bondspeople, women and children in particular, one may legitimately wonder how she must have felt about her husband's hiring eight-year-old Mary Jane to one E. D. Peyton, in 1853, for the trifling sum of ten dollars. Regardless of the contract clause requiring that she be treated kindly, and not be sublet without the owner's consent, Mary Jane was only a child and would suffer from the separation from her mother and other familial attachments for what would surely seem to her an interminable year. So far as we can gather from extant sources, Mary Jane was the youngest among the enslaved persons ever hired out by the Grigsbys, suggesting that after that experience, Susan may have set a minimum age limit for children, along with the rule that their prospective situations be carefully selected and closely monitored.[44]

Not until 1858 was John Grigsby's own position vis-à-vis Susan's properties clarified, and he did this by filing a second "instrument in writing" in which he reiterated his 1852 deed of conveyance to her, thus allowing Susan's name to finally show in the tax records. With his financial circumstances at a nadir, we can surmise that he may have been prompted to do so by a desire to protect his wife's estate from any seizures by his own creditors.[45]

Preceded by her mother's reputation as a considerate and compassionate mistress, early upon her resettling at Traveller's Rest in 1852 Susan Grigsby nurtured her own ability to establish mutually trustful relationships with her enslaved domestics and to secure harmony and collaboration in the management of her household. Toward this end, she endeavored to tease out individual skills and inclinations, with a view to achieving the most satisfactory distribution of tasks among them. This was a complex and challenging feat, for many of them were young and inexperienced. By late 1853, however, Susan Grigsby had formed pretty clear opinions of each of them and spotlighted a few as particularly gifted and dependable. Biddie, for example, seemed to be "a sensible industrious woman," and Susan often tasked her with the incessant going back and forth between Traveller's Rest and Lexington, or Danville, to deliver messages to her mother and collect her replies along with supplies and goods. Of all her domestics, however, Jennie was the apple of Susan's eye, being not only "a clean, systematic, industrious servant" but also "resolved to do as well if not better than she has ever done." Jennie was, above all, "really a superior nurse," and Susan had her "wash and dress the children, clean up [her] room," and maintain it in good fashion in the event she needed to keep them in her quarters.[46]

Evolving notions of domesticity induced mistresses to place greater and greater stress on cleanliness and order, and thus become increasingly intolerant of what they would brand as lazy, shiftless, or filthy habits on the part of their enslaved staff, without realizing that these habits might in fact be expressions of rebellion to bondage. Susan Grigsby was oblivious to this possibility. In her opinion, Judy cooked so badly and was so "indescribably dirty" that Susan took "no pleasure in eating slow." Ambrose, as she reported to her mother, "scarcely amount[ed] to a hand and Autry and Betsy [were] perfectly trifling and good for nothing." Even Sarah, on whom Susan had initially placed great hopes, turned out to be "utterly incapable of attending to several kinds of work together," and thus to function as an alter ego to Jennie. In fact, once, when Susan was sick for several days, Sarah "let everything get in such a sad confusion" that Susan didn't know when she would have been able to straighten up the situation. That incident led her to conclude that "it is useless to require of all servants the same amount of work" and, in particular, that "no one could do more than the half Jennie does from week to week without a word being uttered." She therefore decided not to engage Sarah as a nurse anymore, for she was "too harum scarum for her patience," especially after she had let "everything go to sack," so that one morning not a set of clean clothes could be found for little Alfred.[47]

In the evaluation of a domestic bondswoman's performance, Susan Grigsby attached the utmost importance to cleanliness, especially for those who had access to the nursery and other spaces in the house where her infant and small children might spend time—including her own bedroom. Mary apparently lived up to this fundamental requirement, for Susan at some point assigned this enslaved woman to assisting Jennie in that delicate incumbency. She also contemplated recalling home Walker, whom she considered "a very smart boy," at the expiration of his hiring contract, with a view to training him as a kitchen help. After all, she reasoned, "I don't much think I would have to watch him more than anyone else, except Jennie." The most problematic of Susan's enslaved domestics was perhaps Sarah. Unable to determine how to employ her most proficiently, Susan momentarily applied her to "washing & ironing half the week," and planned on having her assist in the training of Walker as a cook. To her surprise, Sarah revealed instead to be well versed in sewing, and, "as she had succeeded so well with the pantaloons," Susan "intend[ed] to try her upon a sack coat."[48]

Despite her great ability at sewing, Sarah was not enough to fulfill the needs of Susan's growing family. Since 1853, Grigsby had found a solid helpmeet in one Mrs. Peckham, an honest and moderately priced garment maker to whom she would put out her "important work." But Peckham also could be summoned to Traveller's Rest when needed. However, sometime in the mid-1850s the woman secured a good job somewhere out of state and left. In the absence of other reliable alternatives, Susan Grigsby's only resort remained Mrs. Dolbins, whom she continued to hire through the 1850s, despite repeated complaints on how "exorbitant" her fees were.[49]

Misled by the exceptionally good work performance of the enslaved Jennie and Mary, Susan Grigsby did not understand, or refused to admit to herself, that the poor behavior of other enslaved servants, which ranged from indolence and carelessness to sabotage, was not the result of innate inadequacies or ignorance. Although deeply disturbed by them, Susan Grigsby joined other plantation mistresses in minimizing occasional acts of rebellion. Misbehavior, if committed by a hireling, commanded instead more serious attention, for a master/mistress's ability to collect their rents was strictly subordinated to the satisfaction of the lessee. Aware of the measure of empowerment the enslaved enjoyed in decisions concerning their own placements in an increasingly complex market for the hiring of bonded labor, masters and mistresses might want to secure their approvals before stipulating a contract. Susan Grigsby avowedly did so in 1857, in a case concerning Sarah.[50]

Insofar as the records reveal, less than a year of daily interaction with her own bondspeople, since she had resettled at Traveller's Rest, was enough to arouse crises of conscience. Susan believed herself to be fundamentally antislavery in her sentiments. In December 1853, having decided to hire out a number of enslaved servants with whom she was not at all satisfied and did not wish to keep around, Susan confronted a major dilemma. Upon hearing of their mistress's intention, the bondswomen in question, who were all "middle aged women" who had never been much hired, and were thus "violently opposed to quitting their old home," implored her in the most harrowing manner not to hire them out. Their prayers threw Susan in a terrible predicament. Should she keep those bondswomen with her and continue to be in "an everlasting fret"? Or, should she stick to her initial intention and carry the moral burden of having separated them from their children and other attachments, both familial and communal, without their consent? Of the two alternatives, Susan Grigsby concluded that she had better have her temper "sharpened" by the challenge rather than destroy "the happiness of three or four poor dependant [*sic*] creatures." This incident brought her to reflect on what the "duty" of a "conscientious" enslaver ought to be, and she so conveyed her conclusions to her mother: "A great number of persons who own slaves," she reasoned, "endeavor to do their duty by them still it is extremely difficult to say *what is our duty,* for each one has a different sensibility on the subject." Although we don't know which specific examples Susan had in mind, we may conjecture that she was thinking of her husband. Apparently a fair master, he had in fact a thoroughly profit-oriented approach to the destination of the family bondspeople.[51]

Despite her moral qualms, problems connected with her family economy prompted Susan to try and maximize the revenue from the hiring practice. She was willing to lease her Black bondspeople also for short periods of time, even by the day. In the attempt to find suitable situations for those to be hired out, she turned to her mother. Accordingly, sometime around the mid-1850s she asked her to see "if Mrs. Montmullen would like to hire Vicy [the young woman previously hired out to Mr. Batterton] and Bonaparte [a young adolescent of thirteen or fourteen]. Vicy for fifty but sixty [dollars] if you can get it and Bonaparte for what you think him worth." In 1857, not having any sewing for Sarah to do, and upon obtaining her consent, Susan decided to "hire her by the day." Virginia H. Breckinridge, on her part, often relied on the inputs offered by Becky, one of her most trustworthy and experienced bondswomen, who, thanks to her introductions with Lexington's enslaved community, had a pulse on which ones the bondspeople themselves deemed the most recommendable families. Appreciative of Becky's judgment, sometime in 1858 Susan begged her mother to let the enslaved woman go to Mrs. Bowman & Cowan, and "see if they will take Nelson [a child about ten years old]. She knows what he can do & could describe him better than anyone else. $15 or 20 for him."[52]

Despite what she thought to be her special attention for the well-being of her bondspeople, financial imperatives and custom prevailed over Susan's moral qualms, for she continued to hire out children and young adolescents of both sexes through the 1850s. Debt over conscience—a dilemma from Jefferson forward—compelled enslavers in the Upper South to bend their own rules to fill their coffers.

Within the Grigsby Household: Black versus White Labor

Susan Grigsby's second pregnancy, in 1852, was marred by poor health. With her physical strength dwindling, and in the anticipation of a long period of confinement, she became more and more doubtful of her own ability to direct and supervise even routine household activities. During those interminably long days of seclusion, the thought of her possibly bearing more children conjured up even more unsettling scenarios for her. Consequently, well before the birth of her daughter Susan Shelby, on December 1, Grigsby made the resolve to look for a white, responsible woman who might act as an alter ego to herself: someone who could manage every department of the household—from general keeping to cooking, to sewing and to the nursery—with constant control. Yet Susan *also* sought a companion, someone who might render her loneliness more bearable during John's long periods of absence from home. Meeting these disparate demands was no mean feat, and certainly a challenge for her mother and aunts who collaborated in the search.

In late January 1853, aunt Letitia Wallace identified in one Mrs. Anderson the person who most closely approached her niece's requirements. An American-born widow with a little boy to raise, the woman needed to find a situation soon, "because the winter is too hard to be unemployed long." On this account, Letitia urged Susan to promptly let her know "whether she will take her & upon what terms, what she wishes her to do." Greatly annoyed at her niece's persistent unresponsiveness, Letitia finally cut it short and advised Susan that, if she intended to consider Mrs. Anderson's candidacy, she had better contact the woman directly. At that point, Susan immediately followed suit, and, shortly after, Anderson was hired primarily as a nurse.[53]

For a couple of years, and at least until after the birth of Susan's third child in February 1855, the arrangement seemed to work fine. Having acquired a competent white nurse, Susan could temporarily dispense with the services of the bondswoman Jennie—whom she hired out along with Benjamin. All seemed to proceed smoothly at the Grigsbys' until, in the summer of 1855, something absolutely bewildering happened to suddenly interrupt the peace that seemed to reign in their household. One day, while she was about to enter her mother's house in Danville, Susan was assailed "in the most insulting low bred manner" by one Miss Burnett, an Englishwoman who resided in Louisville. Burnett declared herself indignant and resentful for the offensive treatment that Mrs. Anderson, "her apparently superior, high-born friend," received at the Grigsbys'. To Susan's legitimate query of what was the source of her information, the woman replied that Anderson herself had frequently written her "that she was more of a slave than anyone of Mrs. Grigsby's fourteen [domestic] negroes and that she earned her living blacking boots & shoes and was even compelled to eat the crumbs which [fell] from [her] table." Astonished and shocked, Susan maintained the aristocratic demeanor becoming to a lady and, upon her return home, reported to Anderson the words uttered by her "truly dignified English friend." Having signified her bitterness for the "very improper manner" in which Anderson had represented her situation despite the ample compensation she received for her services, Susan ended the conversation by advising the woman that, if she thought that of a nurse a job far beneath her, she had better not engage in it again.[54]

Susan conceded that Anderson's caring for a job "solely for mercenary motives" was to be explained by the many hardships she had suffered in life, but she could not excuse the woman for having disparaged Grigsby, and unjustly spoken of the treatment she received at her hands. It is plausible, however, to surmise that Anderson's complaints may have sprung from disappointment at having been repeatedly applied to tasks that had nothing to do with her competencies and duties as a nurse. Apparently these were too menial for Anderson to perform without feeling wounded in her professional dignity. This conjecture hints at Susan's difficulty in understanding the new concept of "professionalism" in the field of domestic service. Be that as it may, her animus strongly suggested that Mrs. Anderson would be immediately laid off, but the idea of being left alone with three children to tend, two of whom were infants, prompted Susan to follow a conciliatory course. Knowing of Anderson's reluctance to undertake the journey to New York—where she was headed—in the hot summer weather, Grigsby was able to preserve her dignity by magnanimously allowing the woman to stay on until temperatures had dropped enough to make travel bearable for herself and her little son Freddy. In the meantime, Virginia Breckinridge and some of her sisters began to look around for a replacement but apparently with no success. When Anderson finally set out on a Thursday morning in the early fall of 1855, escorted by her "virago friend—Miss Burnett," Susan still prayed "simply to get a girl who can nurse the babe [Mary Ashley] through the day & wash & dress the older children," someone who might stay with her as long as possible.[55]

In the winter of 1855–56, with the search not yet yielding any good result, Susan began to fret about the further difficulties she was to confront in the months ahead on account of her pregnancy. Resigned to face the worst, she wrote her mother: "Don't be uneasy about me but I have determined to let the house and kitchen take care of themselves." Early on, the pressing necessity to secure some kind of white help brought her to hire one Mrs. Queen. This experience proved to be a total failure, however, making Susan feel "very much wounded," and regretful of having been too rushed in taking in that woman, considering "the confusion & filth that reigned sovereign in her house" by the time Mrs. Queen left. Not long after her discharge, the Grigsbys hired one Mrs. Jones for a nurse. Although Susan deemed her "a very proper old woman [who] knows her place," past disappointments with white personnel prompted John to urge his wife to check her enthusiasm and not to spoil her too much before assessing her character and competencies. He therefore exhorted Susan "to treat her kindly but not by any means as a companion," such as she was inclined to do with white employees. John's invitation to cautiousness revealed to be well-grounded, for Mrs. Jones turned out to be not "at all competent to perform such duties as always required of nurses," to say nothing of her complaint that she could not manage Susie, Mary Ashley, and Virginia at the same time. Mrs. Jones's departure from the Grigsby household, on March 1, 1856, confirmed Susan in the opinion that "not many American women in that sphere . . . know what their duty is, although they are especially tenacious of their own rights."

Despite the long series of disastrous experiences with American-born white domestics, Susan Grigsby apparently did not resign herself to the idea that, in a capitalist market economy, labor relations eschewed implications of personal attachment between employer and employee even in the elusive domain of domestic service. In this vein, she wrote her mother, "I wish . . . that I had a quiet respectable woman staying with me who would attend to the children & house—for I have never been in such a predicament before."[56]

Much of Susan's difficulty in securing competent white help was accountable to the reluctance of the most professional women in the field to consider employment in remote areas of the countryside, given that they could find work in the cities. Virginia H. Breckinridge had at least one experience similar to her daughters'. In the summer of 1855, she was unsuccessfully seeking someone to look after her aging mother, her efforts being constantly stymied by the unwillingness of prospective candidates to remove far away from town. At some point, one Miss Margaret Quinton applied for the job and, although she declared herself unhappy with the idea of leaving the city, was nonetheless well-disposed to take it upon certain conditions. First, she was to "be treated with the highest respect due to a free born American," and not in the capacity of a servant. She therefore expected to eat at the table with the family, as she had always done in the homes where she had worked before. Second, but definitely prejudicial, her remuneration was to be liberal enough to compensate for the sacrifice, "the amount of money [Mr. Breckinridge] will give . . . and as much as he can give for money [being] the object."[57]

The fast-paced demands of Kentucky's growing economy in the 1850s allowed less qualified, but pretentious fellow-workers to carve a space for themselves in the labor market. In late 1856, Susan Grigsby was willing to pay even upward of a hundred dollars for a white woman, "provided she would accommodate herself to the requirements that [she] might feel inclined to make of such person." In fact, she wanted someone who would "do up [her] sewing—attend the house—& if necessary take charge of the children." Such demands were latitudinarian enough to intimidate more than one applicant, but not Mrs. Meyers, who, in an interview with Susan, "said she would be willing to do any thing." The woman did not sound very competent, but Susan hired her, regardless. Quite predictably, Mrs. Meyers's performance turned out to be a flop for, sometime between late 1857 and early 1858, Susan sent her mother the following laconic note: "Would you be so kind as to send Mrs. Meyers what I owe her for the time she has been with me."[58]

As a reaction to this umpteenth failure with white personnel, Susan resolved to revert to the exclusive use of her Black domestics' services. Whether this decision was made upon realization that those negative experiences were, at least partly, due to the tensions arising between each new white woman she hired and the enslaved house servants is only conjecture. Be that as it may, Grigsby came to conclude that the most competent and dependable among her bondswomen—Jennie, Mary, and Sarah—could be put in charge of the several departments of ordinary household work: general cleanliness, the kitchen, the nursery, and the care of the older children. Besides, they could train and supervise younger enslaved servants. Although aspiring to the criteria of flexibility and substitutability for scientific household management, this arrangement proved precarious. Any illness or even the occasional unwellness of one of the three most experienced enslaved women easily introduced havoc into the household.[59]

It did not take long for Susan to reconsider the wisdom of her recent decision, and return to cherish the presence of a white woman in her house. With the lessons learned from so many negative past experiences firmly in mind, this time she was determined to "wait very patiently" until the candidate who really matched her desiderata came to hand. Accordingly, she turned down the application of an Irish woman who, although willing to do any kind of work, did not meet the requisites in full, including in her being Catholic. This was perhaps the first instance in which religion openly figured as a discriminating factor in shaping Susan's hiring decisions—a theme that would recur later on.[60]

Having formed clearer and clearer ideas on the profile of her ideal white help, in spring 1858 Susan asked her mother to put an advertisement for her in the *Lexington Observer*—as many used to do—to the effect that she was looking for "a steady respectable middle aged woman" to whom she could "trust the children." With the advertisement not yet having produced any feedback, Susan was in a difficult predicament in the fall of 1858, for she was expecting her fifth child. In early March 1859, Aunt Fishback wrote her about one Mrs. Federici—a woman of Latin, perhaps Italian origin?—who proposed to stay with the Grigsbys a month to see whether each party was satisfied with the arrangement, and "to say nothing about compensation until then." The skills she claimed to be possessed of, as well as her willingness to perform the multiple tasks required by Susan, boded well for the successful conclusion of a deal. Whether Mrs. Federici ever took service at the Grigsbys is only a subject of speculation, for no further reference to her appears in family correspondence. What we know with certainty is that, although with various results, from 1858 Susan never retreated again from the determination to have a white woman on staff.[61]

Susan's many failures with white labor reveal more than unpreparedness to handle relations with free employees under the terms of a capitalist, free-labor market economy. Her proclivity to treat American-born white dependents as members of the household suggests not so much lack of understanding of the influence that Kentucky's rapidly changing economy and demography exerted on the domain of domestic service but, rather, insistence on the belief that only an old-fashioned blend of mutual trust and collaboration could answer her special needs. Susan, in fact, basically looked for a companion who might not only help her cope with the material problems of everyday life but, most of all, provide succor for her own boundless solitude. Confronted with the essentially income- and benefit-oriented approach of the several white women she employed during the 1850s, Susan Grigsby blamed the cultural and social gulf separating her from them for the repeated failures. Class and legal status heavily biased Susan's confused inner search for gender solidarity.

4

Bonds of Womanhood

The transformations Kentucky underwent during the mid-nineteenth century were accompanied by similarly striking changes for women. In the era of shifting gender ideologies and religious awakening, new ideals pertaining to domesticity and morality altered the terrain within which women like Susan Grigsby and her mother navigated choices regarding households, children, and their communities.

For Susan, the uncertainties focused on her mother's marital difficulties, her own inability to find a trustworthy white servant whom she could afford, and how to resist the corrosive aspects of enslaving others, even as her husband brought the family further and further into debt. Susan Grigsby's mostly disastrous experiences with white domestics illuminate her contribution to their invariable dismissals.

The new sense of awareness that was developing among native-born white Americans of the importance of defending the moral values of their communities and their common Protestant heritage, up against the encroachment of papism brought in by immigrants, affected Susan Grigsby's attitudes and decisions in two delicate and closely intertwined areas: the rearing of children and the hiring of white domestics. As a result, Susan became increasingly selective in the evaluation of candidates, especially on matters of religious faith. This approach undercut Susan's chances to develop feelings of sisterhood and gender solidarity with white women of differing classes and ethnic backgrounds.

Repeated failures with white domestic staff reinforced her sense of class pride and superiority. Not surprisingly, when she finally identified the person whose requisites fully matched her desiderata, the woman in question was an Anglo, with an education and a middle-class background.

Evangelical Protestantism, with its racist overtones, also constituted a major obstacle to Susan's feeble attempts to understand the plight of bondswomen, and to truly sympathize with them. When she was confronted with cases of miscegenation, and when facing the sale of an enslaved woman, Susan Grigsby's role as a compassionate, benevolent mistress crumbled under pressure. Her ability to hold onto her moral compass disintegrated into pieces, and she ended up by at least formally acquiescing to the tenets of the prevailing enslaving culture.

My Dear Mother . . . Whom I Almost Worship

As predicted by Letitia Wallace, wealth alone could not guarantee her sister Virginia's happiness in her new matrimonial union.[1] Yet even the most discouraging of the scenarios she conjured up paled in comparison with the series of family tragedies and the psychological hardships that Virginia actually endured during her first four years of marriage to Robert J. Breckinridge.

Although physically taxing, having to handle Robert's large family while she was bearing their first child was amply rewarded by the joy brought by the birth of little Virginia Hart, in February 1848. The baby, however, survived less than a month, leaving both mother and father prostrate with grief. Only the arrival of a new child could possibly mitigate their intense sorrow, and, much to their contentedness, this happened very soon. In the fall of 1848 Virginia was pregnant again and recovered her good spirits. But in December a tragedy of major proportions befell her: the death of both of her sons by her first marriage—Isaac and Alfred Shelby. The shock from these further losses added to Virginia's long-lingering nervous frailty and threw her into a state of deep emotional unbalance. Shaken by the close sequence of so many sad and fateful events, Robert was unable to avoid tension with his wife. On account of their equally strong personalities, frictions degenerated into an endless series of recriminations, which made their marriage a stormy one.[2]

The birth of two more children between July 1849 (Nathaniel Hart) and September 1850 (John Robert) predisposed Virginia to look at her matrimonial crisis in a conciliatory manner. In an attempt to rework the frayed pieces of her marriage, in 1850 she engaged Robert in an ambitious project—the building of a magnificent mansion in the very heart of Lexington, on Broadway Street. Her intention was to seal their renewed alliance, and to prove the seriousness of her commitment by offering to contribute four thousand dollars—a little over half of the estimated total cost—toward this undertaking. By this arrangement, the property of the new residence would be vested in them jointly, and Breckinridge was apparently persuaded to go along with the plan. Begun in 1850, the city home took five years to complete. However, during the protracted construction process, the loss of their second child in 1852 rekindled old wounds so that, when the new mansion was finally ready for occupancy in mid-1855, their relationship again had deteriorated precipitously. Further, unable to collect the monies promised by his wife toward the cost of their new home—which consisted in notes by her brothers—Breckinridge felt cheated by her failure to meet this obligation.[3]

During their frequent altercations, Virginia became increasingly aggressive and litigious. Her outbursts of verbal violence being "apparently connected . . . in many forms & for many years" with the subject of property. On such occasions, she would also openly convey to Robert that, having "lost all affection" for him, it was her wish to split up. Despite his repeated attempts to appease her, and the efforts made by close friends and relatives to convince her of the foolishness and destructiveness of her course, Virginia could not be swayed. In 1854 she made the final decision "that she should not live with [Robert] *as a wife* [italics mine]" anymore. Although no explicit reference to the issue of reproduction was ever made, Virginia's attitude may have been also a desperate desire to avoid further pregnancies—in an age when abstinence was the only effective and even acceptable form of birth control. Be that as it may, she entrusted John Grigsby, her son-in-law and a lawyer, with the unpleasant task of representing her in an interview with her husband, to define the details of their legal separation. The meeting took place in late September 1856 at the office of Major John C. Breckinridge, a nephew of Robert's who, after four years of service in the US House of Representatives, had recently resumed law practice in Lexington.[4]

Assuming that his role would have been limited to the discussion of the financial aspects of separation (mainly dispositions on property and inheritance), Grigsby agreed. However, he was totally discomforted by the more intimate nature of Robert's complaints. "I have been abandoned by my wife without cause," he lamented, and "not knowing the reasons why she wants this separation, I consider myself the injured part [*sic*]." As Breckinridge maintained, the present demand was the most extreme of requests by his wife in "twenty such previous cases." In the past, he had always abstained from exerting any pressure on her, making clear that he would never separate from her and, "if she [saw] fit to *return to her duty* [italics mine]," he would "receive her as [he] had done twenty times before." This time, however, Virginia insisted in her determination for a permanent split, and he demanded that she sign a statement to the effect that "this separation is her act, and the concession I make, is subject to revocation by me, if any time, her conduct should in my opinion, render my further proceedings necessary." To make his position unequivocal, Robert Breckinridge concluded by stating that, once gone into effect, eventual separation would have been irreversible.[5]

How could two bright and resourceful individuals like Virginia and Robert, whose matrimonial union had been based on such sincere attachment and affection—not on social or economic advantage—become so mutually destructive? While their respective characters and personal histories may undoubtedly provide important clues about the aberrant dynamic that triggered their bitterness and animosities, the answer probably lies in a complex combination of factors.[6]

Although Robert admired Virginia's strong-willed and independent personality, which was so similar to his own, he shared attitudes similar to his male contemporaries, championing a husband's authority, even within the most equal of unions. Therefore, he could not tolerate his wife's extreme stubbornness and her challenging his decisions beyond what he found acceptable. Virginia, for her part, had been accustomed to exerting freedom of agency during her long widowhood and could not conceive of bowing to her husband's will on a matter of crucial importance, particularly the distribution of property among heirs.

In light of her substantial wealth, and in consideration of the fact that the couple had by then only one surviving child, in 1854 Robert thought it fair to bequeath most of his holdings (excepting for the properties he meant to will to his wife, and which she would be free to bequeath to her descendants as she saw fit) the entire rest of his estate to his eight children from his first marriage. Virginia Breckinridge deemed such a decision as discriminatory, and detrimental to their only surviving child, John Robert.[7]

To assert the equal right to inheritance by her offspring, twenty years earlier Virginia had waged an extenuating but finally successful legal war against her first husband's testamentary executors. Although still combative by the mid-1850s, she was no longer the rational, sharp woman she had formerly been. Circumstances had increasingly undermined her nervous system, making it harder and harder for her to control her emotions and respond to unsettling situations in a balanced manner. Two people like Virginia and Robert, equally possessed of a strong ego, ended up waging a nerve-racking psychological battle. Nothing can describe the sense of mutual estrangement and betrayal that developed between them better than their own words. In the conclusion of his "memorandum" on legal separation, Robert wrote: "God only, knows what I have endured for this unhappy & deluded woman—what a blessing she might have been to me, to my family & to her own—and how much she has done to make every thing a wreck." Virginia, on her part, prayed: "May God . . . enable him to see & to acknowledge to *Him* the cruel injustice he has done one who has loved him with true affection—and whose heart is still capable of the deepest, the most fervent love for her once tender but embittered and estranged Husband."[8]

Hinging upon issues of authority, companionship, and decision-making—especially insofar as any offspring were concerned—the major tensions that unfolded between them probably expressed larger shifts in marriage going on at midcentury. Although this was a long and tortuous process, by the late antebellum era ideas of "mutuality and egalitarianism" in marriage had made definite headway in Kentucky, and the law responded to change by allowing divorce, if only for "loss of affection." This was precisely Virginia's motivation in asking for legal separation, and Robert verbatim reported it in his separation memorandum. Virginia had, however, underestimated the negative impact that her demand would have exerted on the public profile of a prominent man with high social visibility. Robert numbered himself as a member of a tightly knit, conformist elite within Kentucky. He would never have consented to a separation unless on terms that favored him over her.[9]

Thanks to the good offices of a Dr. Young, her physician and devoted friend, Virginia finally became persuaded that legal separation would disadvantage her only, and she desisted from pursuing that course further. Although frictions between Robert and Virginia persisted, the Breckinridges resumed the appearance of a normal married life, while in practice Virginia spent much of her time at her house in Danville. How long this seemingly viable arrangement would have continued is hard to tell, for sometime in 1858 she developed a heart condition—perhaps angina, likely associated with her nervous fragility. The disease progressed, and she was dead in less than a year.[10]

At the sight of her dear mother stricken by disease and laid low in such a miserable state, Susan was "heart broken & crushed with sorrow." Despite reassurances that people with her condition might still survive for years, she sensed that the end was very near for Virginia. In anticipation of that, on April 3, 1859, she wrote aunt Letitia Wallace urging her to come as soon as possible if she wanted to see her sister alive for a last time. However, the impending birth of a grandchild by daughter Sue Alexander forced Letitia to postpone her trip to Danville by ten days or so. Despite the delay, she probably managed to bid farewell to her sister, for Virginia Hart Breckinridge died on May 8 at the relatively young age of fifty.[11]

The death of her mother meant to Susan the loss of her most precious confidant, her psychological mooring, and, no less significant to her, the only surviving member of her family of origin. The woman whose very existence and loving presence had helped her tolerate the sense of loneliness that permeated her life was no more. However terrible, Virginia Shelby Breckinridge's demise forced Susan to learn how to walk on her own two feet and take an important leap forward by acquiring a measure of self-reliance, which would soon be invaluable to her in confronting the many challenges the Civil War era had in store for her.

Mrs. Drummond . . . and Beyond

Virginia H. Breckinridge's demise coincided with one of several critical moments (either physically and psychologically) that punctuated Susan's married life: a new pregnancy. Although nothing could reduce her grief for her recent loss, she found some consolation in the thought of a new baby adding to the family, which reinforced her faith in Divine Providence. The Lord takes, and the Lord gives. With her deeply religious perspective, Susan may also have interpreted the arrival of Jane Drummond at that particularly delicate time in her life as a gift from God.

In late July 1859, when Mrs. Drummond reached the Grigsby residence, "highly recommended" as a white servant by a plethora of relatives, Susan would have just given birth to her fifth child (Hart Preston) or would have been about to do so. Everybody placed great hopes in Jane's ability to provide the kind of relief Susan had cherished and required for almost a decade. Congratulating their niece on the felicitous birth of Hart, Aunt Fishback and the Voorhies family expressed warmest wishes that Drummond might reveal herself to be the very person they had heard represented. From Crab Orchard, where he was trying to alleviate his chronic respiratory problems, on August 5 John Grigsby wrote his wife, "I hope you have found all the comforts in Mrs. Drummond that we both anticipated and that the dear children have become affectionate to her."[12]

Very little is known about Jane Drummond's background except that she was a Jamaican by birth whose family had at some time removed to the United States—possibly as part of the slow but steady out-migration of whites from the island following the abolition of slavery, in 1834.[13] Assumedly people of some means in Jamaica, Drummond's parents had been able to provide their daughter with a good education. But they may have suffered a major reduction in their fortunes—most probably losing real estate—upon leaving the island and had therefore resettled in Trenton, New Jersey, as a family of modest circumstances. Necessity had therefore compelled Jane to seek an income-generating occupation, to support herself and her elderly parents. By the time she entered service at the Grigsbys', she was thirty-six, and her being referred to as "Mrs. Drummond" suggests that she might have been a widow. This hypothesis may explain the difficulty in identifying any candidates for her parents' household in the population schedules of the 1860 federal census for Trenton, New Jersey.[14]

A woman of refined education and exquisite manners, Drummond soon proved to be the person Susan had always hoped to have around herself and her children. Alfred and Susie, who were aged eight and seven respectively, badly needed instruction, and Drummond gladly agreed to be their governess. At the same time, she seemed to be the person with whom Susan could trust all of her children in case she needed to leave home. An opportunity to test her dependability came soon, when in late October 1859, Susan had to spend several days in Lexington—probably in connection with the settlement of her late mother's estate. During her absence, Jane kept Susan constantly posted on how things were going at home. On the last day of the month, she wrote Mrs. Grigsby, "The children are quite well, take lessons each day, and are behaving nicely." This was enough to convince Susan that Drummond was the perfect coadjutor.[15]

The two women soon established an entente and a satisfying sense of companionship that promised to be long-lasting. Yet, much to their mutual disappointment, in June 1860 news of her father's severe illness forced Jane to make a hasty return to Trenton. Although it was hoped that her absence would be only temporary, her departure caused much desolation for every member of the family. Susan hated the idea that Mrs. Drummond might not be able to return to Traveller's Rest in time for the birth of her next baby—who was due sometime between late November and early December. The children had developed a strong attachment to their mother's genteel and sensitive employee, and they marked the departure of dear "Drummie"—as they had affectionately nicknamed her—as a near-tragedy.

Although unavoidable, separation from the Grigsby family appeared painful for Jane as well. Upon reaching Trenton, by mid-July, she immediately wrote Susan a sweet letter in which she conveyed her attachment to the children and how "lost" she felt "without them around." Not long after, she asked Susan to send a "likeness" of them, which she received toward mid-August and proudly showed to her mother. Reciprocating this affection, little Susie wrote dear "Drummie" a very tender letter.[16]

Unfortunately, the bad health of both of her parents prevented Jane Drummond from returning to Kentucky anytime soon. She could not be of much support to the Grigsbys in mourning Lilie Shelby, who died in late December 1860 after only twenty-five days of life. Nor could she help Susan with the nursing of her next "dear little babe," Letitia Wallace, who was born in late November the following year. The hazards of southbound travel connected with the onset of the Civil War, coupled with pressing financial needs, further postponed Drummond's return to Traveller's Rest.

Although Mrs. Drummond was virtually irreplaceable, Susan needed a replacement. Increasing debilitation and the physical ailments produced by three close consecutive pregnancies between 1859 and 1861 induced Grigsby to look elsewhere for the white helpmeet she required. As many times before, cousin Sue Alexander and Aunt Fishback took over the search. In August 1860, the application of an Irish girl named Mary Cosland was turned down on account of her Catholic faith, which might create problems in the cultural and religious training of the children, especially the older ones. Early on, one Miss Ann, a stout and strong eighteen-year-old girl, "used to hard work in the country," was also rejected. Despite her multitasking credentials, which spanned from sewing to cinder washing, and to the care of children, Ann's most appreciable quality was that of being "an American and Protestant," Sue suggested. Otherwise, she would "do just what a negro would only cleaner and better." Aunt Fishback, for her part, presented the candidacy of one Mrs. Judy Milburn, who, although not a professional nurse, was equipped with good references, and urged her niece to consider her application seriously, for "professed nurses are all so constantly rugged they wont leave home to get so far off." For some reason, this woman was not hired either.[17]

As a result of the scarcity of suitable candidates, by late March 1861 Susan Grigsby was still in want of a steady, white domestic servant. The young daughter of a sick and needy woman recommended by cousin Sue Alexander was unlikely to satisfy her, but by mid-August Susan was considering the application of eighteen-year-old Ottelia Liljebech for a position as a general servant. The girl's polite and unassuming approach, and her smooth writing style suggested that she had some education, and, in fact, Miss Liljebech had just completed her curriculum of studies in a Cincinnati school. Long accustomed to dealing with pretentious yet incompetent women, Susan was favorably impressed by the modesty with which Liljebech described her skills and insufficiencies. "I do not doubt my ability to keep in order and even make the children's plain garments, but would not undertake to cut and make outer garments," the young woman candidly admitted. Also, "I do not venture to say that I could superintend your household affairs to your satisfaction, but with kind instruction from [you] and initiation into your ways and wishes, I should hope soon to gain sufficient knowledge." Had it not been for "some particulars" concerning her physical appearance, Susan might have been seriously tempted to employ Miss Liljebech, regardless of her inexperience. By self-admission, Ottelia was in fact "slightly lame," one of her limbs being shorter than the other, thus requiring the use of "a cork soled shoe." Furthermore, she had "a purple tinge on one cheek" which, "although perfectly harmless," was not pleasant to look at. Doubting that her children could ever develop an attachment for such a disfigured woman in an age when physical disability was looked upon with both pity and embarrassment, Susan finally decided not to hire the hapless Miss Liljebech.[18]

Despite the gravity of the circumstances that prevented Jane Drummond from returning to Kentucky, Susan Grigsby nurtured hopes that a miracle might return this savior to her until, in January 1862, it became crystal clear that this would not happen. "I shall be here," Jane sadly wrote Susan, "as I have applied for a situation in a family who reside in Trenton." Drummond begged Susan to send back the two letters of recommendation she had handed her at the time she was hired, along with a third one signed by herself and Mr. Grigsby. Calling each other "*Friend,*" the two women kept corresponding during the war years, always cherishing the hope of being reunited.[19]

With her model being the idolized Mrs. Drummond, Susan had scant chance of finding a white domestic whose profile could compare. In June 1862 a Cincinnati friend, Mrs. White, reported contact with a French woman, aged fifty-five, who was available to take up service at the Grigsbys. Misunderstandings arose, however, between Susan's rather vague description of her requirements and current definitions of tasks for domestic employees in Ohio—a free state—making it hard for Mrs. White to carry on successful negotiations. Vis-à-vis Susan's demand for "a *general* servant," her friend pointed out that, in Cincinnati, that appellation implied that she would be the only servant in the house. That was not of course the case with Mrs. Grigsby, who had several enslaved domestics at hand. Mrs. White therefore invited Susan to speedily let her know "*what* will be required of the French woman . . . whether it is a chamber girl, cook, or washer-woman." Her unwillingness to take charge of the children was probably decisive in leading Susan to discard this umpteenth opportunity.[20]

This incident illuminates how slavery impinged upon the agreed-upon standards for modern labor relations in neighboring states like Ohio and Kentucky. Although domestic service was becoming increasingly professionalized in the free states, Susan Grigsby continued her search for a versatile white servant who could be a jill-of-all-trades: a housekeeper, a governess, a nurse, and a companion in a home where slave labor could not be eliminated. The new challenges brought about by the Civil War coming to Kentucky, and the personal trials Susan confronted during these war years, combined to revolutionize her perspective and make Susan Grigsby's quest for the perfect white female servant utterly irrelevant.

Reluctant Enslavers

Scores of diaries and letters written by plantation mistresses—the bulk of which remain unpublished—suggest that many of these women generally despised slavery and wished to see it terminated. This attitude rarely stemmed from antipathy to enslaving and antislavery sympathy but, rather, from white women's callous attitudes toward African Americans. Most particularly, much aversion to the peculiar institution has been ascribed to the scabrous reality of miscegenation, which, not infrequently, involved the male members of their own families.[21] Often rage and venom was unleashed against enslaved women who were coerced and victimized by white predators rather than against the predators themselves.

As Thavolia Glymph has amply documented, plantation mistresses often poured out their fury and frustrations, believing themselves to be victims at the mercy of the southern patriarchal order. Many white mistresses, in the illusory hope of affirming their superiority as members of the ruling class, did not hesitate to resort to physical violence. In this regard, Stephanie Jones-Rogers argued that girls of the planters' class borrowed the culture of violence toward the enslaved from their parents' example, which they tended to imitate. When adults, it was up to them whether to insist in their fathers' style of disciplining bondspeople or to reject it.[22]

Despite their alleged sensitivity to the plight of the enslaved, the shameful culture of violence toward them was not unknown among the enslaving women of Kentucky. Yet it does not appear to have belonged to people who, like Susan Grigsby and her extended family, considered themselves sincere in their antislavery persuasion. Although this dark facet of the condition of an enslaver was hardly ever revealed in writing, both Susan and her mother's overt concern for the physical well-being of their domestic bondspeople, whether those residing with them or those hired out, conveys the impression that they eschewed and condemned physical abuse of them. Although they would not easily admit it, pecuniary interest prompted them to protect the integrity of their investment in human beings. However undesirable they declared their reliance on human bondage, the powerful force of economic interest kept them—and Kentuckians of similar persuasion—enthralled. They remained caught in the moral dilemma of enslaving humans.

Being an enslaver with antislavery feelings undoubtedly sounds like an oxymoron to our modern sensibilities, but in the mid-nineteenth-century Upper South the two could and did coexist in elusive and self-deceiving ways. Widespread proclamation of "hatred" for slavery could be coupled with concern for freedpeople's fate in a racist society. This might prevent masters from manumitting their bondspeople, unless they agreed to leave the country under the aegis of the American Colonization Society (ACS) or some other exiling scheme.

Quite understandably, those enslaved held a completely different point of view on the subject. Because the vast majority of them were third- or fourth-generation Americans, they revolted at the idea of being recolonized. This ambitious project, to send enslaved Blacks back to a distant colony that was not even the place from which their ancestors originated, rarely attracted African American support. As a result, only a small number of enslaved Blacks agreed to remove to Liberia as a precondition for emancipation.[23]

The most intelligent and realistic enslavers who thought themselves sincere in their opposition to human bondage strongly doubted the ACS's ability to provide any effective answer to the problem of slavery in the United

States. Among them was Susan's uncle Tobias Gibson, who, despite his being an extensive enslaver, openly condemned the peculiar institution. He once complained, "I am in conscience opposed to slavery—I don't like it, and the older I get the worse it seems—& to entail it upon my children is not very agreeable to think of." His wife, Louisiana Hart, entertained similar feelings and was a member of the antislavery congregation of the Second Presbyterian Church of Lexington. Their home was therefore one of the few in which southern women might freely discuss their opposition to slavery.[24]

Notwithstanding his theoretically strong antislavery opposition to human bondage, Tobias Gibson reasoned that emancipating his nearly three hundred enslaved persons in a state that recorded the second-lowest ratio of enslaved to free population after South Carolina was mere folly. But the fact that Robert J. Breckinridge, who was in the forefront of the antislavery crusade in Kentucky, never honored his proclaimed intention to liberate his three dozen bondspeople reveals how the decision to emancipate the enslaved was challenging even in an allegedly congenial enslaving state.[25]

The patent contradiction between thought and action on the part of enslaving men made the responses of women of this class even more conflicted. No matter how strong and sincere their opposition to the institution, or how dismissed their concern for the financial losses to be suffered from emancipation might be, their legal position as *femes covert* made women bow to their husbands' primarily economic interest. Cultural prescriptions of subordination to male authority meant that women of the enslaving class, however reluctant, still proved accomplices in the continuation of a system that allowed them to enjoy their elated status and elite lifestyles.[26]

Sometimes sentiments of mutual affection might develop between a white girl and a bondswoman about her age. It was in fact customary for enslavers to present young daughters with a personal bondswoman. The case of the relationship between Frances (Fanny) Thurston Ballard of Louisville and her enslaved servant Cecelia illustrates this important point. On her fifteenth birthday, Fanny, the daughter of Charles W. Thurston, a rope manufacturer with antislavery sentiments, was presented with an enslaved girl named Cecelia, who was one of the few bondspeople her father had retained for domestic service. He had sold his business and all the enslaved men engaged in it. The two girls grew up as sisters and, in their youthful speculations about the future, shared the hope that "slavery would be some day abolished," allowing them to enjoy their friendship on an equal footing.[27]

A widower, in the fall of 1845 Thurston decided to take his daughter on a holiday at Niagara Falls, in upstate New York, and Cecelia was of course in their party. The choice of the season was rather curious, for it was definitely not the most enjoyable for vacationers and, as such, certainly the least crowded with southerners. Because of its location near the border with Canada, the place was known for being constantly patrolled by abolitionists who tried to entice, or simply help, enslaved fugitives to cross the state line. Shortly after the family's arrival, Cecelia was, in fact, punctually contacted by some men who promised to guide her to Canada, and she followed them without any hesitation.[28]

Although the Thurstons would never admit it, circumstances suggest that they may have deliberately wanted to offer Cecelia a chance to flee.

For several years afterward, Fanny and Cecelia were out of touch, and when they finally reestablished contact in 1852, they were both married, and Cecelia still resided in Canada. Recollections of the olden times rekindled mutual affection between the two women, who, as they had dreamed in youth, could now enjoy friendship as equals. In one of her letters, Fanny addressed her former enslaved servant: "you were the companion of my childhood . . . and far from reproaching you for leaving me, I think and always thought it a very natural desire of the slave to be free. . . . I am and always will be a friend to the slave, and denounce the system of slavery as diabolical [and] at variance with Christianity."[29]

Their idyll soon precipitated into harsh reality as they came to realize the gulf that still separated the worlds of two women who, although both free, had very different priorities and problems in life, which, inexorably, swung them back to their former inequality. Cecelia strongly desired to be reunited with her old mother, Mary, who was still held in bondage and, upon hearing that her owner was in the process of moving to New York, implored Fanny and her husband, Andrew Ballard, to buy her. He consented but, instead of emancipating the old woman right away, as Fanny expected and Cecelia hoped, Ballard decided that he would only grant her freedom after six years, unless he was reimbursed the six hundred dollars he had paid for her. This was an impossibly steep sum for Cecelia and her mother to get their hands on, but at Fanny's insistence, in 1859 Ballard agreed finally to cut the redemption by half.[30]

Although we don't know whether, amid the convulsions of the Civil War, mother and daughter were ever able to see one other again, the story showcases how limited the influence of a white woman on an enslaving husband might be, as issues always boiled down to property and money. And inevitably commerce rather than conscience prevailed.[31]

Single, white women—a group among southern enslavers long neglected by historians—were in the position to develop autonomy of will and independent agency to far greater extents than those accessible to widows. And some single women actually *had* agency. As opposed to the former, their decisions were in fact free from considerations concerning offspring.[32]

Economic interest in slavery, largely perceived as a means to guarantee a comfortable future to offspring, could also dampen a woman's antislavery impulse. These commercial considerations might make attitudes toward emancipation contradictory. The examples of Virginia H. Shelby Breckinridge and her daughter Susan P. Shelby Grigsby show that, despite their professed desire to see slavery abolished, and any uneasiness caused by its most disturbing immoral and inhumane aspects, they ultimately accepted its continuation precisely on economic grounds. Yet, unlike her mother, who was extremely well-off, Susan had a more immediate stake in the need for the profitability of slavery because of her husband's growing financial embarrassment. So in an effort to contribute to her family's economy, from the mid-1850s, Susan Grigsby consented to hiring out as many enslaved persons as she could spare, regardless of any family or other considerations for the bondspeople she continued to own.

One enslaved girl, Mary, was only fourteen when Susan hired her out in 1859 to the Ronalds, the family of a steamboat captain residing in Louisville. Thanks to the girl's special abilities in the care of children—and the Ronalds had many—the arrangement worked well. Shortly before the expiration of her contract, they wished to secure Mary's service for another year. On account of her need for competent help within her own nursery, Susan wavered and tried to persuade the Ronalds to consider another of her bondswomen for hire, but she found them unyielding: "Please, send Mary down immediately," wrote Kate, the Ronalds' oldest child, "for we are in need of a girl . . . and the children want to see her very much and talk about her often." Finally, their offer to pay for a full year's lease, despite the onset of January (thus they could not expect to have the girl with them until the end of the month at least) provided such a financial windfall that Susan set aside her feelings, and Mary continued in the Ronalds' service until mid-1861.[33]

Florence was barely ten in early 1859, when Grigsby first contemplated hiring her out. Yet she could not do so before the child had received some basic instruction, and, toward this end, Susan turned to her cousin Sue Alexander for help in training. At Nelson Furnace, where they resided, the Alexanders had only one bonded domestic servant, supplemented by "a free negro woman to cook." Although professing to be "not naturally a disciplinarian," and a neophyte in "the management of any servant," Sue yielded to her cousin's insistence and agreed to have Florence sent over for that purpose.[34]

Sometime later, Sue got a letter from her cousin and could not quite understand whether Susan needed Florence back home or wished to relieve her of the inconvenience. Annoyed by her rather cryptic expressions, Sue responded in a very straightforward manner: "if you want her I can easily spare her, but if you don't, it will be no trouble to me to get her a home for the balance of this year & for the next." In the absence of a conclusive answer, she went ahead and looked for a suitable placement for Florence, and, in a short while, two offers came to hand. The first was made by one Mrs. Gordon, but Sue warned her cousin that, although hers was an "excellent home" in many respects, that lady was well known for overworking her servants. The second offer came from one Mrs. Stefah Shortwell, who was actually interested in buying the girl. But in this case Sue's advice was "a decided *no,*" on account of her being known as "a very harsh mistress." Susan Grigsby joined cousin Sue in condemning those who used to overwork bondspeople and might easily become physically abusive of them. Both women were therefore very scrupulous in trying to avoid any such occurrence.[35]

Finally, little Florence was leased to Mrs. Gordon for the balance of 1859 and 1860, but the poor child was so unhappy in her new situation, not just because of the very hard work conditions, but likely homesickness. Thus by the end of August she was again at Nelson Furnace with the Alexanders. In informing cousin Susan of the circumstances, Sue remarked that, most probably, Florence was not to be blamed for the failed arrangement, for she was "a good girl . . . and could make a good servant." Once more confronted with Susan's sluggishness, Sue went on to explore more venues and finally indicated one "Mrs. S." of Louisville as the selected lessee. Was this the Shortwell lady to whom she had previously discouraged cousin Susan from leasing Florence because of her harshness in dealing with enslaved hirelings? If so, Sue's indication may suggest the very limited market that Susan was able to tap for hiring a very young and largely inexperienced girl as, unfortunately for her, constituted the bulk of those she could spare. Be that as it may, the offer of the more than respectable sum of sixty dollars per year convinced Susan Grigsby to strike the deal.[36]

Regardless of her destination, little Florence "hated to go & was much disappointed that she could not go home & see her mother and the rest after such a long absence." Sue Alexander "felt sorry for her" and, knowing how deeply uncomfortable her cousin was with the hiring of the young enslaved girl, tried to console her by expressing the conviction that the arrangement would be satisfactory. She promised to visit with Florence every time she happened to be in Louisville, and report to her owner on "how she seems to be doing."[37]

For reasons unknown, this arrangement did not work out, and in January 1861 Florence was again in the service of the Gordons. In May, however, many middle-class families that had formerly enjoyed a comfortable lifestyle found their financial means curtailed by the onset of the Civil War. All of a sudden, people who had routinely hired one or more enslaved servants, usually for domestic help, feared they would be unable to honor their obligations, and renounced what, under the new circumstances, was increasingly deemed a luxury. Furthermore, rumors of an imminent invasion of Louisville from the river kept everybody on the *qui vive* and prepared to leave the city on short notice. Worried about the uncertainties created by the "unsettled state of affairs of the country [and] our community (not knowing when we have to move our families)," Mr. Gordon signified to Susan Grigsby his resolve that, although "we have no fault to find with the girl she is a good servant . . . we would greatly prefer to send home." The panic initially raised by such fears slowly gave way to more sedate hopes that strict neutrality might spare Kentucky. By January 1862, with the prospect of having to leave home momentarily dispelled, the Gordons rehired Florence for a year term. They were able to offer only forty dollars, due to their diminished resources in lean times.[38]

The Gordons' hopes to be spared major economic losses began to falter in July 1862, when the Confederates launched a massive effort to occupy Kentucky. Their hopes crumbled further still in early September when, with the Falls City virtually under siege and threatened with evacuation, they were forced to remove in haste. Before their departure, they put Florence in the care of one William B. Mold, who, knowing that "She [was] a good servant," wished "to secure her for the coming Year." To that effect, in early December 1862 he contacted Susan Grigsby, who was by then temporarily residing with her Scott cousins in Franklin County, begging her to let him know "immediately" what her terms were "& c. & c." The contract was stipulated for the balance of 1862 and renewed in January 1863 for the sum of forty dollars. Unfortunately, the turmoil that accompanied the enslaved people's transition to freedom in the final phases of the Civil War in Kentucky caused Florence's disappearance from the records.[39]

In the effort to maximize financial returns from the sweat of her bondspeople, in 1859 Susan Grigsby ventured into the new experiment of hiring out as many adult males as could be spared from farm labor. She explored the possibility of employing them on one of the boats, plying the Ohio and Mississippi Rivers between Louisville and New Orleans. To this end, she turned to riverboat captain and longtime acquaintance G. P. Lowitt for advice. Although disarming, his reply was frank and honest: "If any other disposition can be made of your servants," he wrote Grigsby, "don't put them on the river. They will never be worth anything for you except on the River." As Lowitt contended, bondsmen onboard boats contracted habits and tastes that would later make them dissatisfied with any different situation. Regardless, he assured Susan that, if that was really her intention, he would hire them himself, or find them situations "on a good Boat." The captain's straightforward opinion convinced Susan of the difficulties associated with this scheme.[40]

Susan therefore turned to other kinds of employment for her bondsmen and was finally able to place them with some sort of manufacturing establishment in Louisville, though evidently with disastrous results. In early December 1859 she in fact got from their lessee, one W. W. Wells, the following, rather rude note: "Your servants," he dryly wrote, "have already been more trouble to me than all the other negroes we hire," and he invited Grigsby to instruct her lawyer "to collect the balance of the negro hire" and get him rid of them! While the enslaved servants' unruly behavior may have been studied—as the surest and fastest way to return home—this failure probably convinced Susan Grigsby of the impracticality of employing her bondsmen in activities so different from the agricultural ones to which they were accustomed. As far as we know, Grigsby never tried to hire out her farmhands again.[41]

In dealing with such an important income-generating activity as the hiring practice represented for her family economy, Grigsby displayed a good deal of indecision and, as cousin Sue Alexander could attest, at times, costly distraction. These attitudes puzzled the relatives who were trying to help her, and put their patience on trial. Were these behaviors the result of her timid and scarcely self-reliant nature? Did they stem from the depth of the moral conflicts agitating her conscience? The answer probably lies somewhere between. True enough, Susan proved a poor decision-maker with her hiring of white personnel, but that was more understandable, not only because of its crucial connection to the rearing of her children but also because such delicate financial matters were in play.

Hiring out enslaved persons was a different matter entirely, for it would bring in money for Grigsby. Her reactions to even more unsettling facets of enslaving persons, such as interracial sex and the sale of some of her bondswomen, help to unravel the tangle of moral and cultural imperatives that strongly influenced her and allowed her to think of herself as a compassionate enslaver.

Compassion and Reaction

When Susan resettled at Traveller's Rest with her family in mid-1852, her bondspeople hoped that she would be as sympathetic a mistress as her mother had been, and that they could turn to her for help and support. In a short while, she in fact became the compassionate listener of all their travails and pleas, which they took care to present to her only when Mr. Grigsby was not at home.

One Sunday evening, sometime toward the end of February 1853, an enslaved man named Davy, the property of a neighbor and the husband of Rachel, one of Susan's enslaved servants, arrived at her mansion much agitated by his inability to visit with his wife during the weekend. Perhaps the woman was hired out at that time, for Davy begged Susan to write Rachel a letter on his behalf, which she promised to do the next day. Then he could not restrain himself from conveying to Mrs. Grigsby his wrenching pain from being separated from his wife and children, and his utmost desire to be reunited with them. "Miss Susan," he said, "I know white and privileged to think that *we* Can get other wives & husbands, but *that is not* my principal [*sic*]. I want no other wife than Rachel—for she is a good wife, mother & Christian." Because his master had stated several times that "he had never felt so much sympathy for two negroes as Davy and Rachel," Davy had repeatedly implored him to be sold to reunite with his family, but his master seemed more inclined to buy "Rachel & her children *if possible.*"[42]

Susan was deeply moved by Davy's words and, knowing that "both black and white" in the community held him and Rachel in great esteem and looked favorably on their reunion, was willing to help them. In reporting the case to her mother, she praised Rachel as "one of the neatest, most competent and agreeable servants" she had ever seen, and "extremely faithful kind and clean." In a further letter, she openly stated: "I will attend to Rachel things, and think that you will *do well* to take her over. . . . I think it probable you can make any arrangement about her husband who seems to be a *very* respectable man." It does appear that early on Rachel was in Mrs. Virginia Breckinridge's service. Although it is difficult to ascertain due to the absence of complete census information on the number of bondspersons Virginia Breckinridge enslaved at this time period, we may surmise that either all or some of Davy and Rachel's children—Maria, Celia, and Susan—were among them. Had this been the case, Susan Grigsby may have considered her mother's taking Rachel to be the simplest way to achieve the reunion of their family, leaving to Virginia the making an arrangement with Davy's owner for his purchase. But these are only guesses.[43]

On Christmas Day of the same year, Alick, one of Susan's bondsmen, who must have been in his early fifties by then, knowing that Mr. Grigsby was not at home, knocked at the mansion's door asking to be received by his mistress. He was accompanied by his wife, who belonged to a different owner. The reason for their visit was to implore Mrs. Grigsby to buy their child, a boy of fourteen, who was about to be sold by his master and most likely sent downriver "with a drove of negroes." They told her that, of the twelve children they had had, only this last one was still living with them, "the others all sold & sent off to different parts of the country." Susan was much afflicted at seeing Alick and his wife in such a state of despair and, in her heart, sincerely regretted her inability to help them out due to lack of money. The incident, however, brought her to further reflect on the moral ramifications of keeping human beings in bondage and to convey her feelings explicitly, if only in writing. "What a wicked institution," she wrote her mother, "and I [am] very much afraid that we *will all* have too much to answer for at the bar of God." Then, she concluded: "Independant [*sic*] of the subjection we hold them in, they are the cause, directly & indirectly of two thirds [of] the sins we commit and if I know myself there is no sense within my means that I would not give to have the poor creatures *emancipated*." Her inability to be of any service to Alick and his wife angered Susan to such an extent that, besides the simple consideration that it would be better for the enslaved to be sent back to their native soil, "where they are at least held accountable for their own actions," she pushed her critique of the slavery regime so far as to denounce the paradox of the Americans' boasting of freedom as the greatest of all human blessings, while at the same time they held millions of people of another race in shackles.[44]

Susan's theoretical sympathizing with the plight of the enslaved and, in particular, with that of her own bondspeople, was brought to a test in early December of either 1857 or 1858. Upon his return home from one of his trips, John Grigsby "had heard of his negroes stealing the corn and riding the horses" while he was away. Reckoning that "fifty or sixty dollars worth of corn [had] been taken," and finding the horses looking "as if they had been chased down by a pack of wolves," on December 12 he had all the Black hands summoned with the intention of unmasking the culprits. Suspicion rested on George, a young man not even thirty. Although he "acknowledged to have rode [*sic*] the horses repeatedly," nothing could be ascertained about the theft of corn. The stubbornness shown by the enslaved in covering for each other unless the author of the mischief spontaneously came forward—as George finally did—disconcerted Susan. She sadly had noticed that "they would often die at the whipping post [rather] than acknowledge the truth."

Clearly, like many plantation mistresses, she did not understand the master-slave dynamic from the perspective of the enslaved. But also, she interceded on their behalf with her husband, and, thanks to her entreaties, the older people escaped flogging, while "the younger boys were all punished." A deeply religious woman, Susan Grigsby found in this and other incidents occasions to meditate on the degrading effects of slavery, and on the obstacles that enslaving humans posed to whites toward salvation. But she must not have failed to sadly admit to herself that, despite her being the legal owner of many enslaved persons, the "master's power" on them rested with her husband. Pushing her reasoning to its extreme conclusion, Susan increasingly wished she could avail herself of free labor only. "What a life it is," she exclaimed in a letter to her mother, "and I dread the continuation of it until sometimes I feel as if my salvation depends on making *a change for the better and surely we hire not white servants so completely in our power as are those poor degraded unambitious wretches* [italics mine]."[45]

While this inner torment may explain Susan's incessant quest for white domestic help, her gendered sensitivity for the plight of the enslaved was brought to a test whenever some of her bondswomen became pregnant in circumstances that raised suspicion of miscegenation. On such occurrences, Susan never blamed nor penalized the Black woman involved but, like many women enslavers would do, retreated into a dignified silence and accommodating attitude that actually amounted to complicity in the enslaving regime. No matter what the extent of her grasp on the Black women's sexual vulnerability in a system where rape was part of their plight, Susan sadly shared with her enslaving peers a sense that denouncing a white man for rape or any sexual misconduct was fraught with difficulties, and ultimately inconclusive.[46]

For their part, enslaved women felt ashamed of being made pregnant by a white man and, aware of being denied any hope for legal redress, would not reveal the name of their rapist. Most tried to conceal their encumbrance as long as they possibly could, from fear of unleashing wild retaliation from his spouse, which was often the case.[47]

In the summer of 1852, when thirty-two-year-old Sarah consented to be hired out by the day, the woman was promised and soon to be married to a family bondsman. Apparently, during her service away from home, Sarah was raped by a white man but, uncertain of the paternity of her child and in the hope that it would be a Black baby, she became impatient to be married and convinced Mrs. Grigsby to "let the wedding come off" much ahead of the appointed time. She begged for this even though her own mother—one of Virginia Breckinridge's enslaved servants—would be unable to attend, perhaps because she was hired out and would not be granted a leave.[48]

Much to Susan's astonishment, on April 6, 1853, Sarah gave birth to "a very large bright mulatto boy almost as white as [her] own children." Although the possibility that the rapist might be someone of her acquaintance clearly upset her, Susan did not deprive the enslaved woman of all the necessary assistance, but she expressed her disapprobation by refusing to see Sarah, which was itself a form of moral and psychological punishment. In this connection, she wrote her mother the following dry note: "I haven't seen her, and don't intend to but have her nursed and attended to—she is well and sitting up every day." Recent scholarship has contended that the preoccupation that enslaving women usually showed with the physical needs of both enslaved mothers and their newborns sprang from concern about the preservation of their investment in human beings. The incident involving the enslaved Sarah is not conclusive in this regard. Grigsby's assiduousness in caring for mother and child may have been motivated by more than mere economic interest. The two women had in fact grown up together and developed ties of affection in their childhood and youthful years.[49]

Sarah, for her part, was mortified at having unwittingly lost the favor of her mistress and, at the risk of her life, did not reveal her developing postpartum complications until the fact became self-evident. About a month after delivery, she became extremely ill with "violent pain in her bowels," her abdomen having become "black as pit." The doctor, who was immediately called for, "applied a blister to the stomach and put applications to the bowels," which gave her some relief, but the chances of her survival remained feeble. Realizing that Sarah had been "suffering but concealing it since the very birth of child," and had very imprudently continued to do all kinds of work for her, such as washing and sewing, without ever uttering a word caused much distress to Susan, who thought she had never seen anyone suffer so much from "neuralgia in her head." On May 7, Sarah was somewhat relieved of pain and, despite the doctor's worry that her condition was potentially lethal, seemed to be out of danger. In effect, she recovered sufficiently well as to induce Susan to offer her some light sewing in her own room "a part of two days," but the unpleasant symptoms reappeared in the same, violent manner, prompting her to make the serious resolve that Sarah "shall not expose herself in any possible way." Given her still critical health conditions, Sarah was unable to breastfeed her baby, and Susan arranged for "Old Ritta," an enslaved woman more than fifty years old, to take care of her nursing. Lack of further reference in correspondence suggests that Sarah survived.[50]

Another case of a pregnancy surrounded by murky circumstances involved twenty-three-year-old Jennie, whom Susan had always held up as her best domestic servant and, being herself a mother, particularly competent in the running of the nursery. Jennie had in fact borne three children between 1848 (Nelson) and 1851 (Betty and Bell, twin girls). Given Susan's esteem for this enslaved woman, we may surmise that these children were the issue of Jennie's marriage, possibly to a man enslaved by the family.[51] Sometime in 1852, Susan thought she could momentarily spare Jennie and hired her out. It was not to be. During her service away from home, she became pregnant and, apparently, concealed her encumbrance. So when on Tuesday, March 1, Susan was awakened at three o'clock in the morning and notified that Jennie had given birth to twins (Robert and Jenny), the news caused her "utter astonishment and distress." As it usually happened with cases of miscegenation, in reporting the news to her mother Grigsby only laconically mentioned that the two babies were "very large children indeed and she [Jennie] doing remarkably well." But the fact that she felt "sorry for the poor creature," and that Betsy—Virginia's enslaved Black servant who had possibly recommended the leasing family as a reliable one—was "much mortified at the occurrence," suggest that Jennie must have been violated by a white man, probably her lessee.[52]

A further concern arose involving Mary, the young girl Susan had been hiring to the Ronalds since 1859. As a result of the economic crisis engendered by the war, Mr. Ronald's income had been "cut off *very much,*" and, anticipating even harder times to come with the threatened invasion of Kentucky by the Federals, in May 1861, his wife had "left every *comfort*" and removed her family to Elizabethtown, a rural and very quiet location, to live as economically as she possibly could. In the expectation of Mr. Ronald's return from "down the River," hopefully by the end of the month, she was temporarily occupying a small room at a hotel where she had assumed that Mary would do her washing, but, to her puzzlement, the girl refused to do so, and to take care of her own clothes either. For a few weeks she was "so cross and disagreeable with the children" that Mrs. Ronald could not make sense of, until she discovered that Mary was at least five months' pregnant and perhaps more but, having become impudent, "will not answer [her] satisfactorily."[53]

In reporting the occurrence to Susan Grigsby with great embarrassment, Mrs. Ronald tried to disclaim herself from the fault of negligence by stating that, given all the precautions she had taken to protect the young girl's physical integrity by watching her even more closely than the previous year, and that she had never slept out of her children's room, she could not figure out when the execrable fact may have happened. Unfortunately, and against Mrs. Ronald's intention, precisely those details pointed to the possibility that her own husband might have been the predator. This would amply explain Mary's obstinate refusal to talk, her "strange" behavior being possibly accountable to the shock caused to a girl of fourteen by being violated by a white man whom she trusted. Clearly, Mrs. Ronald wanted to get rid of Mary and, protesting that she could not continue to keep her while at the same time having to give out her own washing, asked Mrs. Grigsby's permission to send her back home, and offered to pay the sum corresponding to the entire time the young enslaved woman would still remain with her.[54]

Mary delivered her baby in late summer of 1861, but the sources don't tell whether it was a mixed-race child. All we know is that, after nursing the baby for a while, Mary was ready to be put on the hiring market again, but, due to the drop in the demand for enslaved hirelings in times of economic crisis, Susan had difficulties in finding a placement for her. There were people who could still afford to rent a bondswoman, however, and most certainly did so at a reduced cost, for rates had begun to plummet in mid-1861. Finally, in early 1863, one Mr. Collins offered twenty dollars for Mary, but Mrs. Grigsby aimed for getting thirty. Considering that his was "a good home," she confided that a mutually satisfactory arrangement could be reached, but we don't know whether the bargain was ever struck.[55]

This may have been Susan Grigsby's last experience with the hiring practice. In a little while, word of emancipation spread among her bondspeople, who became increasingly disobedient, and, with the Danville area occupied by the Union army, Susan concentrated on the effort to protect Traveller's Rest from plunder and the confiscation of its wood, crops, and cattle. Her past activity as a lessor of enslaved persons was so removed that, at the end of February 1863, Louisville attorney-at-law William Attwood had to remind her that she still had rents to collect, and urged her to let him know the name of her agent for the collection of the monies that both Mr. Ronald and Mr. Mold owed for the lease of Mary and Florence, respectively, and what was the exact amount due by each of them.[56]

Captives to a Male-Dominated Society

Even women who, like Susan Grigsby, retained legal ownership of their bondspeople within wedlock were often powerless in preventing the consummation of one of the most shameful tragedies of slavery: the separation of families by sale of one or more of their members.

Although indirectly, in the early 1850s Susan Grigsby was exposed to a case of sale concerning the progeny of Alick, one of her bondsmen. Being opposed to it in principle, at that time she was probably convinced that she would never be a party in the odious trafficking of human beings. However, her determination to avoid direct involvement was brought to a test in 1855 or 1856, when her husband found himself in bad financial straits due to the failure of his investment in Chicago real estate underwritten a couple of years earlier to yield the expected return. Susan hated to see John so worried and harassed by dark thoughts, and she tried to convince him to sell his interest in that venture, also turning to her mother for help. "Mr. Grigsby," Susan wrote her, "is considerably in debt . . . makes but little money and does not wish to sacrifice valuable property [perhaps referring to the enslaved]."[57]

No argument could induce John Grigsby to withdraw from the Chicago venture, and his refusal to listen to his wife's input in undertaking important business decisions deeply hurt Susan. Nevertheless, she felt she must do something to help her dear husband honor his debts and, in disregard of

John's open opposition to the possible alienation of some of her properties, finally resolved—or agreed—that only the sale of a bondsperson could spare him from impending ruin. That momentous decision plunged Susan Grigsby into a deep state of prostration—not only for having to break her pledge to never commercialize human beings but also for the consequent unavoidability of consigning one of her bondspeople to an uncertain destiny. Annie's sale was consummated amid outbursts of despair and rebellion on her part at being separated from her home, kin, and other affective relations. Upon learning of her fate, the young woman went wild and, in a fit of anger, destroyed "her own clothes and quilts as many of Charlotte's [probably her mother]." Susan was so emotionally shaken by the event that, once the transaction was over, she could only laconically report to her mother, "Mr. Grigsby sold Annie to Mr. Moore a few days ago and she left here to-day."[58]

Another instance of the sale of an enslaved woman occurred in August 1859—when John Grigsby's financial circumstances were at their nadir—and regarded thirty-four-year-old Vicy, one of Ritta's children. By that time, Susan's position as the legal owner of her estate had been firmly established by John's second deed of conveyance. Consequently, she conducted the transaction in person. This experience literally devastated Susan, who reported to her mother, "The real anguish that I have suffered in consequence of Mr. Ned Huges [*sic*] spending the day in my room bargaining for Vicy . . . *will* in all probability make me sick, for I am perfectly wild and my heart beats so that I can scarcely write." Then, she added: "Well, Vicy is sold to Mr. Ned Huges and if every one who sells a negro feels as I do just now, God forbid that they should have it in their power ever to do the same—Indeed it is my earnest prayer that I may have *no greater* sin to answer for."[59]

The dramatic circumstances that surrounded Vicy's sale took on tragic tones when her buyer, a trader in enslaved people, took her to Lexington with the intention of forwarding her downriver, in open disregard of the Grigsbys' proviso that she be found a suitable placement within the state, or at least in the Upper South, where the material conditions of the enslaved were generally milder than farther South. The poor woman was distraught and, from the jail where she was detained, managed to send a message to Susan's Aunt Fishback through Virginia's trustworthy enslaved servants Becky and Betty, imploring her "for Gods [*sic*] sake to get someone to buy her out of jail and not let her be taken down the river." Like most of the Shelby and Hart women, Susan Fishback deeply sympathized with the plight of the enslaved; she immediately began to look around for someone who would buy Vicy for the $1,200 the trader in the enslaved asked for her release. In effect, several people came forward and proclaimed themselves ready to disburse that much money to prevent Vicy from being deported to the Lower South, but, "having examined the rechord [*sic*] of the paper in the office," not one of them was finally willing to do so, on account of the uncertainty of the property title to her. In reporting the fact to her niece, Susan Fishback pointed out: "Did it ever occur to you that the sale of [Vicy] was not a legal one as your property was all made over in trust to your uncles Evan and Tom [Shelby] *before* your marriage?"[60]

Aunt Fishback's raising of the issue brought havoc for, evidently, John Grigsby's twice-filed instruments in writing, aimed at reverting to his wife full title to her properties, had no legal effect in the absence of his deed to Thomas Shelby, whom Grigsby had chosen as his wife's trustee. Quite mysteriously, the document had disappeared from Susan's drawers and could not be found anywhere in the house. The imperfection of the papers did not constitute a hindrance to the purchase of Vicy by a cunning trader in the enslaved, who, taking advantage of that, felt free to decide about her destination as he pleased. While Vicy could not escape deportation to the Lower South, the tragic incident left Susan and the other white women involved with a bitter taste in their mouths at the umpteenth demonstration of their inability to shield bondspeople from the most extreme trial in their male-dominated, patriarchal slavery-based society.[61]

The thought of the missing document, and of its strange disappearance, constantly tormented Susan. In late summer of 1862 its retrieval became vital to her. With the invasion of Kentucky by the Federals, the whole state prey to the Civil War, and John's enrollment in the Confederate army, hard times were looming large on the horizon. She ought to be prepared to dispose of any single part of her holdings according to necessity, also in light of the possibility that John's many creditors might advance their claims. She therefore resumed the search of the original specimen with alacrity, and, after some exploration, investigation led to the Honorable John Bell, the famous Whig politician and the founder of the Constitutional Union Party. Although with poor execution, from the mid-1850s Bell had been in fact Susan's legal representative and business agent, and Susan assumed—or hoped—that he might be in possession of the original document. She thought he might at least have a clue of where it could be retrieved. Accordingly, in early November 1862 Susan had him contacted by Nat Gaither, probably an attorney. "Mrs. Grigsby says," he wrote Mr. Bell, that "you have a will deed or some article of agreement . . . by which Thos. H. Shelby of Lexington holds the title to her property in trust for herself & the heirs of her body." Although solicitous, Bell's reply was unfortunately negative, but he promised to start a search on the first opportunity he had to go to Lexington. The precipitation of war events probably prevented both Bell from following suit and Susan from investigating further. This meant that John Grigsby was unable to solidify Susan's hold on her property, but this problem was soon superseded by the many wartime challenges.[62]

In early fall of 1862, the winds of war hovering over Kentucky began to batter the little world of Traveller's Rest, too, exposing Grigsby to a whole array of material difficulties. She possibly thought that securing a specimen of the deed proving her legal power to act on any single part of her holdings, as circumstances might require, might be crucial in her primary effort to protect the physical safety and provide for the material comfort of her offspring in dangerous and lean times.

Susan's anticipations, however, were annihilated very soon. Between late September and mid-October, the Grigsbys were hit by a tragedy of major proportions: the death of four of their six children. These incommensurable losses made Susan feel that her world was turned upside down. Folded on herself in the mourning of her dear little ones, the mistress of Traveller's Rest began to look at worldly things—including those of economic import for her family—with detachment, and sometimes indifference. This shift also involved her attitude toward her bondspeople. From 1863, Grigsby's always emotional, yet unresolved inner conflict between conscience and the purse, increasingly gave way to retrenchment into a more subdued acceptance of the inevitability of the course leading up to the liberation of the enslaved—including hers—from the shackles of servitude.

Despite the major financial loss involved, after Jefferson's advice, she was long prepared to "let the wolf loose."

5

The World Turned Upside Down

In 1860, the future of slavery was not the only issue in Kentucky politics. Rather, public debates revolved around the interpretation of the nature of the federal compact in relation to the legitimacy of secession, and on how the impending dismemberment of the Union could be prevented. With the victory of the Republican Party in the presidential race, and Lincoln's call for troops in mid-May 1861, the Kentucky legislature resolved that "this state and the citizens thereof shall take no part in the Civil War now being waged [but will] occupy a position of strict neutrality."[1] This was a vainglorious if not disingenuous moment of wishful thinking.

The Confederate invasion of the southwest quarter of Kentucky in September 1861, soon followed by the occupation of the rest of the state by the Federal army, rendered taking sides with either of the contending forces unavoidable for Kentuckians. Divided in their sectional sympathies, sometimes even within the same household, not even families boasting time-honored unionist and antislavery sentiments like the Shelbys, the Harts, and allied ones were spared the suffering entailed by fratricidal warring within the larger civil conflict.[2]

Most of Susan's kinspeople either stuck to the neutralist stance first taken by the state or elaborated it into allegiance to the Union; others, however, embraced the Confederate cause. Susan entertained mixed feelings on the subject. Despite expectations that she join her most influential relatives—Uncle Will, Aunt Fishback, stepfather Breckinridge, the Voorhieses, and the Wallaces, among others—in following either of the first two courses, John Grigsby's proslavery inclination anticipated the possibility that she might have to clarify her position in the unfolding Civil War. Susan prayed that her husband would not make the extreme resolve to engage himself militarily in the conflict, for this would have necessitated a declaration of allegiance on her part that she was not ready to make. John Grigsby's enrollment in the Confederate army, in late August 1862, left Susan not only alone in confronting the harshness of wartime difficulties but also grappling with the problem of how to navigate divided allegiances. For Susan Grigsby, the war years brought not only uncertainty but many losses. Her equilibrium, beset by indecisiveness at the best of times, was almost wholly undone.

Winds of War

During the first few months of 1861, hopes that professed neutrality might shield Kentucky from involvement in the impending Civil War were at a high pitch. Susan Grigsby shared in this theatrical proclamation. In early January, both reassured and reinforced in her convictions by a speech recently delivered by Robert J. Breckinridge on the subject, Aunt Fishback wrote her niece: "I never could bear the idea of her [Kentucky] going with the South . . . and I can see no reason why she should join the North. . . . *The slave trade ought to be as repugnant to us as abolitionism* [italics mine]."[3] On May 10, right before the approval of the neutrality act by the state legislature, William Preston Hart, Susan's dearest "Uncle Will," so summarized his position: "If we cannot go with the South . . . let's quit the South & not be like a free negro at a Barbecue unable to speak till they have all left."[4]

The invasion of the Bluegrass State by both of the opposing armies, between late summer and early fall 1861, forced Kentuckians to clarify their positions well beyond parlor conversations, thus exposing the ambiguous nature of Unionism in a slavery-based society. Like other people, Susan Grigsby's stepfather, Robert J. Breckinridge, and cousin Morgan Brown Vance worked out their "theoretical" Unionism into staunch support of the federal government, and consistently backed its policies throughout the war.[5] Others, such as Susan's uncle Will Hart, upheld neutrality to the extreme consequence of submitting to arrest and imprisonment. Still others were drawn into the Confederacy's camp, often as a reaction to Lincoln's broken promise to respect Kentucky's neutrality. This response tended to be more typical of young men, thus revealing the true and proper generational gap between fathers and sons. A keen observer of the phenomenon, twenty-one-year-old Johanna Louisa (Josie) Underwood, a resident of Bowling Green, perceptively noted in an early 1861 entry of her diary that many "Union" families in the area had "wild reckless unthinking inexperienced sons—who make so much noise [about] secession as to almost drown their fathers' wiser council [*sic*]."[6]

The case of John (Johnnie) W. Green, although only loosely related to Susan Grigsby by virtue of her friendship with his mother, Louisa Ellen Green, not only corroborates the above point but also shows how bonds of blood could prevail over political persuasion to turn a staunch believer in the Union into an albeit reluctant supporter of the Confederate cause. Born in an enslaving family of Henderson County, Johnnie was raised in the love for the Union but, during 1861, began to manifest pro-southern sympathies. His father, Hector, also blamed Lincoln for falsehood in "any declaration of his inaugural," and for partisanship in dealing with the political crisis opened by South Carolina. But, unlike his son, Hector Green sincerely hoped and prayed that Kentucky's rights be affirmed "in the union, under our national flag." He therefore invited Johnnie "to reflect well before concluding upon a position, throwing off all sectional predilections," and not to be precipitous in volunteering in the Confederate army. "I like not the Southern Confederacy," he stated, "& I like less the Lin's assumptions!" Yet, he added, "if Kentucky is forced to secession and goes North, I shall stand by your side South." Hector Green's conclusion reflected a most humane dimension of the internecine conflict in the Border States, which saw many fathers with abiding Unionist faith drawn into support of the Confederacy in consequence of their sons' choices. In October 1861 Johnnie Green enrolled in the Ninth Kentucky, one of the Confederate regiments composing what would later become known as the "Orphan Brigade," and that was sometime under the command of Benjamin Hardin Helm—son of a Kentucky governor and husband of Susan's cousin Emilie Todd—who was killed in the Battle of Chickamauga in September 1863.[7]

After mid-1862, neutrality was hardly a tenable position for anyone, the alternatives being (1) to take the oath of allegiance to the Union, (2) to be arrested and imprisoned, (3) to voluntarily enroll, (4) to be drafted (something everybody considered tantamount to dishonor), or (5) to seek refuge behind the Confederate lines. By September, Lincoln's recurrent mentions of emancipation in public speeches drew many still-wavering Kentuckians into the Confederate camp. As Josie Underwood commented: "Alas for southern unionists, so many we love are with the rebels. That we look with equal interest and sorrow to the list of wounded and killed on both sides."

At least seven of Susan's cousins (Hart Gibson, George and Charlie Vance, Willie and Tom W. Wallace, Isaac Shelby, and Beriah Magoffin) and two of her half brothers (Willie and Robert Breckinridge Jr.) fought in the Confederate army. Even such an illustrious relative of Susan as Mary Todd Lincoln was exposed to the embarrassing situation of having most of her kin fight for the secessionist South, and she herself was suspected of harboring pro-Confederate sentiments. Of those surviving among her father's fourteen children, only she, a brother, and a half sister openly supported the Union. Her other brother and three half brothers joined the Confederate army, and three half sisters were married to Confederate officers.[8]

Division of loyalties, which affected the majority of Kentucky households, placed a severe strain on women. Wives, with their husbands on the battlefront, and saddled with the great responsibility to provide for offspring and protect family properties, faced insurmountable hurdles in reconciling political beliefs with personal, emotional attachments.

Susan Grigsby's predicament was, in a way, anticipated by her husband's cultural and ideological background, which was much different from hers on matters of slavery and emancipation. A Virginian by birth and education, John Grigsby had never made a mystery of his sectional sympathies and, in the late 1850s, had attended public gatherings in which Beriah Magoffin—a cousin to his wife—featured as a speaker. In September 1859, following his election to governorship, Magoffin had appointed Grigsby a colonel in the Lincoln County state militia, and, in that capacity, he had shown his fundamental understanding of the relation between the enslavers and the enslaved as one of mutual distrust and enmity. In fact, in late April 1861, when many people feared a revolt by the enslaved, Grigsby filed a motion to the effect that "three men in each voting precinct in Lincoln County" be chosen "whose duty it shall be to search the negro cabins of slaves & free negroes in their respective districts for arms and munitions and confiscate such as they may find," and asked "that the negro cabins of the whole county may be visited on the same day."[9]

Besides firmness in his proslavery stance, Grigsby also shared with the majority of Virginians a strong attachment for the Union. A Kentuckian by his own choice, learning of news of a major shift in attitude among his fellow-countrymen in the crucial weeks surrounding the outbreak of hostilities left Grigsby disconcerted. As his brother James reported to him a few days after Fort Sumter, the citizens of Rockbridge County, including himself, had initially elected a "Union" man as a representative to the state convention called to decide upon secession, but, shortly after, many of "the most ardent union supporters . . . lost confidence in the Convention," and turned secessionists for fear that those whom they called "the subjugationists" might succeed in "taking the border states as a tail to the Northern confederacy and thus abolitionize [*sic*] them all." By the time of another presidential election, Virginians would have "open and avowed Natl [*sic*] republicans" in their midst, and James Grigsby prayed that "Virginia and the other Southern states be saved from such degradation."[10]

Although sensitive to his brother's appeal, John Grigsby was reluctant to take up arms with the Confederates. This could have cost him the loss of the esteem he had slowly won over time among Susan's extended family—and, perhaps, the respect of his wife. So he waited for developments until, in mid-1862, with the Danville area swarming with Federal troops, a prosouthern sympathizer could no longer postpone deciding what to do—if he wanted to avoid arrest. Sometime in July, John therefore absconded to Spring Hill, the historic home of the Harts, in Woodford County. There, he hoped to convince Uncle Will, who, although for different reasons, equally opposed the new federal policies, to follow him up to Ohio "until things settle[d] down somewhat." Having failed in this attempt, John made the resolve at the end of the month to leave alone and go off to Lexington, whence he planned to proceed to Cincinnati.[11] That departure was the beginning of a long ordeal for Susan Grigsby, who would not see her husband again until the end of war.

August to December 1862

In August 1862, before the war made correspondence increasingly difficult and sparse, John and Susan Grigsby engaged in a frequent exchange of letters. In those days, Susan's loyalties were literally pulled apart between her "theoretical" political allegiance to the Union as defined by the Founding Fathers—one and indivisible—and far more tangible family concerns. Apparently John had not yet made a final decision about what to do after his escape, but if she knew her husband well enough, Susan could predict that he would soon become actively involved in the warfare. She was agitated by conflicting feelings and did not know how to convey their full complexity to her dear husband. On the one hand, she was not willing to abjure her political convictions and hoped that John might reconsider his stand, for the sake of the attachment he had developed for his new Kentucky home-country. On the other hand, if he decided otherwise, she wanted to reassure John of her unflinching loyalty as a wife. So, in her reply to his August 1 letter, she decided to challenge John on his own turf by touching the inner cords of a man of Virginian ancestry, one who had been reared in the belief that consistency between ideals and actions defined one's honor. "If you are to be taken from us," she boldly stated, "I prefer that you should do it honorably, in the defense [*sic*] of those opinions which have always haunted your fine character with the names of *Rebel! Traitor!* And not in the cheerless comfortless dungeons of Camp Chase [a federal military prison in Ohio]. . . . Oppression & despotism are the main stay & support of this beautiful abolition Government and I pray that you . . . may be induced to seek freedom of speech & protection of person in the genial South."[12]

John's response came sooner than expected, Susan's letter postmarked August 5 having actually crossed with his. Upon realizing that the missive was addressed to the whole family, Susan gathered her five older children—the sixth being only an infant—to have them listen to "Pa's" words. In very simple terms, such as small children could understand, Grigsby explained that, although he considered himself "innocent of any offence save that of opinion," he had been forced to make the painful decision to leave home to protect them in case of his arrest. In all likelihood, that was in fact the fate befalling a Confederate sympathizer in those parts of Kentucky that, like Lincoln County—a veritable Union stronghold—were already occupied by the Federal forces. Having reassured wife and children of his sincere love and devotion, Grigsby concluded his letter by imploring them all to be "strong and courageous," promising to keep them constantly informed of his movements.[13]

How could Susan explain to her five older children, whose ages ranged between three and ten, all the ideological and cultural complexities, as well as the more immediate political reasons that had made Kentucky "a patchwork of divided loyalties" in the present war—even within the same family? Ultimately, how should she convince them to share their father's Confederate allegiance when she herself did not do it wholeheartedly?

For a number of days, Susan attentively scrutinized and scrupulously gathered the children's reactions to their father's letter. Hartie, a boy of three, and Susie, aged nine, seemed to be particularly upset at the idea that their father might never come back, and they sought reassurance from their mother that the Almighty was protecting him and would always do so. Alfred, her oldest child, entertained instead more practical, manly thoughts, which, in their stringent logic, betrayed his being only ten. One day, he told his mother, "Suppose Pa determines to go South, would you give me a pistol & let me go with him?" To which Susan replied, "Why my boy would you leave these four little sisters & myself here alone." "Oh, no," he rejoined, "I would not like to do that, but it would be worse to leave Pa to be shot and die by himself."[14]

Although the scenario lying ahead of her was utterly disquieting, Susan understood how crucial military occupation was in determining people's choices and, in conscience, could not blame her husband if he should decide to stake his fortunes with the Confederacy. So she tried to suppress her uneasiness and wrote: "You tell me to be hopeful & courageous and not let our kin and friends see me low spirited and despairing—I will do so I assure you as far as it is possible. . . . Sometimes I cannot refrain from suppressing my bitterness—for I feel dearest, that you have been guilty of no offense [*sic*] and yet are oppressed and outraged in being obliged to suppress your feelings." Having conveyed to John her dismay for the suppression of freedom of expression that Kentuckians—as well as many other white southerners—were enduring, Susan switched to practical issues. "I suppose" she wrote, "it will be necessary for you Southern sympathizers to take the oath . . . now what will you do, return home and be drafted into the Federal service, or submit to arrest." Knowing well that either one of these alternatives was far too much for John's pride and sense of honor to bear, she summoned all of her courage and offered John the ultimate token of her unconditional love. "Go, go if you can," she gushed, "& stake your life—your all—for my pen has been bad and my brain bewildered—as I shall not be surprised to hear that you have condemned these lines to the flames."[15]

By encouraging John to pursue his own ideals, Susan pledged herself to fully respect the principles of individual liberty they both had cherished, and that had always constituted a solid premise for mutual esteem and trust in their marriage. Although forced separation from him was itself a source of anxiety, Susan also anticipated the further limitations that war was to impose. Females in the country would lose freedom of movement, be they the wives of yeoman farmers or plantation mistresses. Whereas men could come and go as they pleased, women were chained in place as providers for their offspring and custodians of the family estates, which, in many cases like hers, included property in enslaved humans. Being a lone woman in times of war entailed great sacrifice, requiring a good deal of resoluteness and even shrewdness to protect properties and supplies from plunder and confiscation. With this latter ordeal Susan had already had a firsthand experience between mid-July and mid-August, when five horses—including her personal one—had been taken from her for use of the US government by order of Quartermaster R. W. Bradley of the Eighth Kentucky Cavalry. That was a considerable loss, for those horses were worth, collectively, $370.[16]

Initially a colonel in the Sixth Kentucky Cavalry, Company B, under Gen. John H. Morgan's command, John Warren Grigsby was later attached to the First Confederate Cavalry under General Wheeler, and distinguished himself for his bravery in many military actions during the entire conflict.[17] Although his enlistment in the Confederate army marked for Susan the beginning of a long series of tribulations and economic setbacks, in the beginning she did not seem to grasp fully the gravity of the moment and, given Mrs. Drummond's inability to return to Kentucky soon, began to look around for a new governess for Alfred and Susie. By mid-September, Uncle Will recommended the name of Miss Ella Berch, whose credentials were impeccable. "Decidedly an intelligent lady of high principles" and "a graduate of Bullock school," Ella was also related to the Breckinridges through her mother. In all probability, Susan would have hired her, but the importance of the issue was abruptly overridden by the insurgence of major concerns about her children's health. In fact, a few days later both Alfred and Mary Ashley contracted diphtheria and, after a long agony, passed away in early October. The contagion had meantime spread to daughters Susan Shelby and Letitia Wallace, who also died later in the month. At the end of October, only two of Susan's six children—Virginia and Hart—were still alive.[18]

During the terrible weeks of her children's illness, Susan was surrounded by the affectionate support of many relatives and friends, from Rebecca Tevis—who would later become Uncle Will Hart's wife—to cousin Mary B. Scott. Kate Rawling, on October 19 offered to come and help with the nursing of Susan and Letitia and, after their demise, was the one who informed Jane Drummond of the tragedy that had befallen the Grigsby household. Devastated by the incommensurable loss, in late October Susan began to consider taking her two surviving children with her in a southbound journey to look for her husband, who was unaware of the death of four of their children. Considering that she would need a trustworthy companion in the adventure, Susan asked Jane Drummond to join her. Protesting the anxiety that such a decision would have inflicted on her old and weak mother, Jane declined. Yet she expressed with tact the hope that Susan might "alter [her] plans and not go South." Jane's refusal did not stop Susan Grigsby from pursuing her design by applying for a pass to travel south across the Confederate line, and on November 20 she was granted permission "to travel South by way of Cumberland Gap to Knoxville, Tennessee . . . with children and servants and company."[19]

News of Susan's plan upset relatives and close friends alike, who deemed her decision the emotional reaction of a woman traumatized by the loss of four children in little more than a month. They therefore tried to persuade her to desist. On November 4, Aunt Fishback wrote her: "Mrs. [Mary] Voorhies tells me that you sale [*sic*] very soon with a view to going South to join your husband. . . . *I think this would be madness in the extreme* [italics mine]," and begged her niece to be cautious and wait until the spring. Meantime, she urged her: "stay with your friends, *if they can stay with you* [italics mine]," hinting at the suspicion that her husband's sectional allegiance had raised doubts among people about her Unionist sentiments. In this connection, Uncle Will was more straightforward. "I have thought it quite probable dear Susan," he wrote, "that you were in the family again [meaning in confirming her pro-Union sentiments], if so, let this determine you at once not to go South." Expressing more practical, womanly concerns, cousin Letitia H. Vance so addressed her: "Do be advised, Susan by your friends around you, and do not let your desire to see your husband guide you in this matter. If he is safe and well, had you not better remain—where you can be comfortable."[20]

In early November 1862, Susan's physical and psychological states were declining, and all of her relatives concurred in the opinion that she could not protect her estate at a time when Federal confiscations and requisitions were multiplying. Susan's position was made even more delicate by her being the wife of a "Rebel." In the attempt to be of some help, William Voorhies advised his niece not to sell her provisions, for the bad season had already begun, and she was not doing well. He also urged Susan not to wait until Union officers came to her but instead to anticipate them by seeking an encounter, or sending someone to do so on her behalf, and put herself under their protection. Other women whose husbands were likewise enrolled in the Confederate army had successfully done so. Although not an oath of allegiance per se, this step would have enabled Susan to bargain for the supply of wood and other provisions for the militaries at a fair price, the alternative being to have these supplies taken from her anyway, but without compensation. Ultimately, Voorhies and Aunt Fishback agreed with the Scotts and Rebecca Tevis—who lived closer to Traveller's Rest and were thus trying to assist Susan in person. They advised she had better visit family rather than remain home as a woman unprotected, at least temporarily. All of them therefore competed to host her and the children for as long as she wished.[21]

Finally, Susan yielded to the prayers of those who loved her and, postponing her departure, agreed to remove to Spring Hill, the Harts' historic home in Woodford County, where she would stay with Rebecca Tevis, Uncle Will's betrothed. During her time there, Susan's somewhat diminished determination to go south was bolstered by Mary Duncan, cousin Nathaniel Hart Gibson's wife, who urged her to join her party in the southbound journey. Her insistence apparently rekindled Susan's intention for, later in November, Mary wrote her: "Delighted to hear you have decided to go. . . . This time we must go through. Come up and start from here, I shall be ready to leave tomorrow afternoon. . . . [B]e sure to go this time." Despite this explicit direction, Susan did not follow suit.[22]

Because of the haphazard interruptions in communication resulting from the frequent change in territorial control by the Federals and the Confederates, respectively, Susan and John Grigsby had been out of touch since August 1862. In December, when she was sojourning with the Scotts at Locust Hill, in Franklin County, Susan got a letter, postmarked the third of the month. Her husband had been able to send this to her through Uncle Voorhies. Its tenor confirmed Grigsby's ignorance of the demise of four of their little ones. Rather, he talked about Uncle Will's arrest and of the frightening news he had heard of Traveller's Rest having been burned down and Susan having perished in the fire. Praying that none of that was true, John begged his wife not to let herself be overwhelmed by the ordeals of that dire hour but to cope with them "with the courage which becomes your name and mine." Then, he exhorted his wife: "Train up our children to feel the same way and to realize fully the priceless value of an unsullied reputation . . . and tell our son [Alfred] to be a man boy and stand by his mother and little sisters."[23] John's words were wrenching enough to revive Susan's desire to be reunited with him in the joint mourning of their departed offspring, but she was held up from leaving by problems arising from her estate.

Hard Times

With the prospect of an indeterminate and presumably long absence from home, in November 1862 Susan had arranged for the lease of Traveller's Rest to one Judge Irvine. During her stay at Spring Hill, the judge kept her updated on all minutiae concerning the estate. In early December, he reported having paid Mrs. Warren the $1.50 she owed her, and put together the articles she wished "to be taken over by Nelson." Business was "getting on with the wood hauling pretty well," and Mr. Bevel was "getting on with the Corn gathering very well." Although they had not had any outbreak or theft thus far, the presence of nearly three thousand Federal troops at Danville was causing apprehension. The Union soldiers had already begun to cut timber from several neighboring properties to the great annoyance of the owners. Irvine, however, assured Mrs. Grigsby that he was doing his best "to prevent depredations" and, toward that end, had gone to town and "got them to desist." Alas, Irvine's letter also carried the sad news that the child of Mary, the enslaved woman discussed in the previous chapter as a hireling to the Ronalds of Louisville, had died in an accident "caused by burning, supposed to have caught fire by a coal poping [*sic*] into the cradle while all hands were out killing hogs."[24]

The death of enslaved children was a common, tragic loss—economic for the enslaver and irreplaceable for the enslaved mother and her kin. This dreadful occurrence underscores the double trauma of a bondswoman who, despite her having conceived a baby as a result of rape, loved her offspring as intensely as any mother does. She was doubtless agonizing that, had she not been away from home as a hireling, she might perhaps have prevented the tragic death of her child.

On December 17, Judge Irvine conveyed to Mrs. Grigsby that the increased number of Union soldiers stationed in and around Danville—from the original three thousand to between ten and twelve thousand in a mere fortnight—led him to fear probable depredations and, "in the way of *pressing* [*sic*] wood." As he reported, the "frequent changes in the Commanders" had undercut his repeated attempts to establish a dialogue with the military authorities but—and here was the good news—a few days earlier he had had an opportunity to make the personal acquaintance of the new commander, Gen. Absalom Baird, "under very *favorable* Circumstances." The general seemed to be "very much of a gentleman," and the judge had been able to arrange with him that Mrs. Grigsby be paid thirty cents for each cord of wood that had been taken forcefully. In return, Irvine agreed to sell the Federals two hundred cords at the same price. After that, Traveller's Rest would be "exempt from furnishing any more." By Irvine's admission, that was not perhaps the best deal he could strike but, given the circumstances, was better than having wood requisitioned "without one cents [*sic*] pay," as many neighbors, including Susan's agent McFerran, had endured. To add weight to the soundness of his decision, Irvine pointed out that Uncle Isaac (Shelby) gave "is [*sic*] entire approbation as to the wood trade or arrangement [he] made with the Military." With Christmas on the horizon, the judge also took the opportunity to ask a few details concerning supplies for the enslaved. Although "at this *particular time,* as far as I could tell they all seam [*sic*] to be contented . . . unless . . . possibly . . . Ambros [*sic*]," he ventured to suggest that, despite Mrs. Grigsby's well-known liberality in providing for them, the distribution of extra blankets and other goods might keep the bondspeople quiet at a time when rebellion was spreading among them.[25]

As 1862 drew to an end, Susan Grigsby was consumed by conflicting feelings. Even though she continued to cherish the idea of going south in search of her husband, a number of practical concerns suggested a further postponement of the trip. Although Judge Irvine seemed to be a good manager for Traveller's Rest, no important decision could be made without her approval, and McFerran, her new agent, needed to stay in constant touch with her on matters concerning the hirelings. Susan also had to deal with a number of creditors who, having heard of her imminent departure, were pressing for payment. One of them was William Campbell of the disbanded firm Campbell, Yeates & Co., who, in a gracious letter, explained that, with Mr. Yeates having gone south, their creditors were pressing him for the settlement of their claims. While he understood the kind of financial difficulties people were going through in those days, he was, however, forced "to urge those indebted to settle their accounts immediately." He begged Mrs. Grigsby to send him at least part of the $154.60 she owed his firm. Another creditor, Mr. Kinney, was not so delicate and, not having received immediate satisfaction of his claim, wrote McFerran a peremptory note to the effect that he was determined to resort to any means to recover the $420 Colonel Grigsby owed him, for he knew "full well where & how to get the value of every cent of it."[26]

Susan was also much worried about Uncle Will's fate, as she had not heard about him since mid-November. A defiant neutralist, that month she had heard he had been evicted from his home and paroled to stay at the National Hotel in Louisville. Then, ignoring where he would be sent thither, and with scant chance to have a regular trial, on November 17 he had written Gen. William O. Boyle, demanding to be heard by "a Committee of twenty of the most prominent Union men in that part of the state" to represent how he "not only denied but defied any criminal accusation from any quarter."[27]

The year 1863 began under challenging auspices for Susan Grigsby, who was caught between opposing pressures. On the one side, Aunt Fishback and Uncle Arthur Wallace were indefatigable in their attempts to convince their niece not to go south but, rather, to remain in Kentucky and accept the hospitality of either of them. On the other side, cousin Mary D. Gibson reiterated her invitation to join in the adventure down south, "if only to make a visit," considering that "Ladies go constantly from St. Louis to Memphis and return." On February 13, Aunt Fishback reported to her niece of having heard from several sources that John wished to come home and take the Oath of Allegiance. She suggested that the generals in Kentucky were well-disposed to let him do so. This hypothesis would completely change the scenario, but, as it turned out, it was only a rumor. Not many days later, Susan got a long, loving letter from John—also postmarked February 13—in which he, having finally become appraised of their children's demise, joined his wife in mourning.[28]

By the time Susan got this letter, Colonel Grigsby may have already been put in command of the Sixth Kentucky Cavalry Regiment as part of the reorganization of John Hunt Morgan's Cavalry Division, which was known for its extreme mobility in the war theater. This made Susan realize that locating John's regiment from time to time was almost impossible, and, as a consequence, she decided to postpone a little longer. In late June, having secured all the necessary permissions and letters of support from Maj. Gens. Ambrose E. Burnside, James Wheeler, and William S. Rosecrans to also be able to obtain a pass to return home, Susan was finally ready to leave. She was held back, once more, by news of military operations involving her husband's regiment.

In June 1863, Gen. Braxton Bragg, the new commander of the Confederate Army of Mississippi (soon to be known as the Army of Tennessee), launched an invasion of Kentucky to relieve pressure on Mississippi and sent Morgan on a diversionary raid to threaten Louisville. Not contented with his success, Morgan pushed into Ohio but was stopped, on July 19, at the Battle of Buffington Island, Meigs County, which cost the capture of seven hundred of his men. The news quickly spread across Kentucky, along with contrasting renditions of Grigsby's fate, and it was only between August 9 and 14 that Susan received confirmation that her husband had escaped and was safe.[29]

In the second half of 1863, Kentucky became a ruthlessly contested terrain between the two opposing armies. Civilians were exposed to a crescendo of confiscations by either the Confederates, who were trying to mount more infantry, or the Federals, who had occupying troops to support. Times were lean for everyone in the state, and craftspeople who before the war would charge high rates for their work competencies were now reduced to beg for employment in exchange for a handful of pennies. In Lincoln County, such was the case with Mrs. Dolbins, the seamstress Susan had hired in the antebellum days despite her "exorbitant" fees. In March 1863, Dolbins humbly wrote the mistress of Traveller's Rest: "Shelby told me you had not had your servants clothes made up and as I have no work on hand I will be very glad to get the clothes to make. I will doe it verry cheep [*sic*]." Alas, her offer was misplaced for, like scores of Kentuckians, Susan had already begun to experience a slow yet inexorable loss of bondspeople.[30]

Even though, for political reasons, Lincoln's Proclamation did not include specific provisions for the enslaved in Kentucky, they realized that they were virtually free and began to flee to Union lines in greater and greater numbers. In the effort to cope with the emergency, military authorities decided to enroll all able-bodied men in the army as laborers. They would also forward to "contraband" camps especially set up for them, the thousands of other refugees—men, women, and children—who daily flocked to Federal troops asking for protection.[31] Apart from those who left their masters' homes spontaneously, loss of enslaved persons could also result from seizure by Federal recruiting parties. On one of their raids in Lincoln County, Union soldiers abducted a few men who belonged to the Grigsbys, including Nelson, a young domestic servant. Susan immediately sought their release and soon identified the regiments in which they were being kept. However, there is no evidence that she ever followed cousin John Brown's advice "that on proper representation to the Colonel of the Regiment" her bondsmen would be "turned out of camp & [her] civil officer agent must be there to secure them," or that, in the affirmative, her action resulted in their restitution. It seems likely that the men preferred to face the dangers of war as quasi-freemen over any relapse into servitude, no matter how mild.[32]

Meanwhile, Susan had to deal with major problems concerning the tenure of Traveller's Rest. Since March 1863, following an intimation by McFerran, she had been harboring suspicions of Judge Irvine's dishonesty in managing her estate. She had therefore written the judge a diplomatic note in which she praised his "great wisdom & forsight [*sic*] in only making a *temporary* arrangement" for the lease of Traveller's Rest, in the eventuality that he might "vacate" her house. Irvine got the hint and, after suggesting that "some evil spirit" may have influenced Mrs. Grigsby's mind, reiterated his commitment to serve her with complete dedication, even more so in the prospect of her imminent departure. "Your great anxiety to get away and to be absent from the scene of your troubles," he wrote, "together with the liberality manifested toward me and Mrs. Irvine induced me to . . . make such sacrifices as I never should have thought of for a *temporary arrangement.*" In support of his own honesty, the judge declared himself ready at any time to account for the more than one thousand dollars he had thus far collected "from the government to geather [*sic*] with other monies for wood."[33]

During the summer, Susan Grigsby finally reached the conclusion that Judge Irvine was trying to cheat her and, after serious reflection, resolved to engage Dr. C. J. H. Carter—who had been her late mother's physician and, possibly, was also her own—to investigate the soundness of his doings. In early August, Carter reported that, all considered, activities were in full swing at Traveller's Rest, with the flour and sawmills operating incessantly, and tobacco in the fields coming up well. The sewing had been done and the stock properly attended. In this latter regard, however, he remarked that Irvine's pretensions of many heads of cattle having died from privation were false, and part of a scheme of his. As Carter reported to Susan, Irvine had "tried last spring to get persession [*sic*] of everything here when you went south he thought you would not get back during the ware [*sic*] and Mr. McFerran would be sent off and he would have full and compleat persession [*sic*] of everything here." As for hams, he had used five, but two of them were in such a bad state of preservation that he had given them to "the negroes," who had to throw away three-quarters of them. At the moment, there were thirty hams and two shoulders in stock, but he knew no more about this, and respectfully invited Mrs. Grigsby to directly inquire with the Irvines for the balance. That was enough for Susan to relieve Irvine of duties and take over the management of Traveller's Rest again.[34]

After several months of interrupted mail communication, around mid-September 1863, when John was safely in the Confederate capital, he and Susan were able to resume a relatively regular exchange of correspondence. Despite his attempts to dissuade her from further pursuing the design to join him, Susan remained unmoved, firm in her determination. Only in September 1864 did she finally give in, probably persuaded by Uncle Will. Having finally been released by the Federal authorities after a long detention, and returned to Spring Hill, he conveyed his feelings to Susan: "From the unsettled condition of things in Kentucky, I fear that innocent persons are likely to suffer an inconvenience, but can only repeat what I have constantly urged upon you—avoid carefully all political matters—remain quietly at home and devote yourself to the care of your little ones."[35]

Upon learning that Susan "had escaped recent molestations" and that her crops were fair, cousin Scott joined in the opinion "that there was no pressing necessity for [her] to go South."[36] During the next year of war, the Confederate forces were merely retrenching in a last, desperate attempt to check the onslaught launched at them by General Grant's mercilessly destructive campaign across the South. John Grigsby's regiment was in almost daily movement. Perhaps fearing that he might not survive the conflict, John felt the urge to reassure Susan of his unchanged love and constant thoughts. Even as the growing disruption of communications that accompanied the collapse of the Confederacy made mail delivery most uncertain, he took every possible opportunity to write his wife, and especially so on an important date like their fourteenth wedding anniversary—November 5, 1864—when he renewed for his spouse "the vows then made . . . after so many years."[37]

Romantic love seemed to have remained intact between them over the years, and this was enough for Susan to become reconciled with her duties as a wife and a mother in a marriage that, although basically "patriarchal" in nature, found a fresh renewal in the sharing of so many ordeals. Anxiously looking to her husband's return from the war, she quietly resumed her role as the mistress of Traveller's Rest.

Back to Traveller's Rest, Again

In the face of the near-certain impending Confederate defeat, Susan Grigsby returned to her ancestral home in the latter part of 1864. Times were difficult, though, and what meager resources she could draw on for support now exclusively depended on the sale of her crops, wood, and cattle. The demand for these was extremely slack, due to the disarray of the economy and the general poverty in the region. Moreover, the number of Grigsby's enslaved persons had shrunk, not only in consequence of the willful departure or forcible abduction of a number of her bondspeople, but also due to casualties. Thirty-six-year-old Manuel, for example, died from a bladder infection in August 1863.[38]

Apparently Susan could still count on a sufficient number of field hands to carry on routine operations, and, in this connection, she needed to procure a white overseer. She hoped to hire one who was married, so that his wife could help in attending to household chores. Because times were hard everywhere in the country, many people who lived in Ohio were willing to take jobs across the river, in Kentucky, thus presenting Grigsby with the possibility of a number of candidates. The selection process, however, did not prove any easier than her search for a housekeeper had in previous years. As she sadly found out, the new circumstances had not changed the basic principle that competence had a cost. Regretfully, she had to turn down the application of one Mr. Elkins of Cleveland, who, despite his impeccable credentials, demanded an annual salary that was definitely beyond her means. Conversely, the Wilkinsons of Cincinnati, who were more affordable, were not the kind of people accustomed to "laborious work." Once probably members of the urban middle class—Mrs. Wilkinson was a graduate of Franklin College in Tennessee—their fortunes had been eroded during the war, and Mr. Wilkinson, who had been honorably discharged from service in the Second Indiana Cavalry, was not "stout enough to go in the Field." As for his wife, she could do all the sewing, "except Dificult [*sic*] Dressmaking." In a few words, they were willing to engage with Mrs. Grigsby provided she had "any light offices to assign [them]." By this time, however, Susan needed far more substantial help than that offered by people who could only oversee field hands, drive her carriage, and "do any light work about the house." So she discarded the Cincinnati couple's application.[39]

The war was rapidly approaching its conclusion, and, regardless of political allegiances, this meant for white southerners the final demise of the peculiar institution and the full conversion to a system of free labor. Susan had begun to experience a gradual loss of her enslaved people since January 1863. Unfortunately, the sources are silent on the circumstances that surrounded the departure of all of them, but, given her expressed hatred for human bondage, we can only surmise that, when the time came, she parted from them peacefully, possibly wishing them good luck in their journey as free people. Yet confrontation with the new reality deeply disturbed Susan, who perceived that this epochal change, like the collapse of the outer walls of the fortress she had built around herself, would be challenging. Further, she had patiently constructed her self-identity as an enslaving woman who nonetheless condemned human bondage in principle. With "her own" world lying in ashes,

Susan desperately desired to be reunited with her husband, her last bulwark against an onslaught of difficult change. Disregarding the perils entailed by any journey in the waning days of the Confederacy, where the railroads were completely destroyed and travel possible only on horseback or by coach, Grigsby turned to Jane Drummond, once more, for companionship on the trip. Blaming family impediments for her inability to join Susan, Jane actually thought that, however romantic, Susan's plan was utterly unrealistic. In mid-March 1865, she communicated these apprehensions to her: "I am sadly afraid that should you carry out your intention of searching for your husband that you will encounter great difficulties and danger."[40]

On April 11, 1865, General Lee's surrender formally sealed the end of war, and, despite the last resistance by die-hard combatants, by the end of May the South was defeated. The news spread slowly in the Deep South, but, little by little, even enslaved men and women who had been removed to the most secluded areas of the Confederacy—a failed attempt to silence them, to divert them from their stake in the war—increasingly became aware that they were free, at last.[41]

From late April, thousands and thousands of Confederate soldiers began to return to their homes and farms, most of them not knowing what awaited them. Despite his delicate health and the severe wounds inflicted by military actions at Millboro, Tennessee, John Grigsby had survived the conflict. In early May, he wrote his wife from Greensboro, North Carolina, where he was stationed: "The war is virtually at an end. I shall not probably reach Kentucky before some time in June." His arrival at Traveller's Rest, in the early summer of 1865, must have been charged with great emotion and commotion: he and Susan had not seen each other for three long years, and now only two of the six children he had left behind—Virginia and Hart—were there to hug their father. Four of his progeny had been laid to rest in the Shelby family burying ground.[42]

A Confederate veteran returning to a staunchly Unionist Kentucky county was not warmly embraced by many of his fellow citizens. One night, a posse abducted John Grigsby from his home. Whether their action was intended simply to intimidate him or was in preparation for a lynching, the prompt intervention of some friendly neighbors prevented his harm or murder. The frightful incident, however, made Grigsby realize that the scars produced by the fratricidal war would take time to heal. Reconciliation might be possible between people who had fought under opposing flags, but it could take a longer time. Far from discouraged, John Grigsby set himself with alacrity to regain the esteem and consideration of his fellow-citizens. When differences slowly subsided and converged into support of the idea of a white-supremacist New South, myths of the Lost Cause flourished. At this fateful juncture, Grigsby found public recognition and, in 1875, was elected to represent Boyle County in the state legislature.[43]

In the aftermath of the Civil War, most Kentuckians were out of money. This made John's terrible financial situation appear less worrisome to the Grigsbys than had been the case in the antebellum era. Yet they urgently needed cash to pay the wages of the free laborers who worked their lands. To that end, John needed to address financial matters that were of vital importance for his family's future. First and foremost was the hoary issue of his investment in Chicago real estate, which involved extensive travel and a concomitant outlay of money. In an attempt to be as economical as he possibly could, on December 20, 1865, John sadly had to inform his wife he would not be home for the holidays: "If it had not been for questions of finances [I] would have returned until the Christmas holidays are over. It seems [*sic*] to be the most infallible of all speculations [but] Matters do not look so clear to me."[44]

In January 1866, Susan was again alone at Traveller's Rest, with no adequate domestic help and, furthermore, she was pregnant once again. She thought of moving, if only temporarily, into her mother's house in Danville, where the handling of household matters would be easier. She sought her husband's approval for what really was a minor decision compared with the problems he was facing at that time. John found her request of advice redundant and, from Chicago, replied with understandable impatience: "I think if you can make yourself comfortable at Danville for the present it would be better but at this distance I cannot judge so well what is best. . . . [Y]ou must act on your judgement & I shall be satisfied."[45]

In her usual fashion, Susan opted for remaining at Traveller's Rest, and, after some failed attempts between late 1866 and early 1867, was finally able to secure a Black cook, Frances, with the help of Felix Gibson. The girl of fourteen was not "stout enough to stand cooking all the time," and Gibson, who had noticed that her health was on the decline, advised Susan to apply her to "any other kind of work" but cooking, if she wanted to continue to avail herself of the girl's services. Why Gibson laid a claim on determining the terms of her employment is unclear. Maybe Frances was a former domestic servant of his, or perhaps even a formerly enslaved girl of his. In any event, Gibson wished to safeguard her from overwork, much as he would have under the hiring system during slavery. Susan seems to have consented to the request, for in 1870 a seventeen-year-old Black girl by the name of Frances Moore and her twelve-year-old sister, Emma, were reported by the census to be domestic servants at the Grigsbys'. Their household also included three white Kentuckians between twenty-seven and thirty-three, whom they had hired for farmwork.[46]

In 1866, the decimated ranks of the Grigsby family were replenished by the birth of a girl, whom they named Louisiana after Susan's late Aunt Gibson. The arrival of "Lulu," as she soon came to be affectionately called, was hailed as a good auspice for family life, and the Grigsbys looked optimistically to the future. Back from Chicago, John plunged himself into the troubled waters of the Reconstruction economy with new enthusiasm. In 1869 he entered a partnership with E. G. Stagg, James L. Ward, Isaac Shelby, and others to sell dry goods and groceries in Shelby City, and additionally contemplated engagement in more ventures. Susan shivered at the idea for, as she had long thought and sometime openly conveyed to him, John was "*too* fine, credulous & honest" to be "*very* successful in huge speculations." This notwithstanding, Susan continued to profess that she preferred him exactly as he was—and never for a single moment wished to see him changed. Accordingly, she supported John's grandiose vision and, because life seemed to be running in the fast lane for them, gladly resumed a high-maintenance lifestyle, using her husband's new firm to order luxuries, including white French china, a special cheese from Louisville importers, and some velvet.[47]

In 1872, forty-two-year-old Susan Grigsby gave birth to her last child, Susan Shelby, who was named so after the daughter she had lost from diphtheria ten years earlier. The joy procured by her arrival was much enhanced by the cherished return of Mrs. Drummond. Following the death of her mother in 1866, which freed her from family obligations, Drummond discovered the Grigsbys were able to meet her salary demands. Jane stayed with them five years at least, and certainly until sometime after John's death, which occurred in January 1877. Shortly after Christmas Day 1876, John Grigsby had set out for Cincinnati to seek medical advice on his chronic bronchial condition, leaving his wife at home with the children and Mrs. Drummond. After two weeks he had undertaken the return trip, but, as he approached Lexington, he was caught in a snowstorm and sought shelter at the house of Henry T. Duncan, the brother-in-law of Susan's cousin Hart Gibson. There, he unfortunately passed away on January 12, 1877, at the age of fifty-nine.[48]

The colonel's demise was mourned by the citizens of Boyle and Lincoln Counties, as well as by many across the state. Universally known as an honest and upright man, the animosities engendered by the internecine war had begun to heal, and Grigsby had been able to regain a distinguished, prestigious place in his community. He had restored his reputation by involving himself in philanthropic and charitable activities, signally as president of the Board of Commissioners of the Kentucky Institution for the Education of the Deaf and Dumb. In their obituary, its members bade farewell to him in the following accents: "Generous, Noble, High Souled Friend, Adieu!"[49]

John Grigsby always hated the idea of being considered a fortune seeker, living off his wife's money. Despite his desire and determination to provide for his family, he never achieved his goal. Whether out of bad luck or—as Susan sometimes suggested—because he lacked the shrewdness of the speculator, his business ventures invariably met with failure. The will he drafted in 1857 indicates the modesty of his financial legacy: the most valuable property he bequeathed to his several children were his gold watches, asking that his wife distribute them to his heirs at her discretion. He instructed that Alfred, their oldest son, was to receive the one he used to wear all the time. And he left "the balance" of what "his real and personal properties" might be at the time of his death to Susan, whom he named guardian of their children and executrix of his testament. Unfortunately, and contrary to his earnest hopes, he bequeathed only debts.[50]

Jane Drummond's departure, sometime in the latter part of the 1870s, was most likely due to Susan's inability to afford her salary. Grigsby faced serious financial distress following her discovery of the scope of her late husband's indebtedness. In fact, Jane Drummond was no longer listed as a member of the Grigsby household in the population schedules of the 1880 census.[51]

Formerly dependent on a network of family relations for moral support and advice, Susan was now virtually alone in weathering this storm. Both Aunt Fishback and Uncle Will had died in 1868, followed by her Uncle Gibson in 1872. Others had relocated to different states, and most of the trustworthy relatives she still had in Kentucky were old, impoverished, and lacked the political influence to be of any help. In her present circumstances, the vows expressed by a friend in her letter of condolences, that "your business was left in such a way, that it may give you no trouble, and that you have . . . friends who will advise you in any possible way," may have sounded ironic to Susan. By mid-March 1877, she was beginning to discover the full extent of John's debts.[52]

Whether Winners or Losers, Life Goes On

John Grigsby's disastrous financial embarrassment was the result of a series of infelicitous investments and speculations that caused him to become increasingly mired in debt. A very reserved man, the colonel did not confide to anyone, including his legal representative and close friend J. W. Stevenson, the extent of his fiscal distress. Not even his wife knew much of his situation.

In the late 1850s, the failure of the law firm Taylor, Shelby & Co., in which Grigsby was a minority partner, struck a severe blow to his financial assets. The ensuing lawsuit—which was not unusual for a man of his means and class—dragged on for years and was still pending at the time he passed away. In the expectation of having to disburse much in liquidating his share of the creditors' claims, John had borrowed money. In particular, he became indebted to Susan's Uncle Will for a huge sum, amounting to more than twenty-thousand dollars. Before leaving Kentucky in the summer of 1862 to join the Confederacy in the Civil War, Grigsby had placed five notes of five thousand dollars each, endorsed in blank and payable in annual instalments, in the custody of Stevenson, who assumed that they were meant to pay some pressing debt of the former Taylor, Shelby & Co. They were instead drawn for money loaned from William P. Hart. Upon his return from the war, Grigsby directed Stevenson to collect the notes Samuel J. Walker held for real estate he had sold him in connection with the Chicago speculation, and he did so without difficulty. But when the truth came to light, after John's death, Stevenson could not make sense of why a man "so signally upright and sensitively solicitous in all" like Colonel Grigsby had not applied "the twenty thousand dollars collected on the Walker debt . . . to the extinction of his debt to Hart." Whatever the reason, Susan had now to confront the legitimate claims of Uncle Will's widow, Rebecca Tevis Hart.[53]

Stevenson was at first of the opinion that, "If Mrs. Hart agrees to take part of Traveller's Rest at a fair evaluation, it would be . . . a step in the right direction." A subsequent evaluation of the situation of the estate revealed it to be much more complicated than expected. Vis-à-vis Susan's impatience to extinguish that debt as soon as possible, he therefore advised her to "ascertain the entire indebtedness of the estate and by whom held" before making any major decision. Under the circumstances, no bank, either in Lexington or in Louisville, would be willing to loan her money.

In an attempt to dissuade Susan Grigsby from being precipitous in surrendering her real property, he also pointed out that the imminent completion of the Southern Railroad would make Traveller's Rest a very valuable estate in a year or two. Alas, his arguments were not persuasive enough. In early June 1877, he had to reiterate to Susan his belief that it would be unwise "to give a mortgage to Travellers' Rest for the present—& accrued and future interest—! I care not what credit it is proposed to give you—that in my judgement would be a total escheat of the entire estate."[54]

Susan also had to deal with another painful issue connected with John's indebtedness: the lawsuit brought by Rebecca Tevis against James L. Ward of the former Stagg, Ward & Co. merchandizing firm, in behalf of L. W. Tevis—a kin, perhaps a younger brother of hers. A minority partner in the concern, Grigsby had dropped out one year after its forming—perhaps suspecting some kind of irregular behavior on the part of the principal associates. His fears were amply confirmed by Stagg and Ward, who devised ever-new excuses to postpone sending him the money they owed him. Having finally become persuaded that they were trying to defraud him, Grigsby filed a "petition in equity" with the Circuit Court of Boyle County to have all the firm accounts reviewed by decree of the Master of Chancery, and, in March 1875, the court ruled in his favor.[55]

Whatever happened to Mr. Stagg—whether he died or left the state—J. L. Ward apparently remained the only partner against whom claims could be laid, but, alas, he fled Kentucky without honoring his debts. As a party in the lawsuit, it was for Susan to track down Ward and force the issue. The man had moved to California, where he was engaged in mining speculation, and, after prolonged searching, Susan was able to contact him. In the attempt to force him to pay his debt, she threatened to make public some letters in her possession that compromised his position. Ward declared himself innocent of any fraud to the detriment of John Grigsby, whom he pretended to have "esteemed above all other friends," only blaming himself for not having "more fully" laid bare to him the condition of their business. He then tried to convince Susan that, because of his present financial embarrassment, any open action against him would only delay any settlement of the debt he owed her—and Mrs. Rebecca Hart likewise. Ward proposed to pay the amount of the original note of $2,500, with interest at 6 percent per year to May 1877, in three monthly instalments over the following two years. This arrangement sounded acceptable to Susan, but there is no evidence that James Ward ever met his obligation.[56]

The only really successful financial operation the Grigsbys undertook in the postbellum era was the purchase of six thousand dollars' worth of gold from one Leo Hyden, in 1873. The speculation must have been safe enough, for, by mid-June 1875, they had not only repaid their debt in full but more than doubled the initial investment. How was this remarkable sum spent? Given Susan's ignorance of her husband's major exposure, that money might have been applied to the purchase of goods and services she made to return the family to an upper-class lifestyle, and to the payment of a few minor debts.[57]

The fact remains that, after four years of desperate efforts to shield her properties from seizure by creditors, in 1881 Susan Grigsby finally had to surrender them all. To meet the payments of the mortgage on Traveller's Rest and cope with other debts, in February she had to sell the "Warweick" house in Danville she had inherited from her mother. That sacrifice did not suffice to prevent the foreclosure of the mortgage on the Shelbys' ancestral home, which devastated her sometime later that year.[58]

Although some three thousand dollars still accrued to Grigsby from Samuel J. Walker's bankruptcy, in January 1882 Susan's financial prospects looked grim. Homeless and virtually penniless, she momentarily moved into the house of a friend, where she could not remain indefinitely. Most of all, she urgently needed to find a source of income to support herself and her family. Yet, as a woman of aristocratic descent, admired and revered by everyone in the community, Susan Grigsby did not at first consider the possibility of herself engaging in some kind of remunerative work. Rather, she thought of seeking a job for her son Hart, the only male member of the family. To this effect, she contacted Charlie Griggs, an old and dear friend of John, who was superintendent of the Lexington division of the Chesapeake and Ohio Railroad Company. While his reply confirmed the mutuality of their feelings, and conveyed his heartfelt intention to honor John's memory by helping his widow and children, Griggs was regretfully unable to do so immediately, though he eventually kept his promise.[59]

A few months later, Hart was working in some unspecified capacity at the construction of a tract of the railroad lying within Kentucky at a monthly salary of thirty dollars. His income, although very modest, was still essential for his nearly indigent family. In mid-May, he managed to send his mother a little money, but the pay was so small that he despaired to ever "be able to do better." This predisposed Hart to seek better employment, thus he accepted a proposal by cousin Willie Voorhies to take on a commission post. In September, he was working for W. Q. Emisson, "Dealer in Kentucky Whiskies and Imported Wines in Lexington." Although he had hope that the alcohol trade would be lucrative, it was not. Because he was paid in proportion to sales, in late October 1882 Hart had not yet received *any* compensation; his remittances were too modest to contribute significantly to the sustenance of his family. Her son's inability to bring home enough money was decisive in persuading Susan Grigsby to make a momentous decision: she would transform herself from an aristocratic lady to an independent, self-supporting woman. She would join the new American—and southern—middle class.[60]

The Civil War, emancipation, and the loss of protections entailed by *feme covert* status following her husband's death turned Susan's world upside down. Ashamed of living in near-destitution, dependent upon the kindness of others, trapped among those who had known her as the proud mistress of Traveller's Rest, Susan Grigsby found the courage to take a chance and jump over the fence. She would venture into modernity—primarily for her children's sake, but perhaps to prove to herself that autonomy had to be better than the dwindling fate she faced. Although prodded by a necessity that must have been incredibly painful, Grigsby would abandon the emotional fragility that had made her too timid to fight for self-affirmation. She would become more than the wife and mother her class and race had assigned her, and be a woman who sought her own destiny.

Coda

Susan P. Grigsby: From Aristocratic Lady to Middle-Class Woman

Kentucky initially emerged from the devastation of the Civil War with some success, but, unfortunately, the onset of the major depression of 1873 intervened to bring about an economic stagnation, exacerbated by the end of Reconstruction only four years later.[1]

Thus, right at the moment when Susan Grigsby finally had to face her own precarious financial situation, she had to do so within the context of a devastated regional economy, which did not offer much hope or opportunity to women of her age and class. Yet, unimagined possibilities opened up for many of these gentlewomen when the Union government encouraged woman to undertake clerical work, beginning in 1861, as a wartime necessity. This inaugurated a newly emerging attitude about white women's work, which extended into the 1880s with civil service reform. Educated white women with the proper bloodlines and political connections found employment with the federal bureaucracy in Washington, a remedy that so many of these impoverished former elite females gladly welcomed.[2]

Susan Grigsby, who did not lack important connections, found this prospect alluring. Her first cousin Randall Lee Gibson was in fact a prestigious and influential man in Louisiana as well as in national politics. More to the point, Gibson was a staunch supporter of the civil service reform as purported by the Pendleton Bill, which would become law in 1883. In search of a job for herself and Virginia—her oldest daughter—Susan decided to explore this avenue but felt somewhat embarrassed at writing the distinguished politician Randall had become, begging assistance after many years without communication. She trusted that, although circumstances had operated to make contacts between them less and less frequent over time, the bonds of affection established during their youth—when visits were assiduous and frequent—might predispose Randall to look to her request with a sympathetic eye. In her uncertainty, she decided to approach him through his sister, Sarah Gibson Humphreys, with whom she had remained in closer touch. She also knew that Sarah might understand her special difficulties better than anyone else. The two women had shared the worry-free yet intellectually stimulating school years in Philadelphia and together had listened to the "lectures" on racial and gender equality that Uncle Tobias—Sarah's father—used to impart to his children and their cousins during their sojourns in Louisiana. In recent years, their ties were strengthened by the similarity of their experiences with loss and mourning, with struggles to retain properties, and the increasingly burdensome downward spiral of their finances. Susan and Sarah had been raised as carefree heirs of the plantocracy, but with the Confederate defeat, their inheritance dwindled alongside fortunes and dreams.

Contrasting Sarah Gibson's story with her cousin Susan's is particularly meaningful in illuminating how the already diverging paths followed by two kinswomen of similar background and education might become even more at odds in response to the shifting economic and social context of the postbellum period. Whereas Sarah asserted women's rights, seeking autonomy from the beginning, Susan forsook that ideal for a more traditional married life. Yet they remained tied by strong bonds of womanhood, and it is only thanks to their correspondence that we are able to divine many of Susan's feelings and attitudes in the latter part of her life.

Following the death of her husband, Joseph A. Humphreys, from disease, in 1863, Sarah left Kentucky and removed to Louisiana, where her father was trying to retain possession of his remaining lands. The confiscations effected by the federal authorities caused havoc. Tobias Gibson struggled to introduce his former bondspeople to the principles of mutual obligation; he hoped to regulate and influence the relationship between employer and employee in a free labor market. Despite his best exertions, the experiment was largely a failure for, as was happening everywhere else in the South, the freedpeople sought independent employment, spurning wage work, which they associated with their former servile condition. Whites, however, interpreted their reluctance to submit to new rules as a confirmation of their lack of preparation for freedom.[3]

At the end of the war, what remained of the Gibsons' once-thriving sugar plantations was in total disarray. Their formerly prosperous lands were heavily mortgaged and, with the failure of several consecutive crops, they were out of money. Without the resources to pay hands their wages, further decline threatened, and total ruin loomed on the horizon. Sarah was extremely disheartened, and the 1867 death of her daughter, Louisiana Hart (whom she had named after her mother), rendered her even more low-spirited. Five years later her father died suddenly, leaving his offspring in a bad financial situation, save for Randall. He had married into a very wealthy New York family and undertaken a promising political career. Thus he was the only one in a position to help his less fortunate, or irresponsible, siblings—as was the case with Tobe. Randall arrogated to himself the role of the family leader, and this was all right with everyone but Sarah, who, by virtue of her indomitable belief in equality between the sexes, was intolerant of any restrictions on her autonomy. Whether real or imagined, any attempt by a man, even if he was a brother, to encroach on her freedom of agency was met with rancorous resistance.[4]

As a widow in the 1870s and with three children to raise, Sarah G. Humphreys struggled to keep control of her late husband's lands in Kentucky. Yet, sentimental attachment to her own father's estate led her to focus on what remained of his once vast lands in Terrebonne Parish, Louisiana. Randall entertained very conservative views on women's nature and their appropriate place in society. He designated himself the natural protector of his sister's best interests, repeatedly advising her that Kentucky was a far better place for herself and her children to live than the Louisiana bottoms. A staunch feminist, Sarah was deeply hurt and much offended by her brother's intimation that she was not up to the task of taking care of herself and her businesses. She regarded his proffers of financial assistance as attempts to take control of Live Oak plantation, which they owned jointly. Stubbornly, she did not yield to his insistence and resolutely undertook the massive effort to meet the heavy expenditures pertaining to her share of that property without ever asking Randall for a penny.[5]

As late as 1882, up against severe obstacles, Sarah still believed she could stay afloat. However, the following year she was finally compelled to surrender her interest in Live Oak plantation to her brother. She did this in exchange for another property—likely Magnolia—and some much-needed cash. Although the arrangement signified formal reconciliation between the two siblings, it did not stop Sarah from continuing to consider Randall an enemy in the struggle for women's emancipation. She had become a militant member of the Kentucky Equal Rights Association and deplored males who, even with the best of intentions, usurped women's self-determination.[6]

When Susan asked for the favor of intercession, Sarah was at first tempted to refuse; she hated to have to apply to Randall on behalf of any woman—so much the worse if she was a relative. A full decade of fights with her brother over matters of property made her deeply distrustful of him. She doubted the sincerity of his and, for that matter, of any man's intentions. "I have been betrayed by *every man* I ever trusted," she lamented, and "have no faith, none absolutely *none* in a man's unselfish interest in a poor woman—and as for that in a girl [referring to Susan's daughter Virginia] either."

Yet, once she apprehended the severity of Susan's situation, she did not hesitate to comply with her request. To Sarah's surprise, Randall did not claim privilege of interference and resisted any urge to take over their care. Instead, he promptly used his influence to locate jobs for both Susan and her daughter at federal departments in the capital. Between May and June 1883, he kept his cousin Susan constantly updated on the developments of his entreaties. He reassured her that, although he understood that such government employment was "an awful come down" for his female relatives, "many of the descendants of the great men of this Republic" occupied similar positions, and they were "in every way honorable." Finally, on June 11 Randall informed Susan that he had been able to procure employment for her with the Interior Department, and an additional position for Virginia with the Post Office Department. They would each earn an annual salary of one thousand dollars. Both appointments would commence on June 13, and this would offer a decent income for the impoverished Grigsbys.[7]

Elated at the news, Sarah conveyed to Susan her wholehearted wish that the steady source of income she was soon to enjoy might be "the stepping stone" for the recovery of at least part of her properties in Kentucky. Alas, Susan knew well that any such hope was misplaced, for her poverty was so extreme that, on one of her last days in Danville, a compassionate neighbor sent her "a small loaf of bread." She delivered this gift, suggesting her awareness of how busy Mrs. Grigsby was, and how little time she had "remaining for household activities," and in the hope that she might "enjoy it on that day of rest which God has so kindly given us." Despite the reconciliation and financial compromise reached with her brother, Sarah did not fare much better than her cousin and soon found herself in growing economic difficulties. In May 1885, she could not even refund her son Jon the fifty dollars she had borrowed from him sometime earlier.[8] Sarah's story, like Susan's, reveals how Emancipation and southern economic retrenchment following the war left the former enslaving class, and particularly its women, in dire straits.

Susan Grigsby arrived in Washington, DC, with her three daughters around mid-June 1883. She carried with her a few family mementoes: some china and linens she had inherited from her paternal grandmother. She also brought along the "likeness" of her "precious beautiful mother," which, although she considered it a poor one, was the only portrait she had of her. Social life of the US capital, which was by then still far more provincial than Paris, Rome, or London where Susan briefly sojourned as a young bride, was not so tragic for Susan Grigsby. Her major trauma was the very idea that she no longer had a permanent home in Kentucky to which she might return. As an intelligent woman, she understood that the past could not be resurrected and that she was now reduced to a middle-class status, earning her living by wage work. After all, her life story was not dissimilar from those of myriad white southern women of the planter's class who had witnessed the end of an era and courageously entered the transition to a "new" America following the South's defeat in the Civil War. As suggested by Anastasia Sims, the war operated to enhance different elements of a woman's character, depending on the specific circumstances they had to confront. Hence their different responses to postwar realities.[9]

Like scores of women of the old elite, Susan could not reconcile herself to the idea of her children's loss of social advantage. Yet some of them found in the postwar experience of downward mobility a stimulus to come to grips with their never-resolved inner conflicts over the position of white women within the antebellum slavocracy. Once freed from the cultural and psychological constraints of the patriarchal order, they sought to affirm a new understanding of southern womanhood and were determined to fight for their right to participate in every domain of the public sphere—from the world of labor to politics—on the same footing as men. Membership in voluntary associations, such as the League of Women Voters and the Equal Suffrage Association, provided suitable contexts in which to voice their claims. The example of Ella Gertrude Clanton Thomas of Augusta, Georgia—a contemporary of Grigsby with an antebellum background largely similar to hers—illustrates well how critical reconsideration of past experience with slavery, from the vantage point of postwar impoverishment and loss of social status, might turn a former southern belle into a wage-earning woman, and a feminist, in the New South. A delegate from the Women's Christian Temperance

Union at the 1895 Atlanta meeting of the National Woman's Suffrage Association, four years later Thomas became president of its Georgia branch.[10]

Unlike Thomas, Susan Grigsby embraced modernity unenthusiastically, in the belief that her offspring might stand better chances of success in life by moving to a city environment where they could form and cultivate important alliances. She recognized this was preferable to continuing to languish in a remote corner of an impoverished, maimed South. Yet Susan was tormented by the thought of how poor a custodian of the shrine of the Shelbys' glorious past she had been. She was deeply saddened by the realization that, in the place where she presently lived and worked, no one knew or cared about her illustrious forebears. Indeed, these forebears and family connections might be better disguised rather than boasted about in postwar Washington. The last time she recalled anyone showing an interest in her family history had been in distant year of 1868, when Lyman Draper, librarian and historian at the Wisconsin Historical Society, had contacted her seeking materials on her eminent grandfather Isaac Shelby, for his monumental project on the settlement and early history of the trans-Allegheny West.[11]

When cousin Sarah expressed an interest in knowing more about the beginnings of Traveller's Rest and the early history of the Shelbys there, Susan was therefore delighted to fill her in. Although she would have much preferred to do so in the quietness of home, she was forced to answer her letter during work hours for, as she explained, "'t is painfully true that I cannot write, in my only leisure hours, by gas light—my eyes being almost out." Whether real or, perhaps, motivated by the embarrassing fact that she could not afford buying enough oil for lamps to read and write by adequately from home, writing that letter from her office desk was a very unsettling experience for Susan Grigsby. As she got immersed further and further into remembrances of the olden times, full of sweet memories and wrenching pain as well, she became so emotionally drained that tears began to flow from her eyes. Colleagues around her noticed her state of prostration, and some started to ridicule her unmercifully. Their callousness made Susan feel more acutely than ever before that she did not belong to the "modern" world, if modernity meant impersonality and indifference to human tragedies, and in the final lines of her letter, she conveyed to Sarah her acute sense of alienation.[12]

In 1883 Susan Grigsby was a very frail creature, both physically and psychically. "In my intense nervous condition," she confided to Sarah, "my precious children sometime think me deranged—and indeed they are not far mistaken." She felt as if she was merely a spectator in the drama of her own life, and she could barely recognize herself as the main character. All the same, she persevered for eight more years in Washington, seeing her time as a necessary passage to secure a better future for her four surviving children. In her heart, she yearned for everlasting peace, only. "My work will soon be done," she wrote, "and then shant I, Oh, wont I be steered across the Lilley-lined [*sic*] shore of the River of rest! . . . I am almost worn out into life and its disappointments."[13]

Susanna Preston Shelby Grigsby continued at her government post until, in the second half of October 1891, she became ill with pneumonia. She was finally released from her worldly cares on Saturday, November 7. She was sixty-one, but probably felt as if she were nearly a century old. Had her dear John still been alive, they would have celebrated their forty-first wedding anniversary two days before her death, but the man of her life was no longer by her side. Susan perhaps longed to be reunited with him in death. And so she was, at least physically, for her body was interred beside his in the family plot at Lexington cemetery within forty-eight hours of her demise.[14]

Susan Grigsby's lifetime was interlaced with epochal transformations in Kentucky and southern history. She lived through a series of epic shifts: the first important spurt of economic modernization, the crisis of the Union, the Civil War, the abolition of slavery, the defeat of the Confederacy, the emancipation of millions of enslaved persons and constitutional guarantee of citizenship rights—and the difficult adjustment to such new economic and social realities. Each of these important events was a landmark in the long and challenging journey of southern white women toward economic, social, and political autonomy. No improvements came to members of the former enslaving elite without varying degrees of personal crisis as they grappled with emerging identities. All considered, individual character played a significant role in determining a woman's responses to defeat and economic ruin. The majority of them found in associations aimed at preserving the memory of the Lost Cause a way to reaffirm their identity as southerners.[15] Others, like Sarah Gibson Humphreys and Gertrude Thomas, pushed beyond commemoration and nostalgia to engage in feminist activism. Susan P. Grigsby belonged to still another group of women. She was part of a minority who, far from regretting the end of slavery, were nevertheless unable to expunge the trauma produced by the destruction of the enslaving regime. They found their whole world crumbling, they interrogated their former agendas, and, with the Confederate defeat, began to struggle with a new sense of purpose. Even as personal circumstances might have led them to take advantage of some of the blessings that modernity bestowed on women, they never saw these blessings as personal victories.

In her postbellum correspondence, Susan Grigsby never mentioned any of her former bondspeople, and this absence might be attributed to any number of factors. Her personal experience with the increasingly ruthless and acquisitive spirit that reigned in the "new" America may have brought her to reflect on her own former failures to understand the plight of the enslaved. She had often mistaken proximity for intimacy. Even if Black people might have been thought of fondly by their owners, they were nevertheless still regarded as *property* by the master class. And further, among her many regrets, she mourned the loss of the monetary value of her property in human beings. Her consequent reduction to a wage-earning status may have appeared to Susan as minor compared with the cataclysmic demise of her larger world. But her dreams of personal improvement, either material or moral, foundered on the shoals of the Confederate defeat and a depressed southern economy. Her idealization of her family roots could not overcome the reality of irreversible decline.

Although Susan Grigsby undoubtedly welcomed the demise of slavery as a liberation from the burdens she felt the system imposed on her, her unenthusiastic response to modernity leaves us to wonder about any deep-seated motivation. As she witnessed the devastation inflicted on so many of her white fellow-citizens in the post-Reconstruction South, Grigsby realized that the gospel of modernity did not necessarily preach social and economic justice for former enslavers. Instead, modernization heralded the full deployment of the most ruthless manifestations of mature capitalism: greed, wild competition, and a new era of exploitation that targeted the vulnerable without race distinctions. She did not identify with this new scenario, although she definitely benefited from it.

For millions of formerly enslaved African Americans, Emancipation had not marked the end of centuries of sufferings and travails. Rather, it had inaugurated for them a long odyssey to finally obtain the very implementation of the civil and political rights guaranteed to them by constitutional amendments.

In an extremely unfriendly South, dominated by Jim Crow and segregation, Black women were in many ways more vulnerable than men in the face of virulent racism and under the constant threat of physical and sexual violence.

Yet they played a critical role in the community-building effort undertaken by Black Americans. They actively participated in reform movements and, in 1896, founded the National Association of Colored Women (NACW). Young Black women stubbornly sought self-improvement and uplift by pursuing new educational opportunities, going to work, and establishing successful businesses. Susan Grigsby must have been happy to know that the progeny of her formerly enslaved women were finally enjoying some of the fruits of freedom and female self-redress, albeit amid so many difficulties and obstacles.

In the latter part of her life, Grigsby kept her psychological distance from the new regime by clinging to the memories of what she thought was a bygone golden era, the South before the war. For a woman who had struggled so long and hard to exalt her family's reputation, for a woman who had hoped to preserve the Shelbys' status and Traveller's Rest's place in history, for a mother who dedicated herself to her children and their legacy, Susan P. Grigsby's path was littered with obstacles. Instead of sitting by the side of the road and bemoaning her fate, she persisted and became eyewitness to one of the greatest transformations in US history, the decline of southern slavery and the birth of a new freedom. The story of Grigsby's life, and her voice as a storyteller, offer us a window onto the human dilemmas and historical dramas that shaped a newer, more modern South.

Acknowledgments

During this book's long incubation, I have accumulated many debts. I know that I would never have completed this work had it not been for the encouragement and support extended to me in multiple ways by a number of colleagues and friends.

Mark Wetherington, former managing director at the Filson Historical Society, first introduced me to the wealth of its repositories on subjects related to women's participation in the capitalist economy of late antebellum Kentucky. Besides providing a stimulating intellectual counterpoint toward the finalization of my working project, he and his spouse, Glenna Pfeiffer, very generously hosted me at their house during my several sojourns in Louisville. To them both go my deepest sentiments of gratitude.

I am especially appreciative of the help received from the fine staff at the Filson Historical Society, and I wish to thank all of its members for their impeccable professionalism and wonderful assistance. In particular, I want to acknowledge Glenn Crothers, former Director of Research, for deeming my project worth of attention, and Curator James Holmberg, for patiently listening to my daily reports on research, offering useful suggestions on how to proceed, and for reading some of the first draft of the manuscript.

This book draws substance from, and brings together, several lines of research conducted over a considerably long span of time. Too long indeed for me to recall all the names of the archivists and librarians who, with great competence and professional selflessness, assisted my work at the North Carolina Department of Archives and History in Raleigh; the New York Historical Society; the Southern Historical Collection of the University of North Carolina, Chapel Hill; the Tennessee State Library and Archives in Nashville;

the Hodges Library and its Special Collections at the University of Tennessee, Knoxville; the Special Collections of the University of Virginia Library in Charlottesville; the Kentucky Historical Society and the Kentucky Department of Archives and History in Frankfort; the Special Collections of the University of Kentucky, Lexington; and the Manuscript Division of the Library of Congress in Washington, DC. I am deeply thankful to all of them for the many courtesies extended.

At the University of Tennessee, Knoxville—an institution to which I am tied in a special way by virtue of a long history of academic exchanges and fruitful collaboration with my home institution in Genoa, Italy—colleague Flavia Brizio-Skov and former provost Susan D. Martin provided the conditions that allowed me to do the bulk of work on historical literature, and some on primary sources, at the Hodges Library and at its Special Collections. I wish to acknowledge them for being two major contributors to the success of this enterprise. To them both goes my most heartfelt gratitude for the support extended over the years.

I am indebted to Bess Beatty, formerly of Oregon State University, Eugene, for generously hosting me more than once at her house in Washington, DC, in connection with my research at the Manuscript Division of the Library of Congress. She also offered useful comments and suggestions on the first two chapters of the book. The late Loretta Valtz Mannucci, a professor emerita of the Milan (Italy) State University, to whom I owe my early introduction to the US academic community of revisionist historians of the South, offered useful comments on the initial and concluding parts.

At a critical juncture in the finalization of the manuscript, involving language subtleties and nuanced expressions that often escaped the attentive eye of a foreign scholar, two great historians and wonderful friends, Catherine Clinton and Stephanie Cole, came to the rescue. Their professional advice, timely comments, and constructive criticism were fundamental in helping me overcome the impasse. For this, and for more deep-seated reasons concerning the value of woman's mutual loyalty and support, this book is dedicated to them, and to Michele Gillespie. With her intellectual honesty, during our many years of fruitful collaboration, and beyond, she offered a bright example of what true sisterhood is really about.

Many people contributed to the realization of this book, albeit in more indirect, but no less significant, ways. Some of them provided accommodation at their houses; others helped relieve me of the considerable financial burden involved by extended sojourns in the United States by offering opportunities to deliver lectures, thus allowing me to do some research at their respective universities' libraries; still others assisted in my quest for ad hoc funding. The moral support that only a true friend can give, however, is the most enduring legacy of their exertions. For all of this I want to thank Stephen V. and Jean Ash, Todd Diacon, Don H. Doyle, Ernest Freeberg, Valeria Gennaro Lerda, Augusta Molinari, Aleksandra Parker and her late husband, Marcus Parker, Theda Perdue, Vladimir Protopopescu, Philip N. and Frances Racine, and Marjorie Spruill.

At the University Press of Kentucky, acquisition editors Anne Dean and Patrick O'Dowd firmly believed in the relevance of my work and ensured the Press's continued interest in it until Natalie O'Neal finally ferried my manuscript to publication. Without their constant support this book may have never seen the light. But I also wish to acknowledge project editor Sarah Olson, marketing assistant Jewell Boyd, and copyeditor Susan Murray for assisting in the preparation of this book with consummate professionalism and great patience, too.

The steady encouragement lent by my family over the years was fundamental in helping me overcome the moments of discouragement that always accompany the intellectual travail involved in the parturition of a scholarly work. My late husband, Bruno Caviglia, who was a fan of this project, played a crucial role at a critical time. Considerate of the logistic difficulties I was facing, he did not hesitate to drive me even to remote places in Kentucky like Traveller's Rest, or to Oxford, Virginia, in the failed effort to be able to see the only existing portrait of Susan Grigsby. For his unfaltering support, this book is also dedicated to his memory.

Notes

Introduction

1. Susanna Delfino and Michele Gillespie, eds., *Neither Lady nor Slave: Working Women of the Old South* (Chapel Hill: University of North Carolina Press, 2002), and, in it, Susanna Delfino, "Invisible Woman: Female Labor in the Upper South's Iron and Mining Industries," 285–307.

2. US Bureau of the Census, *Compendium of the Tenth Census, 1880* (Washington, DC: Government Printing Office, 1882), 930–31; ibid., *The Seventh Census of the United States, 1850* (Washington, DC: Government Printing Office, 1851), 612–13. In 1850, Kentucky ranked third among the states with legalized slavery, after Virginia and Maryland, for capital invested in manufacturing and industrial production, too. At that time its total population amounted to 982,405 individuals, 761,413 of whom were whites, 10,011 free colored, and 210,981 enslaved. Although the census indicated only one-fifth of the 148,582 whites who were born out of the state as originating from abroad, their number was far higher but went unrecorded for a variety of reasons, including recent immigrant status and impermanence of residence due to the temporary nature of their labor contracts.

Underscoring the capitalistic nature of the US South's slavery-based economy, some recent scholarship has insisted that the wealth generated over time by enslaved labor was instrumental in promoting and sustaining the industrial transformation of the Northeast. See Sven Beckert and Seth Rockman, eds., *Slavery's Capitalism: A New History of American Economic Development* (Philadelphia: University of Pennsylvania Press, 2016); Edward Baptist, *The Half Has Never Been Told: Slavery and the Making of American Capitalism* (New York: Basic, 2014); and Walter Johnson, *River of Dark Dreams: Slavery and the Empire in the Cotton Kingdom* (Cambridge, MA: Belknap Press of Harvard University Press, 2013).

For an overview of the longtime debate on the relationship between slavery and capitalism in the eighteenth and nineteenth centuries' Atlantic economy, and the role of the trade in enslaved humans and enslaved labor in triggering the first industrial revolution in England, France, and the northern United States, see Stanley L. Engerman,

"France, Britain and the Economic Growth of Colonial North America," in *The Early Modern Atlantic,* ed. James J. McCusker and Kenneth Morgan (New York: Cambridge University Press, 2000); Joseph E. Inikori, "Slavery and the Development of Industrial Capitalism in England," in *British Capitalism and Caribbean Slavery: The Legacy of Eric Williams,* ed. B. L. Solow and S. L. Engerman (Cambridge: Cambridge University Press, 1987), and, for a compendium of the debate, Susanna Delfino, *Alla periferia di un impero: Le tredici colonie nordamericane nell'economia atlantica* (Genoa, Italy: Name, 2004).

3. Modernization—as contended by critics of the "modernization theory"—is not an imitative process but an original one, depending on a country or region's distinctive economic, social, and cultural traits. On this assumption, we may look at the process of modernization in the US South as a shift toward rapid economic diversification and industrial development, begun around 1840, that was accompanied by cultural changes that engendered new sensibilities about individual rights, albeit for whites only. The case of Kentucky illustrates well the ensuing tension between the enormous profitability of enslaved labor—also in manufacturing—and the advancing idea of the dignity of free labor (Dean C. Tipps, "Modernization Theory and the Comparative Study of National Societies: A Critical Perspective," *Comparative Studies in Society and History* 15 [1973]: 199–226; Alexander Gerschenkron, *Economic Backwardness in Historical Perspective* [Cambridge, MA: Belknap Press of Harvard University Press, 1962]).

On the origins of an industrial working class in the United States, a classic reference work is Jonathan Prude, *The Coming of Industrial Order: Town and Factory Life in Rural Massachusetts, 1810–1860* (Cambridge: Cambridge University Press, 1982) and, with special regard to the textile industry, Thomas Dublin, *Women at Work: The Transformation of Work and Community in Lowell, Massachusetts, 1826–1860* (New York: Columbia University Press, 1979).

4. The similarity of the South's experience in the process is well illustrated in Bess B. Beatty, *Alamance: The Holt Family and Industrialization in a North Carolina County, 1837–1900* (Baton Rouge: Louisiana State University Press, 1999); Barbara J. Howe, "Patient Laborers: Women at Work in the Formal Economy of West(ern) Virginia"; and Michele Gillespie in "To Harden a Lady's Hand: Gender Politics, Racial Realities, and Women Millworkers in Antebellum Georgia," both in *Neither Lady nor Slave: Working Women of the Old South,* ed. Susanna Delfino and Michele Gillespie (Chapel Hill: University of North Carolina Press, 2002), 121–54 and 261–84, respectively.

5. On middle-class women's engagement in paid work, see Suzanne Lebsock, *The Free Women of Petersburg: Status and Culture in a Southern Town, 1784–1860* (New York: Norton, 1985), 152–54, 175–82; and, for a perspective on women as teachers, Emily Bingham and Penny Richards, "The Female Academy and Beyond: Three Mordecai Sisters at Work in the Old South," in *Neither Lady nor Slave: Working Women of the Old South,* ed. Susanna Delfino and Michele Gillespie, 174–97.

6. All in all, the data on women's participation in the labor market resulting from a verbatim reading of the census should probably be revised upward by several thousands. But even the total figure seems to fall very short of representing the full extent of the working population of late antebellum Kentucky (US Bureau of the Census, *The Eighth Census of the United States* [Washington, DC: Government Printing Office, 1860], Kentucky, Occupations of the Population: 186–88; Kenneth H. Williams and James Russell Harris, "Kentucky in 1860: A Statistical Overview," *Register of the Kentucky Historical Society,* 103 [2005]: 743–64, and 755–56 in particular).

7. On the growing impact of Irish immigrants on the American markets for domestic work, see Daniel E. Sutherland, *Americans and Their Servants: Domestic Service in the United States from 1800 to 1920* (Baton Rouge: Louisiana State University Press, 1981), 51–52. For what concerns the South, see Timothy Lockley, *Lines in the Sand: Race and Class in Lowcountry Georgia, 1750–1860* (Athens: University of Georgia Press, 2001), 35; and, on Kentucky in particular, Stephanie Cole, "Servants and Slaves in Louisville: Race, Ethnicity, and Household Labor in an Antebellum Border City," *Ohio Valley History* 11 (2011): 3–25; Stephanie Cole, "A White Woman, of Middle Age, Would Be Preferred: Children's Nurses in the Old South," in *Neither Lady nor Slave: Working Women of the Old South,* ed. Susanna Delfino and Michele Gillespie, 75–101.

8. Mary P. Ryan, *The Empire of the Mother: American Writing about Domesticity, 1830–1860* (New York: Haworth, 1982), 133–47; Thavolia Glymph, *Out of the House of Bondage: The Transformation of the Plantation Household* (Cambridge: Cambridge University Press, 2008), 65; Randolph B. Campbell, "Slave Hiring in Texas," *American Historical Review* 93 (1988): 108; Keith Barton, "'Good Cooks and Washers': Slave Hiring, Domestic Labor, and the Market in Bourbon County, Kentucky," *Journal of American History* 84, no. 2 (September 1997): 436–60; John Zaborney, *Slaves for Hire: Renting Enslaved Laborers in Antebellum Virginia* (Baton Rouge: Louisiana State University Press, 2012).

9. Cole, "A White Woman, of Middle Age, Would Be Preferred," 90–94; Glymph, *Out of the House of Bondage,* 2. The vast majority of Kentuckians were not enslavers. Moreover, of those who were enslavers, most enslaved very few persons. In 1850, as few as 5 percent of the state's 38,385 enslavers enslaved more than 99 persons, and none enslaved as many as 200. The proportion of Kentuckians enslaving fewer than twenty bondspeople amounted to 18 percent, while those enslaving only one comprised 24 percent of the population. Among the enslaving states, only Missouri averaged fewer enslaved people per enslaver (4.5) than Kentucky (5.4). In 1860, those enslaved constituted 19.5 percent (or 225,486 individuals) of the state's total population of 1,155,684 as opposed to 31 percent in Virginia, 44 percent in Georgia, 55 percent in Mississippi, and 57 percent in South Carolina. The owner of nearly 40 bondspersons, in the early 1850s Susan Grigsby figured among Kentucky's medium-large enslavers (Slavery Documents, folder 346, Grigsby Family Papers, Filson Historical Society, Louisville, Kentucky [hereafter GFP-FHS]). Henceforth, folder numbers will be provided only for undated manuscripts in this collection.

10. Sylvia Wrobel and George Grider, *Isaac Shelby: Kentucky's First Governor and Hero of Three Wars* (Danville, KY: Cumberland, 1974); Joan W. Coward, *Kentucky in the New Republic: The Process of Constitution-Making* (Lexington: University Press of Kentucky, 1979).

11. On southern elite girls' quest for a more equal partnership in marriage, see Anya Jabour, *Marriage in the Early Republic: Elizabeth and William Wirt and the Companionate Ideal* (Baltimore: Johns Hopkins University Press, 1998); and Anya Jabour, *Scarlett's Sisters: Young Women in the Old South* (Chapel Hill: University of North Carolina Press, 2007).

12. Catherine Clinton, *The Plantation Mistress: Woman's World in the Old South* (New York: Pantheon, 1982).

13. Marie S. Molloy, *Single, White Slaveholding Women in the American South* (Columbia: University of South Carolina Press, 2018).

14. Ibid., introduction.

15. Drew Gilpin Faust, "Altars of Sacrifice: Confederate Women and the Narratives of War," *Journal of American History* 76, no. 4 (March 1990): 171; Drew Gilpin Faust, *Mothers of Invention: Women of the Slaveholding South in the American Civil War* (Chapel Hill: University of North Carolina Press, 1996), 79, 214, 247; LeeAnn Whites, *The Civil War as a Crisis in Gender: Augusta, Georgia, 1860–1890* (Athens: University of Georgia Press, 1995), 2–13; LeeAnn Whites, "'Stand by Your Man': The Ladies Memorial Association and the Reconstruction of Southern White Womanhood," in *Women of the American South: A Multicultural Reader,* ed. Christie Anne Farnham (New York: New York University Press, 1987), 133–49; Nina Silber, *Gender and the Sectional Conflict* (Chapel Hill: University of North Carolina Press, 2008), 13, 56; Catherine Clinton and Nina Silber, eds., *Battle Scars: Gender and Sexuality in the American Civil War* (New York: Oxford University Press, 2006), 8–9; Karen Cox, *Dixie's Daughters: The United Daughters of the Confederacy and the Preservation of Confederate Culture* (Gainesville: University Press of Florida, 2004), 1–7.

16. Christine Jacobson Carter, "Indispensable Spinsters: Maiden Aunts in the Elite Families of Savannah and Charleston," in *Negotiating the Boundaries of Southern Womanhood: Dealing with the Powers That Be,* ed. Janet L. Coryell et al. (Columbia: University of Missouri Press, 2000), 110–33, and 112–13 in particular.

17. In 1853 Susan Grigsby enslaved close to forty bondspeople (Slavery Documents, folder 346, GFP-FHS).

18. Stephanie E. Jones-Rogers, *They Were Her Property: White Women as Slave Owners in the American South* (New Haven, CT: Yale University Press, 2019).

1. Kentucky

1. Cass K. Shelby, *A Report of the First Three Generations of the Shelby Family in the United States of America* (Chattanooga, TN: Lookout, 1922), 6–7.

2. Ibid., 7; Archibald Henderson, "Isaac Shelby: Revolutionary Patriot and Border Hero," *North Carolina Booklet* 16 (1917): 109–44, and 109–11 in particular.

3. Henderson, "Isaac Shelby: Revolutionary Patriot and Border Hero," 112–14; John Mack Faragher, *Daniel Boone: The Life and Legend of an American Pioneer* (New York: Henry Holt, 1992), 272–73.

4. In 1748 George Washington was hired by the associates in the Ohio Company of Virginia for the purpose of surveying western lands on their behalf. During his expedition, he located tracts on the Youghiogheny River, in western Pennsylvania, that he later added to his personal holdings. At the end of the Seven Years' War, he was able to secure about 30,000 acres on the Kanawha, Little Miami, and Ohio Rivers, mainly by trafficking in military warrants ("Authorization by [Lord] George W. Fairfax to George Washington to survey four hundred acres of vacant land in Frederick County, Virginia," October 25, 1750; "Descriptive note by George Washington of four tracts of land belonging to himself on the Great Kanawha," George Washington, Miscellaneous Manuscripts, New York Historical Society, New York [hereafter NYHS]; Charles H. Ambler, *Washington and the West* [Chapel Hill: University of North Carolina Press, 1936], 3–14; Archer B. Hulbert, *George Washington and the West* [New York: Century, 1911], 45; Kenneth P. Bailey, *The Ohio Company of Virginia and the Westward Movement, 1748–1792* [Glendale, CA: Arthur H. Clark, 1939], 19–20, 36–70, 164, 264; Bernard Knollenberg, *George Washington. The Virginia Period, 1732–1775* [Durham, NC: Duke University Press, 1964], 93).

5. Daniel Boone to James Breckinridge, March 9, 1781,William Breckinridge to Daniel Boone, January 12, 1786, James Breckinridge Papers, Manuscript Division, University of Virginia, Charlottesville (hereafter UVAC-MD); Lowell H. Harrison, "John Breckinridge of Kentucky: Planter, Speculator, and Businessman," *Filson Club History Quarterly* 34 (1960): 205–25; James A. Ramage, "The Green River Pioneers: Squatters, Soldiers, and Speculators," *Register of the Kentucky Historical Society* 75 (1977): 179–80; Faragher, *Daniel Boone,* 241–45.

6. The Transylvania Land Company was formed in 1775 by nine North Carolinians, among whom were Richard Henderson, John Williams, and Thomas and Nathaniel Hart. The same year, they negotiated a treaty with the Cherokees at Sycamore Shoals by which—they maintained—they acquired from them about 20 million acres, which amounted to most of the organized settlements west of the Appalachians ("Minutes of a Meeting of the Proprietors of Transylvania," September 25, 1775, Vernon E. Howell Collection, Southern Historical Collection, University of North Carolina, Chapel Hill [hereafter SHC-CH]; "To the settlers and inhabitants of that part of Transylvania known by the name of Harrodsburg Greetings: An Address by the Proprietors," December 1, 1775; "Proclamation of the Proprietors of the Transylvania Company," June 26, 1776, John Steele Henderson Papers, SHC-CH).

7. Isaac Shelby and Nathaniel Hart were among the heroes of the Battle of King's Mountain (October 7, 1780), which was decisive in toppling the military fortunes in favor of the American patriots. Susannah Hart was fourteen years younger than her groom, having been born on February 18, 1764 (Faragher, *Daniel Boone,* 216).

8. Both Virginia and North Carolina finally pronounced the Transylvania Company's claims null and void, on grounds of their being a violation of the Royal Proclamation

of 1763 ("Petition of the Proprietors of the Transylvania Company to the General Assembly of North Carolina," May 7, 1782; "An Act passed by the General Assembly of the State of North Carolina," April 18, 1783, Howell Collection, SHC-CH; Peter S. Onuf, *The Origins of the Federal Republic: Jurisdictional Controversies in the United States, 1775–1787* [Philadelphia: University of Pennsylvania Press, 1983], 83–86).

9. Henderson, "Isaac Shelby: Revolutionary Patriot and Border Hero," 134–35; Otis K. Rice, *Frontier Kentucky* (Lexington: University Press of Kentucky, 1975), 118–19.

10. George Washington to Frederick Hill, January 10, 1798, and George Washington to Bushrod Washington, January 19, 1798, in *The Papers of George Washington, Retirement Series,* ed. W. W. Abbott and D. Twohig (Charlottesville: University of Virginia Press, 1998), 2 vols., 2:16, 29–30; John R. Alden, *George Washington: A Biography* (Baton Rouge: Louisiana State University Press, 1984), 94–95, 101–2.

11. Evan Shelby, biographical sketch; Arthur Fox to Isaac Shelby, receipt, 1783; Joseph Barnet to Isaac Shelby, receipt, September 1788, Shelby Family Papers, SHC-CH.

12. "Petition of the Inhabitants of the Western Territories to the General Assembly of North Carolina," 1784; "Petition against the Passage of a Bill repealing an Act commonly called Cession Act," November 25, 1784, North Carolina Governors' and Legislative Papers, North Carolina Department of Archives and History (hereafter NCDAH); Samuel C. Williams, *History of the Lost State of Franklin* (1924; New York: Pioneer, 1933), 38–44.

13. While the radicals' hope to ban slavery from Frankland was rapidly set aside, probably in an effort not to lose consensus in a politically volatile climate, two clauses concerning land ownership were included with the provisional constitution. Article 31 prescribed that the purchase of land and other real estate, as well as other transactions connected with the same, were restricted to permanent residents. Furthermore, to stave off massive speculation, Article 33 pronounced illegal any acquisition of land from the Natives if not made "in the name of the people" and by authority of the General Assembly.

14. "An Act Passed by the General Assembly of the State of Franklin," December 21, 1785, North Carolina Governors' and Legislative Papers, NCDAH; Kevin T. Barksdale, *The Lost State of Franklin: America's First Secession* (Lexington: University Press of Kentucky, 2015), 20.

15. "A Declaration of Rights, also, the Constitution or Form of Government Agreed to, and Resolved upon by the Representatives of the State of Frankland," Philadelphia, 1786; "Remonstrances of the Inhabitants of the Counties of Washington, Sullivan, and Greene to the General Assembly of North Carolina," 1785, North Carolina Governors' and Legislative Papers, NCDAH; William H. Garrett, "The Provisional Constitution of Frankland," *American Historical Magazine* 1 (1896): 48–63.

16. Richard Caswell to Evan Shelby, May 1, 1787, King's Mountain Papers, II, DD, 5, Draper Manuscript Collection, microfilm edition, originals in the University of Wisconsin Library, Madison.

17. Susan P. Grigsby to Sarah G. Humphreys, memoir letter, undated, mid-1880s, folder 187, Grigsby Family Papers, Filson Historical Society (hereafter cited as [GFP-FHS]). Because of his military valor in the Revolutionary War, Isaac Shelby was also known, among whites, as "Old King's Mountain."

18. Isaac Shelby and Susannah Hart had eleven children, three of whom died before their father (Howard H. Galloway, *John Shelby and His Son David Shelby, Pioneers of Tennessee* [Mobile, AL: Printed for the Author by Gill Printing Company, 1864], 57–59; Samuel M. Wilson, *Susan Hart Shelby: A Memoir* [Lexington, KY: printed by the author, 1923], 9; "An Old Kentucky Home," *Ladies' Pictorial Weekly* [Toronto, Canada], 3 [1892], in William J. Campbell Papers, Kentucky Historical Society, Frankfort [hereafter KHS]).

19. Carolyn Murray-Wooley, *Early Stone Houses of Kentucky* (Lexington: University Press of Kentucky, 2008).

20. Henry McMurtrie, *Sketches of Louisville and Its Environs,* sesquicentennial ed. (1819; Louisville, KY: R. G. Clark Press, 1969), 116; "An Old Kentucky Home."

21. Shirley Dunn, *Historic Homes and Old Buildings of Lincoln County,* Kentucky, n.d., n.p., 7–8, FHS; Mary Wingfield Scott, *Old Richmond Neighborhoods* (Richmond, VA: William Byrd Press, 1950), 145. This structure was common in late eighteenth-century Virginia, and Kentuckians apparently borrowed the style from the parent state.

22. John Frederick Dorman, *The Prestons of Smithfield and Greenfield in Virginia* (Louisville, KY: Filson Club Publications, 1982), 2nd ser., no. 3, 256. While the mansion at Traveller's Rest was destroyed by a fire in the early 1950s, the bondspersons' house remained intact.

23. Wilson, *Susan Hart Shelby,* 32.

24. Patricia Watlington, *The Partisan Spirit: Kentucky Politics, 1779–1792* (New York: Atheneum, 1972), 35–44, 66–67; John Mason Brown, *The Political Beginnings of Kentucky* (Louisville, KY: Filson Club Publications, 1889), no. 6, 63–64; Peter S. Onuf, "Liberty, Development, and Union: Visions of the West in the 1780s," *William and Mary Quarterly* 43, no. 2 (April 1986): 179–213 and 207–13 in particular; Thomas Speed, *The Political Club, Danville, 1786–1790,* (Louisville, KY: Filson Club Publications, 1894), no. 9, 107–10, 128–30; George Davidson Todd, "The First Cotton Factory in the West," Todd Family Papers, Filson Historical Society, Louisville, Kentucky (hereafter FHS).

25. Brown, *Political Beginnings,* 107–24; Bennett H. Young, *History and Texts of the Three Constitutions of Kentucky* (Louisville, KY: Courier-Journal Job Print Co., 1890), 35–58, and 27 in particular; Edward Baptist, *The Half Has Never Been Told: Slavery and the Making of American Capitalism* (New York: Basic, 2014), 14–15.

26. Transylvania University had been located in Lincoln County since its founding in 1780. In popular credence, Frankfort prevailed over Danville in the choice of the state capital not so much because of its more central location but thanks to the greater liberality of its elites in meeting the costs involved by the establishment and support of the new government.

27. Sylvia Wrobel and George Grider, *Isaac Shelby: Kentucky's First Governor and Hero of Three Wars* (Danville, KY: Cumberland, 1974), 85, 89; Lowell H. Harrison, *The Antislavery Movement in Kentucky* (Lexington: University Press of Kentucky, 1978), 24.

28. Susan P. Grigsby to Sarah Gibson Humphreys, undated, GFP-FHS; Galloway, *The Shelby Family,* 57–59.

29. Kent T. Dollar, Larry H. Whiteaker, W. Calvin Dickinson, eds., *Sister States, Enemy States: The Civil War in Kentucky and Tennessee* (Lexington: University Press of Kentucky, 2009), 11; Thomas C. Mackay, "Not a Pariah, but a Keystone," ibid., 27.

30. Young, *History and Texts of the Three Constitutions of Kentucky,* 27; Joan Wells Coward, *Kentucky in the New Republic: The Process of Constitution-Making* (Lexington: University Press of Kentucky, 1979), 26–29, 32, 88–89; Asa Martin, *Anti Slavery Movement in Kentucky prior to 1850* (Louisville, KY: Standard Print Company of Louisville, 1918), 27–28; Donald G. Mathews, *Slavery and Methodism: A Chapter in American Morality, 1780–1845* (Westport, CT: Greenwood, 1978), 18–29; Baptist, *The Half Has Never Been Told,* 16.

31. Benjamin F. Cooling, *Fort Donelson's Legacy: War and Society in Kentucky and Tennessee, 1862–63* (Knoxville: University of Tennessee Press, 1997), 35–36; Dollar, Whiteaker, and Dickinson, eds., *Sister States, Enemy States,* 10–11. According to estimates, by 1860 some 65,000 native Kentuckians lived in Indiana, and another 60,000 in Illinois.

32. William McDowell to Green Clay, April 10, 1793, "Statement of taxable property" of Lexington, FHS. The report conveys Lexington's bustling economic life by the time of statehood.

33. Richard Deering, *Louisville: Her Commercial, Manufacturing and Social Advantages* (Louisville, KY: Hanna & Co. Printers, 1859), 10–11, 14–15.

34. H. Denison to unknown addressee, Natchez, October 30, 1800, Tennessee Historical Society; "Early Manufactures in Tennessee and the Western Country," miscellaneous files, Tennessee State Library and Archives, Nashville (hereafter TSLA). The quotation from Cumming is in Deering, *Louisville,* 15.

35. At this time, Louisville counted twenty-four mercantile houses, besides nearly fifty commercial concerns and some ten factories (Deering, *Louisville,* 18–19).

36. McMurtrie, *A History of Louisville,* 16–19, 53–55, 117–18, 127–34, 175–76; Robert H. Gudmestad, "Steamboats and Southern Economic Development," in *Technology, Innovation, and Southern Industrialization: From the Antebellum Era to the Computer Age,* ed. Susanna Delfino and Michele Gillespie (Columbia: University of Missouri Press, 2008), 18–40; Deering, *Louisville,* 21. The population of Louisville soared from 4,500 to 7,063 inhabitants between 1819 and 1827, and reached the number of 10,341 in 1830. The same year, Lexington counted only 6,026 souls (US Bureau of the Census, *Abstract of the Returns of the Fifth Census, 1830,* Population by State and County: Kentucky [Washington, DC: Printed by Duff Green, 1832], 25–26).

37. Nicholas Gautier to brother Etienne, September 20, 1812, Nicholas Gautier, Letter, FHS.

38. Isabel McLennan McMeekin, *Louisville, the Gateway City* (New York: Julian Messner, 1946), 121; Mathews, *Slavery and Methodism,* 18–29; Martin, *Anti Slavery Movement in Kentucky,* 27–28.

39. Mathew Carey, *Essays on Political Economy* (1822; repr., New York: Augustus M. Kelley, 1968), 110–12, 120, 141, 146, 370; Michael O'Brien, *Conjectures of Order: Intellectual Life and the American South, 1810–1860* (Chapel Hill: University of North Carolina Press, 2004), 2 vols., 2:893, 905, 913–17, 935–37; Susanna Delfino, *La fabbrica dei sogni: Dilemmi economici nel sud degli Stati Uniti tra l'età della rivoluzione e la crisi di metà Ottocento* (Milan, Italy: Selene Edizioni, 2008), 172–73, 179–81.

40. Mathew Carey (under pseudonym "Hamilton"), "Some Notices of Kentucky, Particularly of Its Chief Town, Lexington," broadside, Philadelphia, August 23, 1828, FHS.

41. Ibid.

42. Ibid.

43. Anne Royall, *Sketches of History: Life and Manners in the United States* (New Haven, CT: printed for the author, 1826); McLennan McMeekin, *Louisville,* 79 (also for the quotation from Royall), and 95.

44. US Bureau of the Census, *Abstract of the Fifth Census,* 25–26. In 1850, the population of Louisville reached the remarkable figure of 43,194, while Lexington's counted a mere 8,159 souls (US Bureau of the Census, *The Seventh Census, 1850,* Kentucky: Population, 612–13; George H. Yates, *Two Hundred Years at the Falls of the Ohio: A History of Louisville and Jefferson County* [Louisville, KY: 1987], 46–48).

45. Ira Berlin, *Slaves without Masters* (New York: Pantheon, 1974), 28, 202.

46. Mary Kaltenbrun, "The Negro Colonization Movement in Kentucky" (Ph.D. diss., 1941), in Electronic Theses and Dissertations, Paper 1821, University of Louisville, KY; Eric Burin, *Slavery and the Peculiar Solution: A History of the American Colonization Society* (Gainesville: University Press of Florida, 2005), 24–25.

47. Montgomery Bell was the owner of many furnaces and forges, including the renowned Cumberland Furnace. A member of the American Colonization Society, he died in April 1855 (American Colonization Society, Journal of the Executive Committee, December 30, 1853, June 16, 1854, June 25, 1854, Montgomery Bell Papers, TSLA; US Bureau of the Census, Manuscript Returns, 1850, Slaves Schedules, Tennessee: Davidson County; Robert E. Corlew, *A History of Dickson County, Tennessee* [1956; Charlotte, TN: Dickson County Historical and Genealogical Society, 1980], 86).

48. Lowell H. Harrison and James C. Klotter, *A New History of Kentucky* (Lexington: University Press of Kentucky, 1997), 175; Harrison, *The Antislavery Movement in Kentucky,* 18–25, 27–30–39, 50–56; Berlin, *Slaves without Masters,* 202.

49. Marion B. Lucas, *Blacks in Kentucky* (Frankfort: Kentucky Historical Society, 1992), 2 vols., vol. 1: *From Slavery to Segregation, 1760–1891,* 99; Aaron Astor, *Rebels on the Border: Civil War, Emancipation, and the Reconstruction of Kentucky and Missouri* (Baton Rouge: Louisiana State University Press, 2012), 67; Harrison, *The Antislavery Movement in Kentucky,* 3, 6; Harrison and Klotter, *A New History of*

Kentucky, 168; Cooling, *Fort Donelson's Legacy,* 39. According to Walter Johnson, between the 1820s and the advent of the Civil War probably a million people were sold "down the River" through an internal trade in the enslaved larger than Kentucky's (Johnson, *River of Dark Dreams: Slavery and the Empire in the Cotton Kingdom* [Cambridge, MA: Belknap Press of Harvard University Press, 2013], introduction).

50. Stephanie Cole, "Servants and Slaves in Louisville: Race, Ethnicity and Household Labor in an Antebellum Border City," *Ohio Valley History* 11 (2011): 10–11.

51. Gary R. Matthews, "Beleaguered Loyalties: Kentucky Unionism," in *Sister States, Enemy States,* ed. Kent T. Dollar, Larry H. Whiteaker, and W. Calvin Dickinson, 17. For the cases involving Susan Grigsby, see chap. 4, para. 4, in this volume.

52. The two most-used references for Jefferson's phrase are Thomas Jefferson to John Holmes, April 22, 1820, and Thomas Jefferson to Lydia Huntley Sigournay, July 18, 1824. See Paul Leicester Ford, "Writings of Thomas Jefferson," *Magazine of American History* 21 (1891): 418; and Paul Leicester Ford, ed., *The Writings of Thomas Jefferson,* 10 vols. (New York: Putnam, 1892–99), 10:159.

53. Stephanie Jones-Rogers, *They Were Her Property: White Women as Slave Owners in the American South* (New Haven, CT: Yale University Press, 2019).

54. "The Last Will and Testament of Isaac Shelby," date illegible, Lincoln County Court, Wills and Inventories, Kentucky Department of Libraries and Archives (hereafter KDLA).

55. "An Old Kentucky Home"; Angelina Henry to Virginia Shelby, undated, December of probably the late 1840s, Robert J. Breckinridge Papers, box 246, Virginia Shelby Breckinridge folder, Library of Congress, Manuscript Division, Washington, DC (hereafter LC-MD).

56. Dorman, *The Prestons of Smithfield and Greenfield,* 256.

57. Ibid.; "An Old Kentucky Home," William J. Campbell Papers, Kentucky Historical Society, Frankfort [hereafter WCP-KHS]; Susan P. Grigsby to Sarah G. Humphreys, undated, GFP-FHS.

58. Wilson, *Susan Hart Shelby,* 14; Dorman, *The Prestons of Smithfield and Greenfield,* 256–57.

59. Catherine Clinton, *The Plantation Mistress: Woman's World in the Old South* (New York: Pantheon, 1982), 77–78; Marylynn Salmon, *Women and the Law of Property in Early America* (Chapel Hill: University of North Carolina Press, 1986), 158, 183; Angela Boswell, *Her Act and Deed: Women's Lives in a Rural Southern County, 1837–1873* (College Station, TX: A&M University Press, 2001), 68.

60. Alfred Shelby, testament, 1830, KDLA.

61. "Arcadia," typescript, 8–9, Shelby Family Files, KHS.

62. "The Executors of Alfred Shelby deceased against Virginia Shelby," November 6, 1837, June 20, 1839; "Virginia Shelby against Alfred Shelby Executors," May 13, 1841; "The Executors of Alfred Shelby deceased against Virginia Shelby," State of Kentucky, Court of Appeals, May 13, 1842, Robert J. Breckinridge Papers, box 714, Shelby estate folder, LC-MD.

63. Nathaniel Hart Jr. to daughter Virginia H. Shelby, December 26, 1840, January 4, April 7 and 27, 1841, GFP-FHS.

64. Elizabeth Fox-Genovese, *Within the Plantation Household: Black and White Women of the Old South* (Chapel Hill: University of North Carolina Press, 1988), 206–7; Jones-Rogers, *They Were Her Property.*

65. J. P. Mitchell to Susan P. Grigsby, September 25, 1850, and January 2, 1851, GFP-FHS; "An Old Kentucky Home."

66. Lincoln County, Kentucky, Tax Assessment Books, 1833: 47, 1842:42, KDLA.

67. See Kristen E. Wood, *Masterful Women: Slaveholding Widows from the American Revolution through the Civil War* (Chapel Hill: University of North Carolina Press, 2004).

68. Fayette County, Tax Assessment Book, 1849–1855, 1855: 5, KDLA. Virginia's town lot in Danville would be valued at 3,560 dollars in 1855.

2. Looking "Backward" to the Future

1. Susan (as she was called from the beginning) was named for her maternal grandmother, Susanna Preston.

2. John Irwin, Jr., to family, July 8, 1832, John Irwin, Letters, Filson Historical Society, Louisville, Kentucky (hereafter FHS). Louisville's population rose from 10,336 individuals in 1830 to 19,967 in 1835. In 1832, the city counted thirty-three major establishments, but in 1840 their number had soared to well over sixty, among which twelve large foundries for the construction of steam machinery, one large rolling mill, six tobacco stemmeries, and three shipyards, besides a variety of other manufactories. By 1845, the total population had jumped to 37,218 individuals, the vast majority of whom were whites (32,602), 560 free Blacks, and 4,056 enslaved persons (Richard Deering, *Louisville: Her Commercial, Manufacturing and Social Advantages,* 21–22).

3. Deering, *Louisville,* 21–22. The three banks in question were the Bank of Louisville, the Bank of Kentucky, and the Northern Bank of Kentucky.

4. D. McNaughton to John Brunton, March 24, 1840, McNaughton Letter, FHS; Stoddard J. Johnston, ed., *Memorial History of Louisville from Its First Settlement to the Year 1896* (Chicago: American Biographical Publishing Co., 1898), 2 vols., 1:79–80, 83–88.

5. Susanna Delfino, "Running Southern Manufactories: The Antebellum Origins of Managerial Professions," in *The Southern Middle Class in the Long Nineteenth Century,* ed. Jonathan D. Wells and Jennifer R. Green (Baton Rouge: Louisiana State University Press, 2011), 105–34.

6. William E. Ellis, *A History of Education in Kentucky* (Lexington: University of Kentucky Press, 2011), 5.

7. In 1830, the enslaved population of Lincoln County amounted to 3,638 individuals in a total of 7,364. Woodford County recorded however the heaviest concentration of bondspeople in the state, with 6,640 free people and 5,633 enslaved (US Bureau of the Census, *Abstract of the Returns of the Fifth Census,* Kentucky, 25–26).

8. Susan P. Grigsby to Sarah G. Humphreys, undated, Grigsby Family Papers, Filson Historical Society, Louisville (hereafter, GFP-FHS).

9. Susannah Hart Shelby (1791–1868) was the fifth child of Governor Isaac Shelby. She married, in sequence, James McDowell, James Shannon, John McKinney, and, in 1841, Dr. James Fishback. Several years her senior, he unfortunately died only four years after their wedding (Howard S. Galloway, *The Shelby Family: Ancestry and Descendants of John Shelby and His Son David Shelby, Pioneers of Tennessee* [Mobile, AL: printed for the author by Gill Printing Company, 1964], 58).

10. Gibson's wealth was impressive, the value of his real estate in Louisiana alone being estimated at $300,000 dollars, and his personal property at $234,000, by 1860 (John Frederick Dorman, *The Prestons of Smithfield and Greenfield in Virginia* [Louisville: KY: Filson Club Publications, 1982], 2nd. ser. no. 3, 258; Mary McBride and Ann McLaurin, "Sarah G. Humphreys: Antebellum Belle to Equal Rights Activist, 1830–1870," *Filson Club History Quarterly* 65 [1991]: 231–51, and 232, 246–49 in particular). Although the title of the article may suggest otherwise, by admission of the authors, Sarah Gibson never was a "belle" in the conventional meaning of the word. For more on Tobias Gibson's family background, see Christopher Morris, *The Strange Career of Gideon Gibson: An Early American Tragedy* (Gainesville: University Press of Florida, 2011).

11. McBride and McLaurin, "Sarah G. Humphreys," 231–51.

12. Dorman, *The Prestons,* 247.

13. James C. Klotter, *The Breckinridges of Kentucky* (Lexington: University Press of Kentucky, 2006), 68. By 1860, Robert J. Breckinridge was still the owner of thirty-seven enslaved persons (US Bureau of the Census, *The Eighth Census of the United States,* 1860, Manuscript returns, Population Schedules, Kentucky, Boyle County: 26).

14. Letitia P. Wallace to sister Virginia Shelby, January 13, 1842, GFP-FHS.

15. Susan P. Shelby to her mother, June 29, 1842, GFP-FHS.

16. Having been born on May 17, 1830, Sarah Gibson was only three months younger than Susan. She outlived her cousin by sixteen years, however, dying on May 31, 1907 (Dorman, *The Prestons,* 258; Tobias Gibson to Virginia H. Shelby, July 16, 1842, GFP-FHS).

17. Susan P. Shelby to her mother, September 19 and October 20, 1842, GFP-FHS. A different source suggests instead that at the age of fourteen Susan attended Miss Margaret Mercer's school in Virginia along with her inseparable cousin Sarah (McBride and McLaurin, "Sarah G. Humphreys," 233; Catherine Clinton, *Mrs. Lincoln: A Life* [New York: HarperCollins, 2009], 16).

18. The reform was extremely successful: if only one in ten children had ever attended school before 1840, ten years later the proportion was reversed. Between 1847 and 1853, the total number of enrollments in the elementary school alone jumped from ten to seventy-two thousand (Klotter, *The Breckinridges of Kentucky,* 59; Lowell H. Harrison and James C. Klotter, *A New History of Kentucky* [Lexington: University Press of Kentucky, 1997], 147). At higher levels of education, the reform gave impetus to the expansion of female colleges that had been founded between the

late 1830s and the early 1840s such as the Bethel Female College (Baptist) in Hopkinsville, and the Logan Female College in Russellville (Harrison and Klotter, *A New History of Kentucky,* 151; Ellis, *A History of Education in Kentucky,* 25–39). This vast program reached out to include the most neglected children of all: females and free Blacks. As early as 1843, Vermont-born Delia Anna Webster, who was an abolitionist, founded the Lexington Female Academy, and in 1847 William H. Gibson started a school for Blacks in Louisville.

19. For a critical compendium of American treatises on the subject, see Mary P. Ryan, *The Empire of the Mothers: American Writing about Domesticity, 1830–1860* (New York: Haworth, 1982), 133–47.

20. Frances Respess to daughter Evelina, November 20, 1816, Corlis-Respess Family Papers, FHS; Helen D. Irvin, *Women in Kentucky* (Lexington: University Press of Kentucky, 1979), 32–38.

21. Anya Jabour, *Marriage in the Early Republic: Elizabeth and William Wirt and the Companionate Ideal* (Baltimore: Johns Hopkins University Press, 1998), 73, 116, 124; Anya Jabour, *Scarlett's Sisters: Young Women in the Old South* (Chapel Hill: University of North Carolina Press, 2007), 83.

22. Jabour, *Scarlett's Sisters,* 45, 82, 137.

23. Isaac Shelby to his sister, February 6, and March 7, 1846, GFP-FHS. The 1850 federal census did not even list Danville among Kentucky's urban centers for lack of information returned (US Bureau of the Census, *The Seventh Census of the United States, 1850,* Kentucky: 612–13).

24. Isaac Shelby to his sister, March 7, 1846, GFP-FHS.

25. Klotter, *The Breckinridges of Kentucky,* 42–43, 53–56; Kristen Wood, "'The Strongest Ties That Bind Poor Mortals Together': Slaveholding Widows and Family in the Old Southwest," in *Negotiating Boundaries of Southern Womanhood,* ed. Janet L. Coryell et al. (Colombia: University of Missouri Press, 2000), 135–57.

26. Isaac Shelby to sister, October 28, 1845; Mary Breckinridge to Susan Shelby, October 29, 1845; Virginia Shelby to her daughter, November 2, 1845; Robert J. Breckinridge to Susan Shelby, November 4 and 22, 1845; Virginia Shelby to her daughter, February 10, 1846; Isaac Shelby to sister, March 7, 1846, GFP-FHS.

27. Letitia Wallace to Virginia Shelby, March 6, 1846, box 849, Virginia Shelby folder, Robert J. Breckinridge Papers, Library of Congress, Manuscript Division, Washington, DC (hereafter LC-MD).

28. Virginia Shelby to Robert J. Breckinridge, two letters, undated, unsigned, 1846–47, boxes 846, 849, Virginia Shelby and Virginia S. Breckinridge folders, LC-MD.

29. McBride and McLaurin, "Sarah G. Humphreys," 235; Sarah Gibson to Virginia Breckinridge, October 22, 1851, LC-MD.

30. Robert J. Breckinridge to Tobias Gibson, February 11, 1848, John W. Jones Papers, University of Kentucky Library, Special Collections (hereafter UKL-SC). Virginia Hart Breckinridge was born on February 10, 1848 (Daniel J. Sharfstein, *The Invisible Line: The American Families and the Secret Journey from Black to White* [New York: Penguin, 2011], 124).

31. William Voorhies to Isaac Shelby, Jr., undated (1848), box 849, Isaac Shelby folder, Robert J. Breckinridge Papers, LC-MD.

32. Dorman, *The Prestons,* 257–58.

33. W. C. Anderson to Susan Shelby, July 26, 1849, GFP-FHS.

34. Jabour, *Marriage in the Early Republic,* 9–10; Allison D. Fredette, *Marriage on the Border: Law, Mutuality, and Divorce in the Upper South during the Civil War* (Lexington: University Press of Kentucky, 2020), introduction and chap. 1.

35. Susan P. Shelby to mother, undated, Robert J. Breckinridge Papers, box 849, Virginia Shelby Folder, LC-MD; John Warren Grigsby, biographical notes, GFP-FHS.

36. John Warren Grigsby to Susan P. Shelby, May 19, 1850, GFP-FHS.

37. Letitia H. Vance to cousin Susan, September 18, 1850, GFP-FHS.

38. "Permission granted to Susanna P. Shelby to marry John Warren Grigsby," Marriage Records, Fayette County, Kentucky, November 5, 1850, Kentucky Department of Libraries and Archives (hereafter KDLA); *Louisville Daily Journal,* November 18, 1850. According to the terms of her father's will, Susan could receive her dowry only subject to marrying "with her mother's consent."

39. Mary C. Shelby to Susan P. Shelby, October 26, 1850, John H. Todd to Susan P. Shelby, December 20, 1850, GFP-FHS.

40. Susan Wallace to Susan Grigsby, November 20, 1850, GFP-FHS.

41. John W. Grigsby to Susan P. Shelby, October 30, 1850; Susan Wallace to cousin Susan Grigsby, March 9, 1851, GFP-FHS. Susan Wallace was a daughter of Virginia's sister Letitia.

42. Susan Wallace to cousin Susan Grigsby, March 9, 1851, GFP-FHS.

43. Susan Grigsby to mother, two letters, ca. 1853–54, undated correspondence, folders 97 and 100, GFP-FHS.

44. Isaac Shelby to sister, March 7, 1846, GFP-FHS.

45. Susan P. Grigsby to mother, undated, folder 94, undated correspondence, GFP-FHS.

46. On this habit, see also Wood, "The Strongest Ties That Bind Poor Mortals Together," 138–39. The recurrence of this and other themes like loneliness, reliance on the mother, and a physically exacting existence in the letters of plantation mistresses was first highlighted by Catherine Clinton in *The Plantation Mistress.*

47. Susan Grigsby to mother, ca. 1855–56, folder 99, undated correspondence, GFP-FHS.

48. Susan Grigsby to mother, three letters, ca. 1855–56, undated correspondence, folders 97, 103, GFP-FHS. Erysipelas was a skin infection caused by some sort of bacterium that was very difficult to completely defeat.

49. Susan Grigsby to mother, undated correspondence, several letters covering the time period 1853–56 in folders 94–99, GFP-FHS.

50. Judith Walzer Leavitt, *Brought to Bed: Childbearing in America, 1750–1950* (New York: Oxford University Press, 1986), 79; Richard W. and Dorothy Wertz, *Living-In: A History of Childbirth in America* (New York: Free Press, 1977), 108.

According to the US Census mortality statistics, between 17 and 20 percent of infants died under the age of one, and many more deceased within the fifth year of life. An appalling 38 to 43 percent passed away during the 1850s, either from cholera, dysentery, scarlet fever, pneumonia, whooping cough, convulsions, or a variety of other causes.

51. Leigh Fought, *Southern Womanhood and Slavery: A Biography of Louisa S. McCord, 1810–1879* (Columbia: University of Missouri Press, 2003), 1–5, 67, 70; Michael O'Brien, *Conjectures of Order,* 2 vols. (Chapel Hill: University of North Carolina Press, 2004), 2:716–22, 905, 932; McBride and McLaurin, "Sarah G. Humphreys," 239–42; Sharfstein, *The Invisible Line,* 124.

52. Susan to mother, undated correspondence, ca. 1853–54, folder 94, GFP-FHS.

53. Susan to mother, ca. 1854–55, folder 95, GFP-FHS.

54. Susan to mother, two letters, ca. 1855–56, folder 97, GFP-FHS.

55. Susan to mother, ca. 1856–1857, folder 98, GFP-FHS.

56. Susan Grigsby to her husband, undated, ca. 1857, GFP-FHS.

57. Susan to mother, undated correspondence, ca. 1853–54, one letter, folder 94, GFP-FHS.

58. Susan to mother, seven letters, ca. 1855–58, folders 95–100, GFP-FHS. Celery was a prestigious food on the tables of northeastern elites even in the late nineteenth century (Margaret Lynch-Brennan, *The Irish Bridget: Irish Immigrant Women in Domestic Service in America, 1840–1930* [Syracuse, NY: Syracuse University Press, 2014], 63).

59. Susan Grigsby to mother, one letter, ca. 1855, folder 100, GFP-FHS.

60. Susan Grigsby to mother, undated correspondence, ca. 1854–57, folders 95, 99, 100, GFP-FHS.

61. Susan Grigsby, four letters, ca. 1855–57, folders 94, 95, 100, GFP-FHS.

62. Susan Grigsby to her mother, three letters, undated correspondence, ca. 1854–57, folders 94, 100, 103, and May 28, 1858, GFP-FHS.

63. Mrs. H. White to Susan Grigsby, 185(?), June 22, 1862, Susan P. Grigsby to Dearest aunt, April 3, 1859, GFP-FHS.

64. Susan Grigsby to her mother, May 28, 1858, GFP-FHS.

65. H. White to Mrs. Susan Grigsby, July 19, 1859; S. H. S. Fishback to Susan Grigsby, August 1, 1859; Campbell & Krauss visit card; K. Long to Susan P. Grigsby, Lexington, September 8, 1861, GFP-FHS.

66. State of Kentucky, Court of Appeals, May 1841, August 1851, Robert J. Breckinridge Papers, LC-MD. According to my calculations, in 1850 Susan enslaved thirty-seven people (State of Kentucky, Tax Assessment Books, Lincoln County, 1853–1857, and 1858–1866, KDLA; John Warren Grigsby, "Instrument in writing," April 10, 1858, Lincoln County Clerk Office, GFP-FHS).

67. On the gulf between aspiration and reality in the lives of young married southern women, see Jabour, *Scarlett's Sisters,* 154–77 and 194–201.

3. The Bittersweet Taste of Progress

1. Georgia stands as a prominent example in this regard. Although a synthesis is still lacking, a sense of the southerners' thrust toward economic emancipation from the Northeast can be gathered from several monographs. See, for example, Tom Downey, *Planting a Capitalist South: Masters, Merchants, and Manufacturers in the Southern Interior, 1790–1860* (Baton Rouge: Louisiana State University Press, 2006); and Michael J. Gagnon, *Transition to an Industrial South: Athens, Georgia, 1830–1870* (Baton Rouge: Louisiana State University Press, 2012).

2. Lowell H. Harrison and James C. Klotter, *A New History of Kentucky* (Lexington: University Press of Kentucky, 1997), 141; US Bureau of the Census, *Compendium of the Tenth Census, 1880* (Washington, DC: Government Printing Office, 1881), 930–31. Whereas in 1840 the state reported a value of only about $6 million invested in manufacturing, in the span of twenty years that figure more than trebled, reaching the remarkable worth of $20,256,000 in 1860, as compared to $26,935,000 for Virginia and $23,239,000 for Maryland. Still in 1860, industrial production amounted to $50,652,000 in Virginia, $41,735,000 in Maryland, and to $37,931,000 in Kentucky (US Bureau of the Census, *Report of the Superintendent of the Census for December 1, 1852* [Washington, DC: Government Printing Office, 1852], 156–58; J. Winston Coleman, *Old Kentucky Furnaces* [Louisville, KY: Filson Club Historical Society, 1957], reprinted in the *Filson Club History Quarterly* 31 [1957]: 1–16; Lewis Collins, *History of Kentucky* [Covington, KY: Collins & Co., 1874], 68–74).

3. Gary R. Matthews, "Beleaguered Loyalties: Kentucky Unionism," in *Sister States, Enemy States: The Civil War in Kentucky and Tennessee,* ed. Kent T. Dollar, Larry H. Whiteaker, and W. Calvin Dickinson (Lexington: University Press of Kentucky, 2009), 21; Robert E. McDowell, *City of Conflict: Louisville in the Civil War* (Louisville, KY: Louisville Roundtable Publishers, 1962), 13; Isabel McLennan McMeekin, *Louisville: The Gateway City* (New York: Julian Messner, 1946), 115–21.

4. US Bureau of the Census, *The Eighth Census of the United States,* 1860, Manufactures, Manuscript Returns, Kentucky: Jefferson County; Richard Deering, *Louisville: Her Commercial, Manufacturing and Social* Advantages (Louisville, KY: Hanna and Co. Printers, 1859), 69–84; Ben Casseday, *The History of Louisville from Its Early Settlement till the Year 1852* (Louisville, KY: Hull and Brother, 1852), 14, 19, 21, 72, 76–80, and appendix, 3–35. Christopher & Stancliff, manufacturer of railroad cars, sash, blinds, doors &c, was described as an "immense factory." In the manufacturing of furniture, although John M. Stokes's establishment was the largest in the 1850s, an older and renowned firm run by the Cawthon family still retained a reputation as one "among the largest factories of its class in the western country." Isaac Cromie's Paper Mill was described as "the largest . . . in the Western country." The manufacturing of agricultural implements included two large factories, employing a total of 235 operatives. The processing of tobacco also constituted an important branch of the Louisville manufacturing sector, with eight factories.

5. Carl E. Kramer, *Capital on the Kentucky: A Two Hundred Year History of Frankfort & Franklin County* (Frankfort: Historic Frankfort Inc., 1986), 91–94, 117–53.

6. Marli F. Weiner, *Mistresses and Slaves: Plantation Women in South Carolina, 1830–1880* (Urbana: University of Illinois Press, 1998), 43; William Elsey Connelly and E. Merton Coulter, *History of Kentucky,* 5 vols. (Chicago: American Historical Society, 1922), 2:743; C. S. Williams, *Williams' Lexington Directory, City Guide, and Business Mirror, 1859–60* (Lexington: Hitchcock & Searles, 1859), 114–24.

7. James L. Huston, "The Pregnant Economies of the Border South, 1840–1860: Virginia, Kentucky, Tennessee and the Possibilities of Slave Labor Expansion," and Frank Towers, "The Southern Path to Modern Cities: Urbanization in the Slave States," 145–65, both in *The Old South's Modern Worlds: Slavery, Region, and the Nation in the Age of Progress,* ed. L. Diane Barnes, Brian Schoen, and Frank Towers (New York: Oxford University Press, 2011), 120–41, and 123–29 in particular; Susanna Delfino, "Running Southern Manufactories: The Antebellum Origins of Managerial Professions," in *The Southern Middle Classes in the Long Nineteenth Century,* ed. Jonathan D. Wells and Jennifer R. Green (Baton Rouge: Louisiana State University Press, 2011), 105–34, and 111–12 in particular; John Majewski, *Modernizing a Slave Economy: The Economic Vision of the Confederate Nation* (Chapel Hill: University of North Carolina Press, 2009), chap. 2.

8. Mina Conrad Hegewald, "Louisville notes," n.d., Filson Historical Society (hereafter FHS); John Jefferson, Diary, entry for Feb. 6, 1857, FHS.

9. US Bureau of the Census, *The Seventh Census of the United States,* 1850 (Washington, DC: Government Printing Office, 1851), 612–13, 623: Collins, *History of Kentucky,* 56; Harrison and Klotter, *A New History of Kentucky,* 141. In 1860, 19,587 males and 1,671 females were reported to work at Kentucky's 3,450 manufacturing establishments.

10. Matthews, "Beleaguered Loyalties," 19.

11. Coleman, *Old Kentucky Furnaces,* 1–16. There is a discrepancy between Coleman's spelling of his name as "John Irvine" and that appearing in the original correspondence kept at the Filson Historical Society, which is "Irwin."

12. John Irwin Jr. to Father and Mother, September 24, 1836, March 6, 1837; John Irwin Jr. to brother Ellis, May 20, 1839, John Irwin Jr., Letters, FHS.

13. John Irwin Jr. to brother Ellis, May 20, 1839, John Irwin Jr., Letters, FHS. John E. Kleber, ed., *The Kentucky Encyclopedia* (Lexington: University Press of Kentucky, 1992), 456; John P, Lesley, *The Iron Manufacturer's Guide to the Furnaces, Forges, and Rolling Mills of the United States* (New York: John Wiley, 1859), 127. The profitability of enslaved labor in manufacturing was argued for by Robert W. Fogel and Stanley L. Engerman in *Time on the Cross: The Economics of American Negro Slavery* (Boston: Little, Brown, 1974), and its extensive use in that branch of industry first documented by Robert S. Starobin, *Industrial Slavery in the Old South* (New York: Oxford University Press, 1975). The crucial role played by enslaved labor in the early industrial development of the United States is well illustrated by John Bezis-Selfa, *Forging America: Ironworkers, Adventurers, and the Industrious Revolution* (Ithaca, NY: Cornell University Press, 2004).

14. Susan (Sue) H. Wallace was a daughter of Virginia Hart's sister Letitia and Arthur Wallace, and was therefore Susan Grigsby's first cousin.

15. Thomas C. Mackay, "Not a Pariah, but a Keystone," in *Sister States, Enemy States: The Civil War in Kentucky and Tennessee,* ed. Kent T. Dollar, Larry H. Whiteaker, and W. Calvin Dickinson (Lexington: University Press of Kentucky, 2009), 27; McDowell, *City of Conflict,* 129.

16. The amazing complexity and fluidity of the "underworld" of manual labor in antebellum southern cities is masterfully described by Seth Rockman in *Scraping By: Wage Labor, Slavery, and Survival in Early Baltimore* (Baltimore: Johns Hopkins University Press, 2009). On the social "invisibility" of wage-earning women in general, see Delfino and Gillespie, eds., *Neither Lady nor Slave: Working Women of the Old South* (Chapel Hill: University of North Carolina Press, 2002); and, for what concerns an untraditional field of female employment like ironmaking, Susanna Delfino, "Invisible Woman," ibid., 285–307.

17. Jeanne Boydston, *Home and Work: Housework, Wages, and the Ideology of Labor in the Early Republic* (New York: Oxford University Press, 1990), 80–89.

18. The Cawthons had three children: Benjamin F. (1826), Kate (1827) and M. Josephine (1831) (US Bureau of the Census, Manuscript Returns, Population Schedules, Kentucky, Jefferson County–Louisville, 1850). The fact that both Margaret and Benjamin Cawthon reported exactly the same property values raises the suspicion that this may have simply been a repetition by the census taker. *Louisville Weekly Courier,* vol. 7, no. 39, September 28, 1850; *Louisville City Directory and Business Mirror for 1858–59* (Louisville: Hurd and Burrows, 1859), 287. For a useful comparison between the American and the British case, see Alison C. Kay, *The Foundations of Female Entrepreneurship: Enterprise, Home, and Household in London, c. 1800–1870* (London: Routledge, 2009), 80, 90–92, 123.

19. Suzanne Lebsock, *The Free Women of Petersburg: Status and Culture in a Southern Town, 1784–1860* (New York: Norton, 1985), 180–91; Faye E. Dudden, *Serving Women: Household Service in Nineteenth-Century America* (Middleton, CT: Wesleyan University Press, 1983), 72–79 and 75 for the quotation.

20. Timothy J. Lockley, *Lines in the Sand: Race and Class in Low Country Georgia, 1750–1860* (Athens: University of Georgia Press, 2001), 30–37, 47.

21. Anna Irwin to Melissa and Martha Ann Irwin, October 23, 1838, John Irwin, Jr., Letters, FHS; George R. Taylor, *The Transportation Revolution, 1815–1860* (New York: Harper and Row, 1951), 289–90.

22. Betty Joe Wallace, *Between the Rivers: A History of the Land between the Lakes* (Clarksville, TN: Austin Peay State University, 1992), 39, 46.

23. B. Small & C. to Richard Waters, July 6, 1845, B. Small, letter, FHS; "Mechanics and Laborers' Wages North and South," *DeBow's Review* 29 (1860): 381. See also Robert A. Margo, *Wages and Labor Markets in the United States, 1821–1860* (Chicago: University of Chicago Press, 2000), 47–51, 156–57.

24. John Murdaugh, "memoir," fragment, 1840; Temple Bodley, "memoir," typescript, 2 vols., 1:5, FHS.

25. John Jefferson, Diary, May 13–15, 1857; Temple Bodley, "memoir," I: 6, FHS.

26. "The Draymen's Parade," *Louisville Weekly Courier,* March 19, 1859, FHS. *Louisville Daily Courier,* August 16, 1853. Frankfort, Kentucky, is mentioned by

George Rogers Taylor as one of the most active urban centers in workers' unionization and protest movements west of the Appalachians (Taylor, *The Transportation Revolution*.

27. *Louisville Weekly Courier,* April 30, 1853.

28. D. McNaughton to John Brunton, March 24, 1840, McNaughton letter, FHS.

29. "The Wages of Females," March 9, 1850, and "The Seamstress' Prayer," May 14, 1853, both in *Louisville Weekly Courier*.

30. *Louisville Weekly Courier,* January 5, 1850, original specimen, FHS.

31. Ibid.; Mary P. Ryan, *Cradle of the Middle Class: The Family in Oneida County, New York, 1790–1865* (Cambridge: Cambridge University Press, 1981); Harland Hagler, "The Ideal Woman in the Antebellum South: Lady or Farmwife," *Journal of Southern History* 46 (1980): 405–18; Stephanie Cole, "Servants and Slaves in Louisville: Race, Ethnicity and Household Labor in an Antebellum Border City," *Ohio Valley History* 11 (2011): 3–25; Stephanie Cole, "A White Woman, of Middle Age Would Be Preferred: Children's Nurses in the Old South," in *Neither Lady nor Slave: Working Women of the Old South,* ed. Susanna Delfino and Michele Gillespie (Chapel Hill: University of North Carolina Press, 2002), 75–101 and 92–93; Jane H. Pease and William H. Pease, *Ladies, Women, and Wenches* (Chapel Hill: University of North Carolina Press, 1990), 48–50.

32. John Zaborney, *Slaves for Hire: Renting Enslaved Laborers in Antebellum Virginia* (Baton Rouge: Louisiana State University Press, 2012), 163–65; Barton, "Good Cooks and Washers: Slave Hiring, Domestic Labor, and the Market in Bourbon County, Kentucky," *Journal of American History* 84 (1997): 448–49, 454–55.

33. Boydston, *Home and Work,* 57–69; Stephanie McCurry, "Producing Dependence: Women, Work, and Yeoman Households in Low-Country South Carolina," in *Neither Lady nor Slave: Working Women of the Old South,* ed. Susanna Delfino and Michele Gillespie, 55–74 and, for a broader view, see Stephanie McCurry, *Masters of Small Words: Yeoman Households, Gender Relations, and the Political Culture of the Antebellum South Carolina Low-Country* (New York: Oxford University Press, 1995).

34. G. P. Lowitt to Susan Grigsby, October 7, 1859, Grigsby Family Papers, Filson Historical Society (hereafter GFP-FHS).

35. Dudden, *Serving Women,* 126–30, 142–43.

36. Susan Grigsby to her mother, undated correspondence, folder 97, probably the summer of 1855, GFP-FHS.

37. Lucinda B. Helm to daughter Lizzie, February 14, 1857, GFP-FHS.

38. Ibid.

39. Susan Grigsby to her mother, undated letters, ca. 1854–55, folder 97, GFP-FHS.

40. Susan Grigsby to her mother, two letters, ca. 1854–55, undated correspondence, folder 97, GFP-FHS.

41. State of Kentucky, Court of Appeals, May 1841, August 1851, Robert Breckinridge Papers, LC-MD; State of Kentucky, Tax Assessment Books, Lincoln

County, 1853–1857, Kentucky Department of Libraries and Archives (hereafter KDLA). In 1841, the bondspersons Judy, Sarah, and William were decreed to Susan as a distribute of her late sister Sarah. Following the death of Isaac, she was allotted Betsey, Anthony, Walzer, Isaac, Shelby, Woodford, Jeney, Nelson, Betty, Bell, Alick, Little George, Dick, and Margaret. Following Alfred's death, Susan inherited Manuel, Henry, John, Charlotte, Charles, Ambrose, Frederick, Ritta, and Sarah. The balance of her bondspeople constituted the direct inheritance from the father (Lincoln County Clerk Office, "Instrument in writing," April 10, 1858, KDLA). In this deed, Grigsby stated that "no portion of [his wife's estate] having been produced or purchased with the private and personal funds of the said J. Warren Grigsby," his wife was the sole owner of "all and singular the personality of every form and description now on the farm of the said Susan P. Grigsby occupied by me . . . with all the rents and profits arising . . . including stock of all kinds."

42. James P. Mitchell to Susan Grigsby, January 2, 1852; "List of slaves belonging to the Grigsbys," undated, probably second half of 1853, Slavery Documents, folder 346, GFP-FHS.

43. James P. Mitchell to Susan Grigsby, January 2, 1852, GFP-FHS.

44. Contract between John W. Grigsby and D. E. Peyton for the hiring of an enslaved woman named Mary Jane, 1853, GFP-FHS.

45. John Warren Grigsby, "Instrument in writing," KDLA; Lincoln County, Tax Assessment Books, 1858–1866, KDLA.

46. Susan Grigsby to her mother, undated, probably 1854–55, folder 96, GFP-FHS.

47. Susan Grigsby to her mother, two undated letters, probably 1854–55, folders 95, 100, GFP-FHS; Thavolia Glymph, *Out of the House of Bondage: The Transformation of the Plantation Household* (Cambridge: Cambridge University Press, 2008), 5, 66.

48. Susan P. Grigsby to her mother, three letters, undated correspondence, probably 1852–54, folder 96, GFP-FHS; Dudden, *Serving Women,* 126–30, 142–43.

49. Susan P. Grigsby to her mother," undated, probably 1855–1856, folders 95 and 99, GFP-FHS.

50. Cole, "Servants and Slaves," 10–11.

51. Susan P. Grigsby to her mother, two undated letters, December 25, 1853 and 1857, folder 94, GFP-FHS.

52. Susan P. Grigsby to her mother, undated, 1858, folder 98; Slavery Documents, folder 346, GFP-FHS.

53. Letitia P. Wallace to Virginia H. Breckinridge, January 23, 1853; Susan P. Grigsby to her mother, undated, spring 1855, folder 100, GFP-FHS.

54. Susan Grigsby's third child, Mary Ashley, was born on February 28, 1855 (Susan P. Grigsby to her mother, undated correspondence, one letter, summer 1855, folder 100, GFP-FHS).

55. Susan P. Grigsby to her mother, one letter, folder 95, GFP-FHS.

56. Susan P. Grigsby to her mother, undated correspondence, several letters, winter and spring 1855–57, folders 96, 100, GFP-FHS.

57. Margaret Quinton to Mrs. Breckinridge, August 21, 1855, GFP-FHS.

58. Mary Voorhies to Susan Grigsby, probably 1856; Susan Grigsby to her mother, two letters, probably 1857–58, undated correspondence, folder 98, GFP-FHS.

59. Susan Grigsby to her mother, two letters, folder 100, GFP-FHS.

60. Susan Grigsby to her mother, one letter, 1857–58, folder 103, GFP-FHS.

61. Susan Grigsby to her mother, undated, 1858, folder 100; and Susan H. S. Fishback to Susan Grigsby, March 7, 1859, GFP-FHS.

4. Bonds of Womanhood

1. See Letitia Wallace to Virginia Shelby, March 6, 1846, GFP-FHS.

2. Virginia and Robert Breckinridge had three children: Virginia Hart (February 1848), Nathaniel Hart (b. July 1849–d. 1852), and John Robert (b. September 1850–d. 1873) (John Frederick Dorman, *The Prestons of Smithfield and Greenfield in Virginia* [Louisville, KY: Filson Club Publications, 1982], 2nd. ser., no. 3, 114).

3. "Cost and Expenses of the house on Broadway, Lexington," Account Books, 1850–55, Robert J. Breckinridge Papers, Library of Congress, Manuscript Division (hereafter LC-MD); Dorman, *The Prestons,* 114.

4. Born in 1821 of Joseph Cabell Breckinridge and Mary Clay Smith, John Cabell Breckinridge had earned the rank of major through participation in the Mexican-American War. After serving as a Democratic representative first in the Kentucky General Assembly and then in the US Congress, in 1854 he had momentarily abandoned politics and returned to Lexington to practice law. Yet this did not mean the end of his political career for, in November 1856, he became President Buchanan's vice president, and in 1860 was one of Abraham Lincoln's competitors in the presidential race.

5. John Warren Grigsby to Rev. Dr. Breckinridge, September 22, 1854, and Robert J. Breckinridge, "Memorandum of an interview with Col. Grigsby on behalf of Mrs. Breckinridge, held in Lexington on the 20th of September, 1856," September 24, 1856, legal separation folder, Robert J. Breckinridge Papers, LC-MD.

6. Lincoln County, Kentucky, Tax Assessment Books, Virginia Shelby, 1842: 42; Fayette County, Kentucky, Tax Assessment Books, 1849:4, Robert J. Breckinridge, Kentucky Department of Libraries and Archives (hereafter KDLA); Taxable property of Robert J. Breckinridge, March 16, 1849, Robert J. Breckinridge Papers, LC-MD.

7. Breckinridge, "Memorandum," legal separation folder, Robert J. Breckinridge Papers, LC-MD.

8. Breckinridge "Memorandum," legal separation folder, Robert J. Breckinridge Papers, LC-MD; Virginia Breckinridge, note, 1856, Virginia Breckinridge folder, Robert J. Breckinridge Papers, LC-MD.

9. Anya Jabour, *Marriage in the Early Republic Marriage in the Early Republic: Elizabeth and William Wirt and the Companionate Ideal* (Baltimore: Johns Hopkins University Press, 1998); Allison Fredette, "'One Pillar of the Social Fabric May Still Stand Firm': Border South Marriages in the Emancipation Era," in *Rethinking*

Emancipation Legacies of Slavery and the Quest for Black Freedom, ed. William A. Link and Jones J. Broomwall (Cambridge: Cambridge University Press, 2016), 93–118, and 96–97, 99, 103 in particular.

10. Although by that time the connection was not known, recent medical research has established that one form of angina may be provoked by prolonged physical or emotional stress affecting the ventricular activity of the heart.

11. Susan Grigsby to Letitia Wallace, April 3, 1859; Letitia Wallace to Susan Grigsby, April 15, 1859; Susan H. S. Fishback to Susan Grigsby, April 16, 1859; Eliza A. H. Sayre to Susan Grigsby, June 3, 1859, Grigsby Family Papers, Filson Historical Society, Louisville, Kentucky (hereafter GFP-FHS).

12. Cousin L. W. B. to Susan, July 19, 1859, S. H. S. Fishback to Susan Grigsby, August 4, 1959, John Grigsby to his wife, August 5 and 24, 1859, GFP-FHS.

13. James C. Riley, *Poverty and Life Expectancy: The Jamaican Paradox* (Cambridge: Cambridge University Press, 2005), 2–4.

Distribution of the population by racial and ethnic groups, 1844–1861

Year	Blacks	Colored	Whites	Total
1844	293,128	68,529	15,776	377,433
13. 1861	346,374	81,065	13,816	441,264

14. In 1860 Jane Drummond was listed as a member of the Grigsbys' household (US Bureau of the Census, *The Eighth Census, 1860,* Manuscript Returns, Population Schedules, Lincoln County, Kentucky: 41).

15. Jane Drummond to Susan Grigsby, October 31, 1859, GFP-FHS.

16. William Hart to Susan Grigsby, June 7, 1860; Jane Drummond to Susan P. Grigsby, July 16, August 9, 1860; S. H. S. Fishback to Susan, December 11, 1860, GFP-FHS.

17. Sue Alexander to Susan Grigsby, August 26, 1860, S. H. S. Fishback to Susan Grigsby, December 11, 1860, GFP-FHS.

18. Ottelia Liljebech to Susan Grigsby, August 17, 1861, GFP-FHS; Kim E. Nielsen, *A History of Disability in the United States: Re-Visioning American History* (Boston: Beacon, 2012), chapter 4.

19. Jane Drummond to Susan Grigsby, January 20, 1862, GFP-FHS.

20. Mrs. H. White to Susan Grigsby, June 22, 1862, GFP-FHS.

21. Catherine Clinton, *The Plantation Mistress: Woman's World in the Old South* (New York: Pantheon, 1982), 199–222; Catherine Clinton and Michele Gillespie, eds., *The Devil's Lane: Sex and Race in the Early South* (New York: Oxford University Press, 1997) is especially incisive in placing this delicate issue in the cultural/psychological perspective of white women as masters ruthlessly cut through race and gender lines to disrupt already delicate equilibriums between mistresses and their bondswomen.

22. Thavolia Glymph, *Out of the House of Bondage: The Transformation of the Plantation Household* (Cambridge: Cambridge University Press, 2008), 16; Stephanie Jones-Rogers, *They Were Her Property: White Women as Slaveowners in the American South* (New Haven, CT: Yale University Press, 2019), introduction and chap. 1.

23. On the American Colonization Society, see the wider discussion in chapter 1. Notable is the above-reported case of Tennessee iron manufacturer Montgomery Bell, the largest enslaver in Dickson County, and one of the most substantial in the state. A member of the ACS, between 1853 and 1854 he was able to forward to Liberia only eighty-eight of his three hundred bondsmen (Journal of the Executive Committee of the American Colonization Society, December 30, 1853, June 16 and 25, 1854, Montgomery Bell Papers, Tennessee State Library and Archives, Nashville [hereafter TSLA]; Robert E. Corlew, "Some Aspects of Slavery in Dickson County," *Tennessee Historical Quarterly* 10 [1951]: 228–35).

24. Mary G. McBride and Ann M. McLaurin, *Randall Lee Gibson of Louisiana: Confederate General and New South Reformer* (Baton Rouge: Louisiana State University Press, 2007), 25 for the quote, and 33.

25. James C. Klotter, *The Breckinridges of Kentucky* (Lexington: University Press of Kentucky), 68–70; Luke E. Harlow, "Religion, Race, and Robert J. Breckinridge: The Ideology of an Antislavery Slaveholder, 1830–1860," *Ohio Valley History* 16, no. 3 (Fall 2006): 1–24.

26. On the immense source of wealth that slavery represented for the South compared with that generated in the free states by commerce and manufacturing, see James L. Huston, *Calculating the Value of the Union: Slavery, Property Rights, and the Economic Origins of the Civil War* (Chapel Hill: University of North Carolina Press, 2003), 24–41.

27. Rogers Clark Ballard Thurston, "Memoir letter," Louisville, KY, June 5, 1899, Ballard Family Papers, Filson Historical Society (hereafter FHS); Brad Asher, *Cecelia and Fanny: The Remarkable Friendship between an Escaped Slave and Her Former Mistress* (Lexington: University Press of Kentucky, 2011), 1–28. Mary Eliza Churchill, Fanny's mother, passed away in February 1842.

28. Asher, *Cecelia and Fanny,* 1–28.

29. Fanny Thurston Ballard to Cecelia R. Holmes, August 2, 1855, Ballard Family Papers, FHS; Asher, *Cecelia and Fanny,* 54–55, 61, 75–79.

30. Asher, *Cecilia and Fanny,* 88–93.

31. Fanny Thurston Ballard to Cecelia R. Holmes, January 25, 1857, Ballard Family Papers, FHS; Asher, *Cecelia and Fanny,* 93–96, 99–100, 122, 127–31, 141, 171–73. The reconstruction of the relationship between Cecelia Holmes Larrison and Frances Thurston Ballard owes much to the work of Brad Asher, to whom I am indebted for wonderfully supplementing and shedding important light on the information I gathered from the perusal of the Ballard Family Papers at the Filson Historical Society. Frances Thurston Ballard died in 1896, and Cecelia Larrison in 1909.

32. On this important point, see Marie S. Molloy, *Single, White Slaveholding Women in the American South* (Columbia: University of South Carolina Press, 2018).

33. Ibid.; Kate M. Ronald to Susan Grigsby, November 29, 1860 and January 5, 1861, GFP-FHS.

34. Sue Alexander to Susan Grigsby, 1859, GFP-FHS. Although this letter does not carry the indication of the month and day in which it was written, its content places it between late spring and early summer of 1859.

35. Sue Alexander to Susan Grigsby, undated letters, 1859, GFP-FHS.

36. Sue Alexander to Susan Grigsby, October 7, 1859, GFP-FHS.

37. Sue Alexander to Susan Grigsby, August 26, December 11, 1860, GFP-FHS.

38. William Lewis Breckinridge to John Warren Grigsby, January 4, 1862, GFP-FHS.

39. A. A. Gordon to Mrs. J. W. Grigsby, May 10, 1861; William Lewis Breckinridge to John Warren Grigsby, January 4, 1862; William B. Mold to Robert. W. Scott, December 8, 1862, William B. Mold to Susan Grigsby, same date, GFP-FHS; "Report," Boyle County, January 17, 1863, GFP-FHS.

40. G. P. Lowitt to Susan Grigsby, October 7, 1859, GFP-FHS.

41. W. W. Wells to Susan P. Grigsby, December 6, 1859, GFP-FHS.

42. Susan P. Grigsby to Virginia H. Breckinridge, undated correspondence, GFP-FHS. Reference, in the same letter, to the birth of Jennie's twins the previous day, suggests this letter was written on March 2, 1853.

43. Susan P. Grigsby to "My dear Mother," three letters, 1853, undated correspondence, folders 94, 98, 99, GFP-FHS.

44. Susan P. Grigsby to "My dear Mother," presumably December 25, 1853, undated correspondence, folder 94, GFP-FHS.

45. Susan P. Grigsby to "my dear mother," December 13 of either 1857 or 1858, undated correspondence, folder 100, GFP-FHS.

46. Catherine Clinton, "'With a Whip in His Hand': Rape, Memory, and African-American Women," in *History and Memory in African-American Culture,* ed. Genevieve Fabre and Robert O'Meally (New York: Oxford University Press, 1994), 206.

47. Nell Irvin Painter, introduction to *The Secret Eye: The Journal of Ella Gertrude Clanton Thomas, 1848–1899,* ed. Virginia Burr (Chapel Hill: University of North Carolina Press, 1990), 55–65.

48. Susan Grigsby to "My dear Mother," two letters, 1852–1853, undated correspondence, folders 102, 103, GFP-FHS. The fortunate indication of the month and day allows us to precisely identify the date of the letter included with folder 103 as April 10, 1853. From another source, we know in fact that Sarah's son, Theodore, was born on April 6, 1853 (List of slaves, Slavery Documents, folder 346, GFP-FHS).

49. Susan Grigsby to "My dear Mother," April 10, 1853, GFP-FHS; Jones-Rogers, *They Were Her Property,* chap. 1.

50. Susan Grigsby to her mother, six letter, undated correspondence, folders 97, 98, 100, 102, GFP-FHS.

51. Slavery Documents, folder 346, GFP-FHS.

52. Susan P. Grigsby to "My dear Mother," early March, 1853, undated correspondence, folder 95, GFP-FHS. Jennie's twins were born on March 1, 1853 (Slavery Documents, folder 346, GFP-FHS).

53. M. J. Ronald to Mrs. Grigsby, May 1861, GFP-FHS.

54. Ibid.

55. "Report," Boyle County, GFP-FHS.

56. William Attwood to Susan Grigsby, February 28, 1863, GFP-FHS.

57. Susan Grigsby to "My dear Mother," ca. 1855, undated correspondence, folder 94, GFP-FHS.

58. Ibid.

59. Susan Grigsby to "My dear Mother," August 1859, undated correspondence, folder 94, GFP-FHS. The month is derived from the content of another letter written by Aunt Fishback in the same days (S. H. S. Fishback to Susan P. Grigsby, August 1859, GFP-FHS).

60. Susan Grigsby to "My dear Mother," August 1859, undated correspondence, folder 94, GFP-FHS.

61. John W. Grigsby, "instrument in writing," KDLA.

62. Nat Gaither to Hon. John Bell, November 4, 1862, Hon. John Bell to Nat Gaither, same date, GFP-FHS. For an introduction to John Bell's professional and business activity, see Joseph H. Parks, *John Bell of Tennessee* (Baton Rouge: Louisiana State University Press, 1950).

5. The World Turned Upside Down

1. Lowell H. Harrison, *The Civil War and Kentucky* (Lexington: University of Kentucky Press, 1975), 9.

2. Following President Lincoln's call for a special session of Congress, on June 20 special congressional elections were held in Kentucky. On August 5, the regular elections for the state legislature then took place. Both elections gave Unionists ample majorities (J. Stoddard Johnston, *Memorial History of Louisville from Its First Settlement to the Year 1896,* 2 vols. [Chicago: American Biographical Publishing Co., 1898], 159–62; James M. McPherson, *Battle Cry of Freedom: The Civil War Era* [New York: Oxford University Press, 1988], 293–95).

3. Susan H. S. Fishback to Susan P. Grigsby, January 10, 1861, Gibson Family Papers in Grigsby Collection, Filson Historical Society (hereafter GFP-FHS).

4. William Preston Hart to Susan Grigsby, May 10, 1861, GPF-FHS.

5. John Frederick Dorman, *The Prestons of Smithfield and Greenfield in Virginia* (Louisville, KY: Filson Club Publications, 1982), 2nd. ser., no. 3, 247.

6. Lorri Glover, *Southern Sons: Becoming Men in the New Nation* (Baltimore: Johns Hopkins University Press, 2007), 4, 172–79; Josie Underwood, *Josie Underwood's Civil War Diary,* ed. Nancy Disher Baird (Lexington: University Press of Kentucky, 2009), entry for February 5, 1861, 60; Daniel W. Crofts, *Reluctant Confederates:*

Political Origins of Upper South's Unionism (Chapel Hill: University of North Carolina Press, 1989), 334–38.

7. Hector Green to son John W. Green, May 12 and August 14, 1861, Green Family Papers, Filson Historical Society, Louisville, Kentucky (hereafter FHS); Underwood, *Josie Underwood's Civil War Diary,* entries for August 1 and November 26, 1861, 88. Underwood's remarks about the prevalence of family attachments in determining parents' sectional siding in contrast with their heartfelt allegiance are also conveyed in an interview released by an inhabitant of Hickman County, Tennessee, to a local newspaper twenty years after the end of the war (see "Hickman Pioneer," Centerville, TN, December 24, 1886, Small Collections, Tennessee State Library and Archives, Nashville [hereafter TSLA]). A. D. Kirwan, ed., *Johnnie Green of the Orphan Brigade: The Journal of a Confederate Soldier* (1956; Lexington: University of Kentucky Press, 2002), vii–xiii, 5–7.

8. John W. Grigsby to wife Susan, Richmond, December 3, 1862, GFP. Beriah Magoffin resigned from the governorship in August 1862 and joined the Confederacy (Biographical notes, Emilie Todd Helm Papers, Kentucky Historical Society, Frankfort [hereafter KHS]). Catherine Clinton, *Mrs. Lincoln: A Life* (New York: HarperCollins, 2009), 223–24; Helen D. Irvin, *Women in Kentucky* (Lexington: University Press of Kentucky, 1979), 62–65.

9. Susan P. Grigsby to her mother, undated (ca. 1859), GFP-FHS; Family Files, Shelby family, Shelby-Magoffin genealogy, Kentucky Historical Society, Frankfort (hereafter KHS). Beriah Magoffin was married to Anna Wilson Shelby, daughter of Isaac Shelby Jr. (one of Governor Shelby's sons) and Maria Warren. State of Kentucky, the Governor's Office, "Certificate of Appointment of John Grigsby as Colonel of the State Militia," September 1859, GFP-FHS; "John Warren Grigsby's motion to search negro cabins," County Clerk Records, Fayette County, April 25, 1861, 336, KDLA.

10. James S. Grigsby to John W. Grigsby, April 14, 1861, GFP-FHS; Crofts, *Reluctant Confederates,* 338–40.

11. John W. Grigsby to wife Susan, August 1, 1862, GFP-FHS.

12. Susan Grigsby to John Grigsby, August 5, 1862, GFP-FHS.

13. John W. Grigsby to Susan Grigsby, August 7, 1862, GFP-FHS.

14. Susan P. Grigsby to her husband, August 16, 1862, GFP-FHS.

15. Ibid.

16. Receipts for horse confiscations, July 19 and August 14, 1862, GFP-FHS.

17. W. H. Perrin et al., *Kentucky: A History of the State,* 5th ed. (Louisville, KY: F. A. Battey & Co., 1887), 779.

18. William Hart to Susan Grigsby, September 14, 1862; S. H. S. Fishback to Susan Grigsby, October 2 and November 4, 1862; Jane Drummond to Susan Grigsby, November 5, 1862; Louisa W. Green to Susan Grigsby, December 20, 1862; William H. White to "Sue," November 30, 1862, GFP-FHS.

19. Jane Drummond to Susan Grigsby, January 20, 1862; "Pass issued to Susan P. Grigsby to travel South," November 12, 1862, by order of Brigadier General William O. Boyle from the Head-Quarters in Louisville, "Permission granted to Susan P. Grigsby to travel South," November 20, 1862, GFP-FHS.

20. S. H. S. Fishback to Susan Grigsby, November 4, 1862, William P. Hart to Susan Grigsby, November 4 1862, Letitia H. Vance to Susan Grigsby, November (?) 1862, GFP-FHS.

21. William Voorhies to Susan Grigsby, November 2, 1862, S. H. S. Fishback to Susan Grigsby, November 2, 1862, GFP-FHS.

22. Mary Duncan to Susan Grigsby, November 1862, date incomplete, folders 173, 276, GFP-FHS.

23. John W. Grigsby to his wife, December 3, 1862, GFP-FHS.

24. J. H. Irvine to Susan P. Grigsby, December 2, 1862, GFP-FHS.

25. J. H. Irvine to Susan P. Grigsby, December 17, 1862, GFP-FHS.

26. G. H. M. Kinney to Susan Grigsby, November 3, 1862, William Campbell to Mrs. Grigsby, November 26, 1862, GFP-FHS. In the absence of more information, we may surmise that "Campbell, Yeates, & Co." was essentially the same firm as "Campbell & Krauss," dealers in carpet, curtains, and drapery, which Susan had patronized since the 1850s (see chap. 2, para. 5).

27. William P. Hart to Susan Grigsby, November 17, and Robert W. Scott to Susan Grigsby, November 21, 1862, GFP-FHS.

28. Mary D. Gibson to Susan Grigsby, January 1863, S. H. S. Fishback to Susan Grigsby, January 3, February 13 and March 12, 1863, Arthur Wallace to Susan Grigsby, February 9, 1863, John W. Grigsby to his wife, February 11, 1863, GFP-FHS.

29. Communication by telegraph from General Burnside to Susan P. Grigsby, April 20, 1863, Major General James Wheeler to William B. Hazen, June 9, 1863, Permission granted to Mrs. Susan Grigsby by Major General Rosecrans, June 19, 1863, Henrietta Rochester to Susan Grigsby, July 23 and 25, August 14, 1863, William H. White to Susan Grigsby, August 9, 1863, GFP-FHS; McPherson, *Battle Cry of Freedom,* 515–18, 763.

30. Mary D. Gibson to Susan Grigsby, January 1863, R. H. Dolbins to Mrs. Grigsby, March 20, 1863, GFP-FHS.

31. Benjamin F. Cooling, *Fort Donelson's Legacy: War and Society in Kentucky and Tennessee, 1862–63* (Knoxville: University of Tennessee Press, 1997), 36–37, 107, 238–39; Marion B. Lucas, "Freedom Is Better than Slavery: Black Families and Soldiers in Civil War Kentucky," in *Sister States, Enemy States: The Civil War in Kentucky and Tennessee,* ed. Kent T. Dollar, Larry H. Whiteaker, and W. Calvin Dickinson (Lexington: University Press of Kentucky, 2009), 191–201; I. Berlin et al., eds., *Free at Last: A Documentary History of Slavery, Freedom, and the Civil War* (New York: New Press, 1992), 386–400. It is worth noting that, after the granting of freedom to them and their families by act of Congress on March 3, 1865, Kentucky Black men joined the Union army in the largest proportion of any enslaving state (almost 60 percent).

32. Robert W. Scott to Susan Grigsby, undated, 1863, folder 182, GFP-FHS.

33. L. H. Irvine to Susan Grigsby, March 16, 1863, GFP-FHS.

34. C. J. H. Carter to Susan Grigsby, August 9, 1863, GFP-FHS.

35. John W. Grigsby to wife Susan, September 17, 1863, January 11, 1864, September 8, 1864, GFP-FHS.

36. William Preston Hart to Susan Grigsby, September 13, Robert W. Scott to "My dear Cousin," September 27 1864, GFP-FHS.

37. John W. Grigsby to wife Susan, November 5, December 15 and 25, 1864, January 1, 22, 29, and February 19, 1865, GFP-FHS; Mark Grimsley, *The Hard Hand of War: Union Military Policy toward Southern Civilians, 1861–1865* (Cambridge: Cambridge University Press, 1995), 171–221; Stephen V. Ash, *When the Yankees Came: Conflict and Chaos in the Occupied South, 1861–1865* (Chapel Hill: University of North Carolina Press, 1995), 38–75; Scott Nelson and Carol Sheriff, *Of People at War: Civilians and Soldiers in America's Civil War* (New York: Oxford University Press, 2007), 260–94.

38. R. H. Dolbins to Mrs. Grigsby, March 20, 1863, and C. J. H. Carter to Susan Grigsby, August 9, 1863, GFP-FHS.

39. Phillis Elkins to Susan P. Grigsby, January 2, 1865, S. W. W. Wilkinson to Mrs. Grigsby, January 4, 1865, GFP-FHS.

40. Mary D. Duncan to Susan Grigsby, January 1863, Gibson Family Papers in Grigsby Collection, GFP-FHS; Jane Drummond to Susan Grigsby, March 1, 1864 and March 14 and 30, 1865, GFP-FHS.

41. Ira Berlin et al., *Slaves No More: Three Essays on Emancipation and the Civil War* (New York: Cambridge University Press, 1992), 71.

42. John W. Grigsby to wife Susan, May 2, 1865, GFP-FHS; Cass K. Shelby, "Shelby Family Cemetery at Traveller's Rest Lincoln County, Kentucky," *Filson Club History Quarterly* 30 (1856): 31–44.

43. John W. Grigsby's biography, typescript, GFP-FHS; Aaron Astor, *Rebels on the Border: Civil War, Emancipation, and the Reconstruction of Kentucky and Missouri* (Baton Rouge: Louisiana State University Press, 2012), 8.

44. John W. Grigsby to wife Susan, October 30 and December 20, 1865, GFP-FHS.

45. John W. Grigsby to "My dear Wife," January 24, 1866, GFP-FHS.

46. Felix Gibson to Susan Grigsby, June 3, 1868, GFP-FHS; US Bureau of the Census, *The Ninth Census, 1870,* manuscript returns, population schedules, Kentucky, Lincoln County, 53.

47. Dorman, *The Prestons,* 254; Susan Grigsby to husband John, June 9 (?), undated correspondence, folder 292, GFP-FHS; D. H. Cowan, Manufacturers and Distillers' Agent, to Mrs. Grigsby, September 20, 1869, J. L. Ward to Mrs. Grigsby, October 8, 1896, Walton & Brother, Importers, to Mrs. Grigsby, December 4, 1869, GFP-FHS.

48. Henry Timberlake Duncan, biographical sketch, Duncan Family Papers, UKL-SC.

49. Obituaries and newspaper clippings, Kentucky Deaf and Mute, Danville, January 20, 1877; John W. Grigsby, biography; Felix G. Fox to Mrs Grigsby, March 3, 1877, Octavia Sutherland to Mrs. Grigsby, March 7, 1877, GFP-FHS.

50. "Will of John Warren Grigsby," March 18, 1857, GFP-FHS.

51. Jane Drummond to Susan Grigsby, June 15, 1866, Ella Scott to "My dear Cousin," December 28, 1875, "Susie" Grigsby to "Ma," undated correspondence,

1880, folder 361, GFP-FHS; US Bureau of the Census, 1880, Manuscript Returns, Population Schedules, Kentucky, Boyle County.

52. William Preston Hart and Susannah Hart Shelby Fishback were, respectively, sixty-one and seventy-six at the time of their deaths in 1868 (Dorman, *The Prestons*, 254; Samuel M. Wilson, *Susan Hart Shelby: A Memoir* [Lexington, KY: by the author, 1923], 33, 38; A. L. Higgins to Susan Grigsby, March 15, 1877, GFP-FHS).

53. J. W. Stevenson to John Cowan, March 26, 1877, "promissory note" by John Warren Grigsby to William P. Hart, January 2, 1862, GFP-FHS.

54. J. W. Stevenson to John Cowan, cit., Samuel. J. Walker to John Grigsby, April 11, June 8, 1861, July 28, 1862, GFP-FHS.

55. Draft of a "Petition in Equity" by John W. Grigsby, undated, early 1870s. The assumption of the favorable conclusion of the suit derives from a communication by Fox and Twyman, attorneys at law in Louisville, on March 11, 1875, GFP-FHS. L. W. Tevis was a close relative, perhaps a younger brother, of Rebecca who, having married William P. Hart in 1865 at the age of twenty-one, was widowed three years later.

56. Boyle County Circuit Court, Rebecca C. Hart vs. James L. Ward, 1877, James L. Ward to Susan Grigsby, April 9 and May 9, 1877, William F. Edgar to Susan Grigsby, April 12, 1877, GFP-FHS.

57. Indenture between Susan P. Grigsby and Leo Hayden, April 6, 1873, F. W. Alcorn to Susan Grigsby, June 22, 1875, GFP-FHS.

58. "Sale of 'Warweick' home of Mrs. Grigsby at Danville," February 26, 1881; "Mortgage foreclosure on Traveller's Rest," 1881, GFP-FHS.

59. Henry Waller, counsellor at law, to Susan P. Grigsby, January 20, 1882; Charlie Griggs to Susan P. Grigsby, January 28, 1882, GFP-FHS.

60. W. Q. Emisson to Mrs. Susan Grigsby, September 22, 1882; Hart Grigsby to "mother," May 15 and 28, October 20, 1882, GFP-FHS.

Coda

1. Ross A. Webb, *Kentucky in the Reconstruction Era* (Lexington: University Press of Kentucky, 1979), 62. On the postbellum southern economy, see Eric Foner, *Reconstruction: America's Unfinished Revolution, 1863–1877* (New York: Harper and Row, 1988), 512–34.

2. Jane Turner Censer, *The Reconstruction of White Southern Womanhood, 1865–1895* (Baton Rouge: Louisiana State University Press, 2003), 153–55; Cindy Sondik Aron, *Ladies and Gentlemen of the Civil Service: Middle-Class Workers in Victorian America* (New York: Oxford University Press, 1987), 3, 6, 40–41.

3. Mary McBride and Ann McLaurin, "Sarah G. Humphreys," *Filson Club History* Quarterly 65 (1991). Sarah Gibson and Joseph Humphreys had married in 1853 and, between 1854 and 1859, had had five children, four girls and finally a boy. Two daughters died in childhood: Isabella Hart (1860) and Louisiana Hart (1867). Daniel J.

Sharfstein, *The Invisible Line: The American Families and the Secret Journey from Black to White* (New York: Penguin, 2011), 124, 135, 46–47, 190. On the freedmen's attitude on work, see Eric Foner, *Reconstruction*, 77–79 and 132–36. For a fundamental work on the Black people's attitudes and feelings in the aftermath of Emancipation, see Leon F. Litwack, *Been in the Storm So Long: The Aftermath of Slavery* (New York: Knopf, 1980).

4. Mary McBride and Ann McLaurin, *Randall Lee Gibson of Louisiana: Confederate General and New South Reformer* (Baton Rouge: Louisiana State University Press, 2007).

5. Ibid.

6. Sarah G. Humphreys to Susan P. Grigsby, January 10, 1882, Gibson Family Papers in Grigsby Collection, GFP-FHS; Webb, *Kentucky in the Reconstruction Era,* 70–71, Sharfstein, *Invisible Line,* 224–25. The Kentucky Equal Rights Association was founded in 1879.

7. Sarah G. Humphreys to Susan P. Grigsby, May 6, 1883, R. Lincoln to Randall L. Gibson, June 9, 1883, Randall L Gibson to Susan P. Grigsby, June 9 and 11, 1883, GFP-FHS.

8. Sarah G. Humphreys to Susan P. Grigsby, May 6 and June 13, 1883; "Anonymous" to Mrs. Grigsby, June 16, 1883, Sarah G. Humphreys to son Jon, May 19, 1885, GFP-FHS.

9. See Anastasia Sims, *The Power of Femininity in the New South: Women's Organizations and Politics in North Carolina, 1880–1930* (Columbia: University of South Carolina Press, 2018), 2.

10. Susan Grigsby, memoir letter to Sarah G. Humphreys, undated, GFP-FHS; Censer, *The Reconstruction of White Southern Womanhood,* 100, 276; LeeAnn Whites, "'Stand by Your Man': The Ladies Memorial Association and the Reconstruction of Southern White Womanhood," in *Women of the American South: A Multicultural Reader,* ed. Christie Anne Farnham (New York: New York University Press, 1997), 133; LeeAnn Whites, "Rebecca Latimer Felton (1835–1930): The Problem of Protection in the New South," in *Georgia Women: Their Lives and Times,* ed. Ann Short Chirhart and Betty Wood (Athens: University of Georgia Press, 2009), 224–44; Nell Irvin Painter, introduction to *The Secret Eye: The Journal of Ella Gertrude Clanton Thomas, 1848–1899,* ed. Virginia Burr (Chapel Hill: University of North Carolina Press, 1990), 12–19. See also Carolyn Newton Curry, *Suffer and Grow Strong: The Life of Ella Gertrude Clanton Thomas, 1834–1907* (Macon, GA: Mercer University Press, 2014). On southern women's reshaping of the ideal of "femininity" in postwar society, see Sims, *The Power of Femininity.*

11. Lyman Draper to Susan Grigsby, May 5, 1868, GFP-FHS. Draper's imposing project never materialized, but he left to the Wisconsin Historical Society an impressive collection of documents, letters, and other records. Organized in fifty volumes, those materials came to constitute the Draper Manuscript Collection, which is, to this day, a fundamental reference for historians of the first trans-Allegheny West. Susan P. Grigsby to Sarah G. Humphreys, undated, GFP-FHS.

12. Susan Grigsby to Sarah G. Humphreys undated, GFP-FHS.

13. Ibid.

14. "Death of Mrs. Susan Grigsby," typescript, biographical notes of the Grigsby family, GFP-FHS.

15. See Karen Cox, *Dixie's Daughters: The United Daughters of the Confederacy and the Preservation of Confederate Culture* (Gainesville: University Press of Florida, 2004); and Drew Gilpin Faust, "Altars of Sacrifice: Confederate Women and the Narratives of War," *Journal of American History* 76, no. 4 (March 1990): 1200–28; Catherine Clinton, *Tara Revisited: Women, War, and the Plantation Legend* (New York: Abbeville, 1995), 184–87.

Bibliography

Primary Sources

Manuscript Collections

Filson Historical Society, Louisville, Kentucky

Ballard Family Papers
Bodley Family Papers
Bodley, Temple, Memoir
Carter, Horace, Letters
Corlis-Respess Family Papers
Gautier, Nicholas, Letter
Gibson Family Papers
Green Family Papers
Grigsby Family Papers
Hegewald, Mina Conrad, Louisville notes
Irwin, John Jr., Letters
Jefferson, John, Diary
M'Cullough, Samuel D., Reminiscences of Lexington
McDowell, William, Letter
McNaughton, D., Letter
Murdaugh, John, Memoir
Shelby, Isaac, Papers
Small, B., Letter
Statement of Taxable Property of Lexington
Todd Family Papers

Kentucky Historical Society, Frankfort

American Colonization Society
Campbell, William J., Papers

Shelby Family Files
Todd Helm, Emilie, Papers

University of Kentucky Library, Special Collections, Lexington

Duncan Family Papers
Jones, John W., Papers

Library of Congress, Manuscripts Division, Washington, DC

Breckinridge, Robert J., Papers

New York Historical Society

Washington, George, Miscellaneous Manuscripts

Southern Historical Collection, Chapel Hill, North Carolina

Henderson, John Steele, Papers
Howell, Vernon E., Collection
Shelby Family Papers

Tennessee State Library and Archives, Nashville

Bell, Montgomery, Papers
Small Collections
Tennessee Historical Society, Miscellaneous Files

University of Virginia Library, Manuscripts Division, Charlottesville

Breckinridge, James, Papers

Unpublished Government Records

Kentucky Department of Libraries and Archives, Frankfort

Circuit Court and Court of Appeals, Records
County Clerk Records, Lincoln and Fayette Counties
Marriage Records, Fayette County
Tax Assessment Books, Lincoln and Fayette Counties
Wills and Inventories, Lincoln County

North Carolina Department of Archives and History, Raleigh

North Carolina Governors' and Legislative Papers

Primary Sources on Microfilm

King's Mountain Papers, Draper Manuscript Collection (originals in the University of Wisconsin Library, Madison)

U.S Census Returns, Kentucky: Lincoln, Boyle, and Jefferson, Counties, Population Schedules, 1860–1880

———, Kentucky: Jefferson County, Manufactures, 1860

———, New Jersey: Trenton, Population schedules, 1850 and 1860

———, Tennessee: Davidson County, Slave schedules, 1850

———, Tennessee: Stewart, Montgomery, and Dickson Counties, Population schedules, 1860

Published Government Records

US Bureau of the Census. *Abstract of the Returns of the Fifth Census, 1830.* Washington, DC: printed by Duff Green, 1832.

———. *Compendium of the Tenth Census, 1880.* Washington, DC: Government Printing Office, 1881.

———. *Report of the Superintendent of the Census for December 1, 1852.* Washington, DC: Government Printing Office, 1852.

———. *The Seventh Census of the United States, 1850.* Washington, DC: Government Printing Office, 1851.

Printed Primary Sources

Abbott, W. W., and D. Twohig, eds. *The Papers of George Washington. Retirement Series.* 2 vols. Charlottesville: University of Virginia Press, 1998.

Carey, Mathew. *Essays on Political Economy.* 1822. Reprint, New York: Augustus M. Kelley, 1968.

——— [Hamilton, pseud.]. *Some Notices of Kentucky, Particularly of Its Chief Town, Lexington.* Broadside. Philadelphia, August 23, 1828.

Casseday, Ben. *The History of Louisville from Its Early Settlement till the Year 1852.* Louisville, KY: Hull and Brother, 1852.

Collins, Lewis. *History of Kentucky.* Covington, KY: Collins and Co., 1874.

"A Declaration of Rights, also, the Constitution or Form of Government Agreed to, and Resolved upon by the Representatives of the State of Frankland." Philadelphia, 1786.

Deering, Richard. *Louisville: Her Commercial, Manufacturing and Social Advantages.* Louisville, KY: Hanna and Co. Printers, 1859.

Ford, Paul Leicester, ed. *The Writings of Thomas Jefferson.* 10 vols. New York: Putnam, 1892–99.

Lesley, J. P. *The Iron Manufacturer's Guide to the Furnaces, Forges, and Rolling Mills of the United States.* New York: John Wiley, 1859.

Louisville City Directory and Business Mirror for 1858–59. Louisville, KY: Hurd and Burrows, 1859.

The Louisville Directory and Annual Business Advertiser for 1855–56. Louisville, KY: W. Lee White and Co., 1856.

McMurtrie, Henry. *Sketches of Louisville and Its Environs.* 1819. Sesquicentennial ed. Louisville, KY: G. R. Clark, 1969.

Perrin, W. H., et al. *Kentucky: A History of the State.* 5th ed. Louisville, KY: F. A. Battey and Co., 1887.

Royall, Anne. *Sketches of History: Life and Manners in the United States.* New Haven, CT: printed for the author, 1826.

Williams, C. S. *Williams' Lexington Directory, City Guide, and Business Mirror, 1859–60.* Lexington, KY: Hitchcock and Searles, 1859.

Young, Bennett H. *History and Texts of the Three Constitutions of Kentucky.* Louisville, KY: Courier-Journal Job Print Co., 1890.

Newspapers and Periodicals

Hickman Pioneer (Centerville, Tennessee), 1886
Ladies' Pictorial Weekly (Toronto), 1891
Louisville Daily Journal, 1850
Louisville Weekly Courier, 1850–59
DeBow's Review, 1860

Historical Literature

Ambler, Charles H. *Washington and the West.* Chapel Hill: University of North Carolina Press, 1936.

Aron, Cindy Sondik. *Ladies and Gentlemen of the Civil Service: Middle-Class Workers in Victorian America.* New York: Oxford University Press, 1987.

Ash, Stephen V. *When the Yankees Came: Conflict and Chaos in the Occupied South, 1861–1865.* Chapel Hill: University of North Carolina Press, 1995.

Asher, Brad. *Cecelia and Fanny: The Remarkable Friendship between an Escaped Slave and Her Former Mistress.* Lexington: University Press of Kentucky, 2011.

Astor, Aaron. *Rebels on the Border: Civil War, Emancipation, and the Reconstruction of Kentucky and Missouri.* Baton Rouge: Louisiana State University Press, 2012.

Bailey, Kenneth P. *The Ohio Company of Virginia and the Westward Movement, 1748–1792.* Glendale, CA: Arthur H. Clark, 1939.

Baptist, Edward. *The Half Has Never Been Told: Slavery and the Making of American Capitalism.* New York: Basic, 2014.

Barksdale, Kevin T. *The Lost State of Franklin: America's First Secession.* Lexington: University Press of Kentucky, 2015.

Barnes, L. Diane, Brian Schoen, and Frank Towers, eds. *The Old South's Modern Worlds: Slavery, Region, and Nation in the Age of Progress.* New York: Oxford University Press, 2011.

Barton, Keith C. "'Good Cooks and Washers': Slave Hiring, Domestic Labor, and the Market in Bourbon County, Kentucky." *Journal of American History* 84, no. 2 (September 1997).

Beatty, Bess. *Alamance: The Holt Family and Industrialization in a North Carolina County, 1837–1900.* Baton Rouge: Louisiana State University Press, 1999.

Beckert, Sven, and Seth Rockman, eds. *Slavery's Capitalism: A New History of American Economic Development.* Philadelphia: University of Pennsylvania Press, 2016.

Berlin, Ira. *Slaves No More, Three Essays on Emancipation and the Civil War.* New York: Cambridge University Press, 1992.

———. *Slaves without Masters: The Free Negro in the Antebellum South.* New York: New Press, 1974.

Berlin, Ira, Barbara J. Fields, Steven F. Miller, and Joseph Reidy, eds. *Free at Last: A Documentary History of Slavery, Freedom, and the Civil War.* New York: New Press, 1992.

Bezis-Selfa, John. *Forging America: Ironworkers, Adventurers, and the Industrious Revolution.* Ithaca, NY: Cornell University Press, 2004.

Bingham, Emily, and Penny Richards. "The Female Academy and Beyond: Three Mordecai Sisters at Work in the Old South." In *Neither Lady nor Slave: Working Women of the Old South,* edited by Susanna Delfino and Michele Gillespie. Chapel Hill: University of North Carolina Press, 2002.

Boswell, Angela. "Married Women Property Rights and the Challenge to the Patriarchal Order: Colorado County, Texas." In *Negotiating Boundaries of Southern Womanhood: Dealing with the Powers That Be,* edited by Janey L. Coryell, Thomas H. Appleton, Anastasia Sims, and Sandra Gioia Treadway. Columbia: University of Missouri Press, 2000.

———. *Her Act and Deed: Women's Lives in a Rural Southern County, 1837–1873.* College Station, TX: A & M University Press, 2001.

Boydston, Jeanne. *Home and Work: Housework, Wages, and the Ideology of Labor in the Early Republic.* New York: Oxford University Press, 1990.

Brown, John Mason. *The Political Beginnings of Kentucky.* Louisville, KY: Filson Club Publications, no. 6, 1889.

Burin, Eric. *Slavery and the Peculiar Solution: A History of the American Colonization Society.* Gainesville: University Press of Florida, 2005.

Campbell, Randolph B. "Slave Hiring in Texas." *American Historical Review* 93, no. 1 (February 1988).

Carter, Christine J. "Indispensable Spinsters: Maiden Aunts in the Elite Families of Savannah and Charleston." In *Negotiating Boundaries of Southern Womanhood: Dealing with the Powers That Be,* edited by Janet L. Coryell., Thomas H. Appleton, Anastasia Sims, and Sandra Gioia Treadway. Columbia: University of Missouri Press, 2000.

———. *Southern Single-Blessedness: Unmarried Women in the Urban South, 1800–1865.* Urbana: University of Illinois Press, 2006.

Censer, Jane Turner. *The Reconstruction of White Southern Womanhood, 1865–1895.* Baton Rouge: Louisiana State University Press, 2003.

Clinton, Catherine. *Mrs. Lincoln: A Life*. New York: HarperCollins, 2009.

———. *The Plantation Mistress: Woman's World in the Old South.* New York: Pantheon, 1982.

———. *Tara Revisited: Women, War, and the Plantation Legend.* New York: Abbeville, 1995.

———. "'With a Whip in His Hand': Rape, Memory, and African-American Women." In *History and Memory in African-American Culture,* edited by Genevieve Fabre and Robert O'Meally, 205–18. New York: Oxford University Press, 1994.

Clinton, Catherine, and Michele Gillespie, eds. *The Devil's Lane: Sex and Race in the Early South.* New York: Oxford University Press, 1997.

Clinton, Catherine, and Nina Silber, eds. *Battle Scars: Gender and Sexuality in the American Civil War.* New York: Oxford University Press, 2006.

———. *Divided Houses: Gender and the Civil War.* New York: Oxford University Press, 1992.

Cole, Stephanie. "Servants and Slaves in Louisville: Race, Ethnicity and Household Labor in an Antebellum Border City." *Ohio Valley History* 11 (2011).

———. "A White Woman, of Middle Age, Would Be Preferred: Children's Nurses in the Old South." In *Neither Lady nor Slave: Working Women of the Old South,* edited by Susanna Delfino and Michele Gillespie. Chapel Hill: University of North Carolina Press, 2002.

Coleman, J. Winston. *Old Kentucky Furnaces.* Louisville, KY: Filson Club Historical Society, 1957. Reprinted in *Filson Club History Quarterly* 31 (July 1957).

Connelly, William E., and Merton E. Coulter. *History of Kentucky*. 5 vols. Chicago: American Historical Society, 1922.

Cooling, Benjamin F. *Fort Donelson's Legacy: War and Society in Kentucky and Tennessee, 1862–63.* Knoxville: University of Tennessee Press, 1997.

Corlew, Robert E. *A History of Dickson County, Tennessee.* Charlotte, TN: Dickson County Historical and Genealogical Society, 1980.

———. "Some Aspects of Slavery in Dickson County." *Tennessee Historical Quarterly* 10, no. 3 (September 1951).

Coryell, Janet L., Thomas H. Appleton, Anastasia Sims, and Sandra Gioia Treadway, eds. *Negotiating Boundaries of Southern Womanhood: Dealing with the Powers That Be.* Columbia: University of Missouri Press, 2000.

Coward, Joan W. *Kentucky in the New Republic: The Process of Constitution-Making.* Lexington: University Press of Kentucky, 1979.

Cox, Karen. *Dixie's Daughters: The United Daughters of the Confederacy and the Preservation of Confederate Culture.* Gainesville: University Press of Florida, 2004.

Crofts, Daniel W. *Reluctant Confederates: Upper South Unionists in the Secession Crisis.* Chapel Hill: University of North Carolina Press, 1989.

Curry, Caroline N. *Suffer and Grow Strong: The Life of Ella Gertrude Clanton Thomas, 1834–1907.* Macon, GA: Mercer University Press, 2014.

Delfino, Susanna. *Alla periferia di un impero: Le tredici colonie nordamericane nell'economia atlantica.* Genoa, Italy: Name, 2004.

———. "Invisible Woman: Female Labor in the Upper South's Iron and Mining Industries." In *Neither Lady nor Slave: Working Women of the Old South,* edited by Susanna Delfino and Michele Gillespie. Chapel Hill: University of North Carolina Press, 2002.

———. *La fabbrica dei sogni: Dilemmi economici nel Sud degli Stati Uniti tra l'età della rivoluzione e la crisi di metà Ottocento.* Milan, Italy: Selene Edizioni, 2008.

———. "Running Southern Manufactories: The Antebellum Origins of Managerial Professions." In *The Southern Middle Class in the Long Nineteenth Century,* edited by Jonathan D. Wells and Jennifer R. Green. Baton Rouge: Louisiana State University Press, 2011.

Delfino, Susanna, and Michele Gillespie, eds. *Global Perspectives on Industrial Transformation in the American South.* Columbia: University of Missouri Press, 2005.

———. *Neither Lady nor Slave: Working Women of the Old South.* Chapel Hill: University of North Carolina Press, 2002.

———. *Technology, Innovation, and Southern Industrialization: From the Antebellum Era to the Computer Age.* Columbia: University of Missouri Press, 2008.

Dollar, Kent T., Larry H. Whiteaker, and W. Calvin Dickinson, eds. *Sister States, Enemy States: The Civil War in Kentucky and Tennessee.* Lexington: University Press of Kentucky, 2009.

Dorman, John Frederick. *The Prestons of Smithfield and Greenfield in Virginia.* Louisville, KY: Filson Club Publications, 1982, 2nd. ser., no. 3.

Downey, Tom. *Planting a Capitalist South: Masters, Merchants, and Manufacturers in the Southern Interior, 1790–1860.* Baton Rouge: Louisiana State University Press, 2006.

Dublin, Thomas. *Women at Work: The Transformation of Work and Community in Lowell, Massachusetts, 1826–1860.* New York: Columbia University Press, 1979.

Dudden, Faye E. *Serving Women: Household Service in Nineteenth-Century America.* Middleton, CT: Wesleyan University Press, 1983.

Ellis, William E. *A History of Education in Kentucky.* Lexington: University Press of Kentucky, 2011.

Engerman, Stanley L. "France, Britain, and the Economic Growth of Colonial North America." In *The Early Modern Atlantic,* edited by James J. McCusker and Kenneth Morgan. New York: Cambridge University Press, 2000.

Faust, Drew Gilpin. "Altars of Sacrifice: Confederate Women and the Narratives of War." *Journal of American History* 76, no. 4 (March 1990).

———. *Mothers of Invention: Women of the Slaveholding South in the American Civil War.* Chapel Hill: University of North Carolina Press, 1996.

Fogel, Robert, and Stanley Engerman. *Time on the Cross: The Economics of American Negro Slavery.* Boston: Little, Brown, 1974.

Foner, Eric. *Reconstruction: America's Unfinished Revolution, 1863–1877.* New York: Harper and Row, 1988.

Fought, Leigh. *Southern Womanhood and Slavery: A Biography of Louisa S. McCord, 1810–1879.* Columbia: University of Missouri Press, 2003.

Fox-Genovese, Elizabeth. *Within the Plantation Household: Black and White Women of the Old South.* Chapel Hill: University of North Carolina Press, 1988.

Fredette, Allison D. *Family, Law, and Inheritance in America: A Social and Legal History of Nineteenth Century Kentucky*. New York: Cambridge, 2013.

———. "'One Pillar of the Social Fabric May Still Stand Firm': Border South Marriages in the Emancipation Era." In *Rethinking Emancipation Legacies of Slavery and the Quest for Black Freedom,* ed. William A. Link and Jones J. Broomwall. Cambridge: Cambridge University Press, 2016.

Gagnon, Michael J. *Transition to an Industrial South: Athens, Gorgia, 1830–1870.* Baton Rouge: Louisiana State University Press, 2012.

Galloway, Howard S. *The Shelby Family: Ancestry and Descendants of John Shelby and His Son David Shelby, Pioneers of Tennessee.* Mobile, AL: printed for the author by Gill Printing Company, 1964.

Garrett, William H. "The Provisional Constitution of Frankland." *American Historical Magazine* 1 (January 1896).

Gerschenkron, Alexander. *Economic Backwardness in Historical Perspective.* Cambridge, MA: Belknap Press of Harvard University Press, 1962.

Gillespie, Michele. "To Harden a Lady's Hand: Gender Politics, Racial Realities, and Women Millworkers in Antebellum Georgia." In *Neither Lady nor Slave: Working Women of the Old South,* edited by Susanna Delfino and Michelle Gillespie, 261–84. Chapel Hill: University of North Carolina Press, 2002.

Glover, Lorri. *Southern Sons: Becoming Men in the New Nation.* Baltimore: Johns Hopkins University Press, 2007.

Glymph, Thavolia. *Out of the House of Bondage: The Transformation of the Plantation Household.* Cambridge: Cambridge University Press, 2008.

Green, Johnny. *Johnny Green of the Orphan Brigade: The Journal of a Confederate Soldier*. Edited by A. D. Kirwan. 1956. Lexington: University Press of Kentucky, 2002.

Griffin, Richard W. *Newspaper Story of a Town: A History of Danville, Kentucky.* The Danville Advocate-Messenger and the Kentucky Advocate, 1965.

Grimsley, Mark. *The Hard Hand of War: Union Military Policy toward Southern Civilians, 1861–1865.* Cambridge: Cambridge University Press, 1995.

Gudmestad, Robert H. "Steamboats and Southern Economic Development." In *Technology, Innovation, and Southern Industrialization: From the Antebellum Era to the Computer Age.* edited by Susanna Delfino and Michele Gillespie. Columbia: University of Missouri Press, 2008.

Hagler, Harland. "The Ideal Woman in the Antebellum South: Lady or Farmwife." *Journal of Southern History* 46, no. 3 (August 1980).

Harlow, Luke E. "Religion, Race, and Robert J. Breckinridge: The Ideology of an Antislavery Slaveholder, 1830–1860." *Ohio Valley History* 16, no. 3 (Fall 2006).

Harrison, Lowell H. *The Antislavery Movement in Kentucky.* Lexington: University Press of Kentucky, 1978.

———. *The Civil War and Kentucky.* Lexington: University Press of Kentucky, 1975.

———. "John Breckinridge of Kentucky: Planter, Speculator, and Businessman." *Filson Club History Quarterly* 34 (1960).

Harrison, Lowell H., and James C. Klotter. *A New History of Kentucky.* Lexington: University Press of Kentucky, 1997.

Henderson, Archibald. "Isaac Shelby: Revolutionary Patriot and Border Hero." *North Carolina Booklet* 16, no. 3 (January 1917).

Howe, Barbara J. "Patient Laborers: Women at Work in the Formal Economy of West(ern) Virginia." In *Neither Lady nor Slave: Working Women of the Old South,* edited by Susanna Delfino and Michele Gillespie. Chapel Hill: University of North Carolina Press, 2002.

Hulbert, Archer B. *George Washington and the West.* New York: Century, 1911.

Huston, James L. *Calculating the Value of the Union: Slavery, Property Rights, and the Economic Origins of the Civil War.* Chapel Hill: University of North Carolina Press, 2003.

———. "The Pregnant Economies of the Border States, 1840–1860: Virginia, Kentucky, Tennessee, and the Possibilities of Slave-Labor Expansion." in *The Old South's Modern Worlds: Slavery, Region, and Nation in the Age of Progress,* edited by L. Diane Barnes, Brian Schoen, and Frank Towers. New York: Oxford University Press, 2011.

Inikori, Joseph E. "Slavery and the Development of Industrial Capitalism in England." In *British Capitalism and Caribbean Slavery: The Legacy of Eric Williams,* edited by B. L. Solow and S. L. Engerman. Cambridge: Cambridge University Press, 1987.

Irvin, Helen D. *Women in Kentucky.* Lexington: University Press of Kentucky, 1979.

Jabour, Anya. *Marriage in the Early Republic: Elizabeth and William Wirt and the Companionate Ideal.* Baltimore: Johns Hopkins University Press, 1998.

———. *Scarlett's Sisters: Young Women in the Old South.* Chapel Hill: University of North Carolina Press, 2007.

Johnson, Walter. *River of Dark Dreams: Slavery and the Empire in the Cotton Kingdom.* Cambridge, MA: Belknap Press of Harvard University Press, 2013.

Jones-Rogers, Stephanie. *They Were Her Property: White Women as Slaveowners in the American South.* New Haven, CT: Yale University Press, 2019.

Johnston, J. Stoddard, ed. *Memorial History of Louisville from Its First Settlement to the Year 1896.* 2 vols. Chicago: American Biographical Publishing Co., 1898.

Kay, Alison C. *The Foundations of Female Entrepreneurship: Enterprise, Home, and Household in London, c. 1800–1870.* London: Routledge, 2009.

Kleber, John E., ed. *The Kentucky Encyclopedia.* Lexington: University Press of Kentucky, 1992.

Klotter, James C. *The Breckinridges of Kentucky.* Lexington: University Press of Kentucky, 2006.

Knollenberg, Bernard. *George Washington. The Virginia Period, 1732–1775.* Durham, NC: Duke University Press, 1964.

Kramer, Carl E. *Capital on the Kentucky: A Two Hundred Year History of Frankfort & Franklin County.* Frankfort: Historic Frankfort Inc., 1986.

Leavitt, Judith W. *Brought to Bed: Childbearing in America, 1750–1950.* New York: Oxford University Press, 1986.

Lebsock, Suzanne. *The Free Women of Petersburg: Status and Culture in a Southern Town, 1784–1860.* New York: Norton, 1985.

Litwack, Leon. *Been in the Storm So Long: The Aftermath of Slavery.* New York: Knopf, 1980.

Lockley, Timothy J. *Lines in the Sand: Race and Class in Low Country Georgia, 1750–1860.* Athens: University of Georgia Press, 2001.

———. "Spheres of Influence: Working White and Black Women in Antebellum Savannah." In *Neither Lady nor Slave: Working Women of the Old South,* edited by Susanna Delfino and Michele Gillespie. Chapel Hill: University of North Carolina Press, 2002.

Lucas, Marion B. *Blacks in Kentucky.* 2 vols. Frankfort: Kentucky Historical Society, 1992.

Lynch-Brennan, Margaret. *The Irish Bridget: Irish Immigrant Women in Domestic Service in America, 1840–1930.* Syracuse, NY: Syracuse University Press, 2014.

Mackay, Thomas C. "Not a Pariah, but a Keystone." In *Sister States, Enemy States: The Civil War in Kentucky and Tennessee,* edited by Kent T. Dollar, Larry H. Whiteaker, and W. Calvin Dickinson. Lexington: University Press of Kentucky, 2009.

Majewski, John. *Modernizing a Slave Economy: The Economic Vision of the Confederate Nation.* Chapel Hill: University of North Carolina Press, 2009.

Margo, Robert A. *Wages and Labor Markets in the United States, 1821–1860.* Chicago: University of Chicago Press, 2000.

Martin, Ann S. *Buying into the World of Goods: Early Consumers in Backcountry Virginia.* Baltimore: Johns Hopkins University Press, 2008.

Martin, Asa. *Anti Slavery Movement in Kentucky prior to 1850.* Louisville, KY: Standard Print Company of Louisville, 1918.

Mathews, Donald G. *Slavery and Methodism: A Chapter in American Morality, 1780–1845.* Westport, CT: Greenwood, 1978.

Matthews, Gary R. "Beleaguered Loyalties: Kentucky Unionism." In *Sister States, Enemy States: The Civil War in Kentucky and Tennessee,* edited by Kent T. Dollar, Larry H. Whiteaker, and W. Calvin Dickinson. Lexington: University Press of Kentucky, 2009.

McBride, Mary, and Ann McLaurin. *Randall Lee Gibson of Louisiana: Confederate General and New South Reformer.* Baton Rouge: Louisiana State University Press, 2007.

———. "Sarah G. Humphreys: Antebellum Belle to Equal Rights Activist, 1830–1870." *Filson Club History Quarterly* 65, no. 2 (April 1991).

McCurry, Stephanie. *Masters of Small Worlds: Yeoman Households, Gender Relations, and the Political Culture of the Antebellum South Carolina Low Country.* New York: Oxford University Press, 1995.

———. "Producing Dependence: Women, Work, and Yeoman Households in Low-Country South Carolina." In *Neither Lady nor Slave: Working Women of the Old*

South, edited by Susanna Delfino and Michele Gillespie. Chapel Hill: University of North Carolina Press, 2002.

McDowell, Robert E. *City of Conflict: Louisville in the Civil War.* Louisville, KY: Louisville Roundtable, 1962.

McMeekin, Isabel McLennan. *Louisville: The Gateway City.* New York: Julian Messner, 1946.

McPherson, James M. *Battle Cry of Freedom: The Civil War Era.* New York: Oxford University Press, 1988.

Molloy, Marie S. *Single, White Slaveholding Women in the American South.* Columbia: University of South Carolina Press, 2018.

Morris, Christopher. *The Strange Career of Gideon Gibson: An Early American Tragedy.* Gainesville: University Press of Florida, 2011.

Murray-Wooley, Carolyn. *Early Stone Houses of Kentucky.* Lexington: University Press of Kentucky, 2008.

Nelson, Scott, and Carol Sheriff. *Of People at War: Civilians and Soldiers in America's Civil War.* New York: Oxford University Press, 2007.

Nielsen, Kim E. *A History of Disability in the United States: Re-Visioning American History.* Boston: Beacon, 2012.

Oakes, James. *The Ruling Race: A History of American Slaveholders.* New York: Vintage, 1983.

O'Brien, Michael. *Conjectures of Order: Intellectual Life and the American South, 1810–1860.* 2 vols. Chapel Hill: University of North Carolina Press, 2004.

Onuf, Peter S. "Liberty, Development, and Union: Visions of the West in the 1780s." *William and Mary Quarterly* 43, no. 2 (April 1986).

———. *The Origins of the Federal Republic: Jurisdictional Controversies in the United States, 1775–1787.* Philadelphia: University of Pennsylvania Press, 1983.

Parks, Joseph H. *John Bell of Tennessee.* Baton Rouge: Louisiana State University Press, 1950.

Pease, Jane H., and William H. Pease. *Ladies, Women, and Wenches.* Chapel Hill: University of North Carolina Press, 1990.

Perkins, Elizabeth A. "The Consumer Frontier: Household Consumption in Early Kentucky." *Journal of American History* 78, no. 2 (September 1991).

Prude, Jonathan. *The Coming of Industrial Order: Town and Factory Life in Rural Massachusetts, 1810–1860.* Cambridge: Cambridge University Press, 1982.

Ramage, James A. "The Green River Pioneers: Squatters, Soldiers, and Speculators." *Register of the Kentucky Historical Society* 75, no. 3 (July 1977).

———. *Rebel Raider: The Life of General John Hunt Morgan.* Lexington: University Press of Kentucky, 1986.

Riley, James C. *Poverty and Life Expectancy: The Jamaican Paradox,* Cambridge: Cambridge University Press, 2005.

Rice, Otis K. *Frontier Kentucky.* Lexington: University Press of Kentucky, 1975.

Rockman, Seth. *Scraping By: Wage Labor, Slavery, and Survival in Early Baltimore.* Baltimore: Johns Hopkins University Press, 2009.

Ryan, Mary P. *Cradle of the Middle Class: The Family in Oneida County, New York, 1790–1865.* Cambridge: Cambridge University Press, 1981.

———. *The Empire of the Mother: American Writing about Domesticity, 1830–1860.* New York: Haworth, 1982.

Salmon, Marylynn. "Women and Property in South Carolina: The Evidence from Marriage Settlements, 1730–1830." *William and Mary Quarterly* 39 (1982).

———. *Women and the Law of Property in Early America.* Chapel Hill: University of North Carolina Press, 1989.

Scott, Mary Wingfield. *Old Richmond Neighborhoods.* Richmond, VA: William Byrd Press, 1950.

Sharfstein, Daniel J. *The Invisible Line: The American Families and the Secret Journey from Black to White.* New York: Penguin, 2011.

Shelby, Cass K. "Shelby Family Cemetery at 'Traveller's Rest' Lincoln County, Kentucky." *Filson Club History Quarterly* 30 (January 1956).

Silber, Nina. *Gender and the Sectional Conflict.* Chapel Hill: University of North Carolina Press, 2008.

Sims, Anastasia. *The Power of Femininity in the New South: Women's Organizations and Politics in North Carolina, 1880–1930.* Columbia: University of South Carolina Press, 1997.

Speed, Thomas. *The Political Club, Danville, 1786–1790.* Louisville, KY: Filson Club Publications, no. 9, 1894.

Starobin, Robert S. *Industrial Slavery in the Old South.* New York: Oxford University Press, 1975.

Streater, Kristen L. "'Not Much a Friend to Traiters No Matter How Beautiful': The Union Military and Confederate Women in Civil War Kentucky." In *Sister States, Enemy States: The Civil War in Kentucky and Tennessee,* edited by Kent T. Dollar, Larry H. Whiteaker, and W. Calvin Dickinson. Lexington: University Press of Kentucky, 2009.

Sutherland, Daniel E. *Americans and Their Servants: Domestic Service in the United States from 1800 to 1920.* Baton Rouge: Louisiana State University Press, 1981.

Taylor, George R. *The Transportation Revolution, 1815–1860.* New York: Harper and Row, 1951.

Thomas, Ella Gertrude Clanton. *The Secret Eye: The Journal of Ella Gertrude Clanton Thomas, 1848–1899.* Edited by Virginia Burr. With an introduction by Nell Irvin Painter. Chapel Hill: University of North Carolina Press, 1990.

Tipps, Dean C. "Modernization Theory and the Comparative Study of National Societies: A Critical Perspective." *Comparative Studies in Society and History* 15, no. 4 (October 1982).

Towers, Frank. "The Southern Path to Modern Cities: Urbanization in the Slave States." In *The Old South's Modern Worlds: Slavery, Region, and Nation in the Age of Progress,* edited by L. Diane Barnes, Brian Schoen, and Frank Towers. New York: Oxford University Press, 2011.

———. *The Urban South and the Coming of the Civil War.* Charlottesville: University of Virginia Press, 2004.

Underwood, Josie. *Josie Underwood's Civil War Diary.* Edited by Nancy Disher Baird. Lexington: University Press of Kentucky, 2009.

Vaughan, William H. *Robert J. Breckinridge as an Educational Administrator.* Nashville, TN: Peabody College for Teachers, 1937.

Wallace, Betty Joe. *Between the Rivers: A History of the Land between the Lakes,* Clarksville, TN: Austin Peay State University, 1992.

Watlington, Patricia. *The Partisan Spirit: Kentucky Politics, 1779–1792.* New York: Atheneum, 1972.

Webb, Ross A. *Kentucky in the Reconstruction Era.* Lexington: University Press of Kentucky, 1979.

Weiner, Marli F. *Mistresses and Slaves: Plantation Women in South Carolina, 1830–1880.* Urbana: University of Illinois Press, 1998.

Wells, Jonathan D. *The Origins of the Southern Middle Class, 1800–1861.* Chapel Hill: University of North Carolina Press, 2004.

Wells, Jonathan D., and Jennifer R. Green, eds. *The Southern Middle Class in the Long Nineteenth Century.* Baton Rouge: Louisiana State University Press, 2011.

Wertz, Richard W. and Dorothy Wertz. *Living-In: A History of Childbirth in America.* New York: Free Press, 1977.

Whites, Lee Ann. *The Civil War as a Crisis in Gender: Augusta, Georgia, 1860–1890.* Athens: University of Georgia Press, 1995.

———. "Rebecca Latimer Felton (1835–1930): The Problem of Protection in the New South." In *Georgia Women: Their Lives and Times,* edited by Ann Short Chirhart and Betty Wood. Athens: University of Georgia Press, 2009.

———. "'Stand by Your Man': The Ladies Memorial Association and the Reconstruction of Southern White Womanhood." In *Women of the American South: A Multicultural Reader,* edited by Christie Anne Farnham. New York: New York University Press, 1987.

Williams, Kenneth H., and James R. Harris. "Kentucky in 1860: A Statistical Overview." *Register of the Kentucky Historical Society* 103, no. 4 (Autumn 2005).

Wilson, Samuel M. *Susan Hart Shelby: A Memoir.* Lexington, KY: by the author, 1923.

Wood, Kristen E. "'The Strongest Ties That Bind Poor Mortals Together': Slaveholding Widows and Family in the Old Southeast." In *Negotiating Boundaries of Southern Womanhood: Dealing with the Powers That Be,* edited by Janet L. Coryell, Thomas H. Appleton, Anastasia Sims, and Sandra Gioia Treadway. Columbia: University of Missouri Press, 2000.

Wrobel, Sylvia, and George Grider. *Isaac Shelby: Kentucky's First Governor and Hero of Three Wars.* Danville, KY: Cumberland, 1974.

Yates, George H. *Two Hundred Years at the Falls of the Ohio: A History of Louisville and Jefferson County.* Louisville, KY: Filson Club, 1987.

Zaborney, John. *Slaves for Hire: Renting Enslaved Laborers in Antebellum Virginia.* Baton Rouge: Louisiana State University Press, 2012.

Unpublished Secondary Sources

Dunn, Shirley. "Historic Homes of Lincoln County." Undated typescript, Filson Historical Society.

Kaltenbrun, Mary. "The Negro Colonization Movement in Kentucky." Ph.D. diss. (1941). In Electronic Theses and Dissertations, Paper 1821, University of Louisville, KY.

Laurence, James R., "Forest History." Undated typescript, Filson Historical Society.

Mather, O. A., "Aetna Furnace." Undated typescript, Filson Historical Society.

Index

ACS. *See* American Colonization Society
Alexander, Richard, 62–63
Alexander, Susan (Sue) Wallace, 46–47, 62, 91, 98, 99
American Colonization Society (ACS), 24–25, 94
Anderson, W. C., 44
antislavery movement, 24–25
Arcadia (estate), 30
Attwood, William, 107

Baird, Absalom, 121
Ballard, Andrew, 96
Ballard, Frances (Fanny) Thurston, 95–96
Barton, Keith, 69
Battle of Buffington Island, 123
Bell, John, 109–10
Bell, Montgomery, 25
Berch, Ella, 118
Birney, James G., 25
Blacks: as enslaved labor (*see* enslaved labor); in postbellum period, 137, 143–44; violence targeting free Blacks, 66–67
Black women: as enslaved domestics (*see* enslaved domestics); interracial sex/rape and, 93–94, 103–7; in postbellum period, 143–44
Bloody Monday, 66
bondspeople. *See* enslaved labor
Boone, Daniel, 13
Boyle, William O., 122
Bradley, R. W., 118
Bragg, Braxton, 123
Breckinridge, John, 20, 41
Breckinridge, John Cabell, 86, 169n4
Breckinridge, John Robert, 87
Breckinridge, Mary, 41
Breckinridge, Robert, Jr.: conflicted antislavery views, 37, 95; marriage to Virginia, 32, 40–42, 43, 85–88; personality of, 41–42; profession of, 38, 41; Union sympathies, 112
Breckinridge, Virginia Hart, 43, 85
Breckinridge, Virginia Hart Shelby: as businesswoman, 30–32; correspondence with Susan, 48–49; death of, 88–89; enslaved domestics and, 73, 77, 101–2; marriage to Alfred and early widowhood, 28–32; marriage to Robert, 32, 40–42, 43, 85–88; sons' deaths, 85; white domestics and, 81
Breckinridge family, 13
Brevard, Keziah, 31
Burnside, Ambrose E, 123
butter-making, 69–70

Cabell, Mary Hopkins, 41
Campbell, William, 122
Carter, C. J. H., 125
Carey, Mathew, 23
Cawthon, Margaret, 64
census records: women's labor participation and, 2, 3, 63, 65
childbearing, 50

Chinese labor, 66
cholera, 49
civil service reform, 136
Civil War period: divided loyalties, 112–15; John Grigsby's departure and military service, 115–20, 123; Susan Grigsby's return to Traveller's Rest, 126–31; impact on women, 7, 114, 117–18; Kentucky's neutrality, 111, 112; leasing of Traveller's Rest, 120–26. *See also* postbellum period
class divisions, 67
Clay, Cassius Marcellus, 61
Clay, Henry, 24
cleanliness, 70, 75–76
Clinton, Catherine, 6
clothing, 54–55, 71–72
Cole, Stephanie, 3–4
colonization project, 24–25, 37, 94
companionate marriage, 45, 56–57, 88
Confederate army: confiscations and, 123–24; Grigsby's service in, 118, 123
confiscations, 123–24
cooking, 70
Cosland, Mary, 91
Cox, Letitia, 12
cult of domesticity, 39, 64
Cumming, F., 21

Danville, 17–18, 35, 48
Danville Female Institute, 38
Danville Political Club, 18
Deering, Richard, 59
Denison, H., 21
divorce, 88
domesticity: cult of, 39, 64
domestic service: Black versus white labor in Grigsby household, 78–83; Susan Grigsby's hiring of help in Civil War period, 127, 129–30; Susan Grigsby's hiring of white domestics, 4–5, 68–69, 72, 78–83, 89–93; Susan Grigsby's hiring out of enslaved domestics, 72–74, 77–78, 97–101; labor relations and, 80–81, 83, 93; political/moral economy of in Grigsby household, 72–78; popularity of white domestics, 3–4, 68–69; religion as hiring criteria, 82, 91
domestic work: in a modernizing enslaving society, 68–72; plantation mistresses and, 69–71. *See also* domestic service
Draper, Lyman, 141
draymen's strike, 67
Drummond, Jane, 89–92, 118–19, 128, 130, 131
Dudden, Faye, 65
Duncan, Henry T., 130
Duncan, Mary. *See* Gibson, Mary Duncan

economic modernization. *See* modernization
education: Susan Grigsby and, 37–40, 42; reform of, 38, 160–61n18; women and, 38–40
emancipation: enslavers' conflicted views on, 94–97; in Kentucky, 124
Emisson, W. Q., 135
enslaved children: death of, 121; hiring out of, 74
enslaved domestics: Black versus white labor in Grigsby household, 78–83; friendship with white women, 95–96; Susan Grigsby's hiring out of, 72–74, 77–78, 97–101; interracial sex/rape involving, 93–94, 103–7; labor market for, 69; political/moral economy in Grigsby household, 72–78; subtle rebellion of, 70, 75, 76
enslaved labor: culture of violence and, 93–94; death of enslaved children, 121; domestic service and (*see* enslaved domestics); emancipation in Kentucky, 124; Grigsbys' gradual loss of, 126–27; Susan Grigsby's responses to plight of, 101–7; hiring out of adult males, 100; housing of, 16–17, 30; importance to labor market, 25–26; interracial sex/rape involving, 93–94, 103–7; postbellum employment and, 137; rejection of colonization, 94; sale of, 26, 107–9; seizure of by Union army, 124; treatment of, 26; use of in iron industry, 62–63
enslavers: compatibility of slavery with modernization and, 1–2, 20–26, 61–63; conflicted antislavery views, 26–27, 36–37, 93–101; conflicted views on

emancipation, 94–97; culture of violence and, 93–94; domestic work in a modernizing enslaving society, 68–72; Kentucky as an enslaving state, 19–22, 151n9; plantation mistresses (*see* plantation mistresses); treatment of enslaved labor, 26
erysipelas, 49
ethnic divisions, 66

farmers: economic investment in slavery, 63
Fayette County, 24
female agency: single women and, 97; in US South, 6–7, 27, 64. *See also* male dominance
financial panic of 1837, 34
Fishback, James, 37
Fishback, Susannah Hart Shelby: death of, 131; Susan Grigsby and, 36, 55, 91, 119, 123; on Kentucky's neutrality, 112; on sale of Grigsbys' enslaved domestic, 108–9
food preservation, 70
Frankfort, 18, 59–60
Frankland (proposed state), 14–15, 154n13
free Blacks: in postbellum period, 137, 143–44; violence targeting, 66–67

Gaither, Nat, 109–10
Galt House, 34
Gautier, Nicholas, 22
Gerschenkron, Alexander, 2
Gibson, Claude, 43
Gibson, Felix, 129
Gibson, Louisiana Hart, 38, 43, 95
Gibson, Mary Duncan, 120, 123
Gibson, McKinley, 43
Gibson, Randall Lee, 136–37, 138, 139
Gibson, Sarah. *See* Humphreys, Sarah Gibson
Gibson, Tobias, 36, 38, 95, 137
Gillespie, Michele, 1
Glymph, Thavolia, 93
government employment: white women and, 136, 139
Green, Hector, 113
Green, Johnnie W., 113
Griggs, Charles, 134
Grigsby, Alfred, 47, 116–17, 118
Grigsby, Hart Preston (Hartie), 48, 116, 118, 134–35
Grigsby, James, 47, 52, 114–15
Grigsby, John Warren: absences of, 51; Breckinridges and, 86; courtship and marriage, 45–47; death of, 130–31; departure and military service during Civil War, 115–20, 123; finances and debts of, 54, 55, 56, 107, 122, 129, 130, 131, 132–34; marital dynamics, 6–7, 56–57; "master's power" and, 103; in postbellum period, 128–30; southern sympathies of, 114–15; Susan's estate ownership and, 56, 73, 74, 109–10; on Susan's hiring of white domestics, 80, 89; Virginia family of, 47, 51–52
Grigsby, Joseph, 45
Grigsby, Letitia Wallace, 91, 118
Grigsby, Lilie Shelby, 91
Grigsby, Louisiana (Lulu), 130
Grigsby, Mary Ashley Shelby, 48, 118
Grigsby, Susanna (Susan) Preston Shelby: antebellum lifestyle and finances, 52–57; attachment to family history, 5–6, 32, 35–37, 47–48, 141; birth of, 28, 33; Black versus white labor and, 78–83; brothers' deaths, 43–44; childhood milieu, 33–37; children born in postbellum period, 130; children's deaths, 110, 118; conflicted antislavery views, 27, 36–37, 77–78, 100–101, 102–3, 143; in context of social and economic changes, 58, 84–85; courtship and marriage, 45–47; culture of violence and, 94; death of, 142; description of Traveller's Rest, 19; determination to travel south during Civil War, 118–20, 125–26; divided loyalties of family during Civil War, 112–15; domestic work and, 70, 71–72; education and family role of, 37–44; estate ownership, 56, 73, 74, 109–10; foreclosure on Traveller's Rest, 134; hiring of domestic help in Civil War period, 127, 129–30; hiring of white domestics, 4–5, 68–69,

72, 78–83, 89–93; hiring out of enslaved domestics, 72–74, 77–78, 97–101; inheritance from father, 30; John's death, 130–31; John's departure and service during Civil War, 115–20, 123; John's finances and debts, 54, 55, 56, 107, 122, 129, 130, 131, 132–34; John's Virginia family and, 47, 51–52; leasing of Traveller's Rest during Civil War, 120–26; marital dynamics, 6–7, 56–57; as middle-class woman in postbellum period, 136–44; mother's death, 89; political/moral economy of domestic service and, 72–78; postbellum financial difficulties, 132–35; pregnancies and illnesses of 1850s, 48–50; responses to slavery limited by male dominance, 103, 107–10; response to interracial sex/rape, 103–7; response to plight of enslaved labor, 101–7; return to Traveller's Rest during Civil War, 126–31; sale of enslaved labor, 107–9; settling at Traveller's Rest, 47–52
Grigsby, Susan Shelby, 130
Grigsby, Susan (Susie) Shelby, 48, 116, 118
Grigsby, Virginia Shelby, 48, 118
Grigsby household: antebellum lifestyle and finances, 52–57; Black versus white labor in, 78–83; children born in postbellum period, 130; death of children, 110, 118; domestic work in, 70, 71–72; Jane Drummond and, 89–92, 118–19, 128, 130, 131; foreclosure on Traveller's Rest, 134; gradual loss of enslaved labor, 126–27; hiring of white domestics, 4–5, 68–69, 72, 78–83, 89–93; hiring out of enslaved adult males, 100; hiring out of enslaved domestics, 72–74, 77–78, 97–101; interracial sex/rape involving enslaved domestics, 103–7; John's departure and service during Civil War, 115–20, 123; John's finances and debts, 54, 55, 56, 107, 122, 129, 130, 131, 132–34; leasing of Traveller's Rest during Civil War, 120–26; political/moral economy of domestic service in, 72–78; postbellum financial difficulties, 132–35; responses to plight of enslaved labor in, 101–7; sale of enslaved labor from, 107–9; settling at Traveller's Rest, 47–52; Susan's return to Traveller's Rest during Civil War, 126–31
Grover & Baker, 60

Hart, Louisiana. *See* Gibson, Louisiana Hart
Hart, Nathaniel, 5, 13
Hart, Nathaniel, Jr., 28
Hart, Rebecca Tevis, 120, 132, 133
Hart, Susannah. *See* Shelby, Susannah Hart
Hart, Virginia. *See* Breckinridge, Virginia Hart Shelby
Hart, William Preston: death of, 131; Susan Grigsby and, 35–36, 119, 125–26; John Grigsby's debts to, 132; neutrality and, 112, 122–23
Helm, Benjamin Hardin, 113
Helm, Lucinda, 71
Henry, Angelina, 28
housing, 16–17, 30
Humphreys, Joseph A., 137
Humphreys, Sarah Gibson, 36, 38, 40, 50, 137–40
Hyden, Leo, 134

immigrants, 60–61, 65–66
industrialization. *See* modernization
interracial sex/rape, 93–94, 103–7
Irish immigrants, 65–66
iron industry: immigrants in, 66; takeoff and expansion of, 34, 59; use of enslaved labor in, 62–63
Irwin, John, Jr., 61–62

Jabour, Anya, 40
Jefferson, John, 61
Jefferson, Thomas, 27
Jefferson County, 24, 59
Jones-Rogers, Stephanie, 9, 94

Kelly, William, 66
Kentucky: as an enslaving state, 19–22, 151n9; during Civil War, 111, 112–15, 123–24; compatibility of slavery with

modernization in, 1–2, 20–26, 61–63; conflicted antislavery views and, 22–27; diverse labor market in, 63–68; early debates on future of, 17–18; early land acquisitions, 13–14; establishment of Traveller's Rest, 15–19; frontier housing, 16; immigrants and, 60–61, 65–66; manufacturing in, 164n2; modernization during 1830s, 34; modernization during 1850s, 59–63; treatment of enslaved labor and, 26
Kentucky Abolition Society, 24

labor activism, 67–68
labor market: domestic service and (*see* domestic service); enslaved domestics and (*see* enslaved domestics); enslaved labor and, 25–26, 62–63; formerly elite women in postbellum period, 136–44; immigrants and, 60–61, 65–66; labor conflicts/activism, 66–68; postbellum employment of Blacks, 137; white domestics and (*see* white domestics); white women's participation in, 2–3, 63–68
land acquisition, 12–15
land surveyors, 12–13
Lebsock, Suzanne, 64–65
legal separation, 85–88
Lexington: availability of luxury goods, 53; construction of Breckinridge home, 85–86; modernization/manufacturing and, 20–21, 23–24, 60
Liljebech, Ottelia, 92
Lincoln, Mary Todd, 38, 114
Louisville: immigrants and, 60–61, 65; labor conflicts and, 66–68; modernization/manufacturing and, 21–22, 24, 34, 59, 156n35; population growth, 159n2; use of stone in, 16
Louisville Courier, 66
Louisville Examiner, 61
Louisville Galt, 66
Louisville Journal, 34
Louisville Weekly Courier, 64, 69
lower-class white women, 2, 64
Lowitt, G. P., 70, 100

Magoffin, Beriah, 114
male dominance: Grigsbys' marital dynamics and, 6–7, 56–57; women's responses to slavery limited by, 95–97, 107–10. *See also* female agency
manual laborers, 61
manufacturing: expansion of, 59–60; white women's participation in, 3. *See also* iron industry
marriage: Breckinridges' legal separation case, 85–88; Grigsbys' marital dynamics, 6–7, 56–57; shifting ideal of, 45, 56–57, 88; women's postponement of, 40, 44
McCord, Louisa S., 50
McMurtrie, Henry, 16, 21
McNaughton, D., 67–68
meat preservation, 70
Mrs. Mentelle's school, 38
middle-class white women: formerly elite women in postbellum period as, 136–44; hiring of enslaved domestics, 69, 99; hiring of white domestics, 4; labor market participation of, 2–3, 65
Milburn, Judy, 91
military warrants, 14
Miller, William and Mordecai, 61
miscegenation. *See* interracial sex/rape
Mitchell, J. P., 73–74
modernization: during 1830s, 34; during 1850s, 59–63; compatibility of slavery with, 1–2, 20–26, 61–63; domestic work in modernizing enslaving society, 68–72; early debates on future of Kentucky and, 17–18; Frankfort and, 59–60; Lexington and, 20–21, 23–24, 60; Louisville and, 21–22, 24, 34, 59; postbellum period and, 136–44; as Susan Grigsby's childhood milieu, 33–37
Mold, William B., 99
Moore, Frances and Emma, 130
Morgan, Catherine Davies, 12
Morgan, John Hunt, 118, 123

National Association of Colored Women, 144
National Woman's Suffrage Association, 141
Native Americans, 15–16

nativism, 66
needle trades. *See* sewing trades
Nelson Furnace, 61–63, 98
neutrality, 111, 112
North Carolina land politics, 14–15

panic of 1837, 34
Picot, Charles, 40
plantation mistresses: culture of violence and, 93–94; domestic work and, 69–71; estate management as widows, 29, 30–32; impact of Civil War on, 7, 114, 117–18; marital stress of, 6; as middle-class women in postbellum period, 136–44; responses to slavery limited by male dominance, 95–97, 107–10
postbellum period: formerly elite women in, 136–44; formerly enslaved labor and, 137, 143–44; John Grigsby and, 128–30; Susan Grigsby's financial difficulties, 132–35
pregnancy: involving Grigsbys' enslaved domestics, 103–7; risks of, 50
Prentice, George D., 34
Preston, Ann Sophonisba (Sophy), 41
Preston, Francis, 41
Preston, Susanna, 28
property rights, 29

rape. *See* interracial sex/rape
Rawling, Kate, 118
religion: as hiring criteria, 82, 91
repatriation. *See* colonization project
Respess, Frances, 39
Robertson, James, 12
Rosecrans, William S., 123
Royall, Anne, 24

Sapling Grove (estate), 12, 14
Scott, Mary Ashley Warren, 45
Scott, Winfield, 45
separate spheres doctrine, 64
Sevier, John, 12
sewing, 54–55, 71–72
sewing machines, 60
sewing trades: diverse workers in, 67–68; white women in, 3
Shelby, Alfred (brother), 28, 30, 43, 85
Shelby, Alfred (father), 27–30
Shelby, Evan, 12
Shelby, Evan (guardian), 46, 56, 109
Shelby, Evan, II, 11–15
Shelby, Isaac (brother): birth of, 28; on Robert Breckinridge, 41–42; death of, 44, 85; inheritance of, 29–30; Susan and, 35, 40
Shelby, Isaac (grandfather): antislavery views, 19–20; birth of, 12; death and will of, 19, 27–28; establishment of Traveller's Rest, 15–19; land acquisitions, 13–14; reputation of, 5–6, 18–19
Shelby, James, 16
Shelby, Mary C., 46
Shelby, Sarah, 16, 30
Shelby, Susannah Hart: death of, 29; marriage/married life, 13, 16, 17, 27; mementoes of, 35; weaving skills of, 28
Shelby, Susanna (Susan) Preston. *See* Grigsby, Susanna (Susan) Preston Shelby
Shelby, Thomas (guardian and trustee), 29, 109
Shelby, Virginia Hart. *See* Breckinridge, Virginia Hart Shelby
Shortwell, Stefah, 98
Sims, Anastasia, 140
single women, 97
slavery: colonization project, 24–25, 37, 94; compatibility with modernization, 1–2, 20–26, 61–63; early debates on future of Kentucky and, 17–18; enslavers' conflicted antislavery views, 22–27, 36–37, 93–101 (*see also* enslavers); Susan Grigsby's conflicted antislavery views, 27, 36–37, 77–78, 100–101, 102–3, 143; Kentucky as an enslaving state, 19–22; Isaac Shelby's antislavery views, 19–20. *See also* enslaved domestics; enslaved labor
Stevenson, J. W., 132–33
Suwanee Furnace and Union Forge, 66

teaching, 3
Tevis, Rebecca. *See* Hart, Rebecca Tevis
Thomas, Ella Gertrude Clanton, 140–41

Thurston, Charles W., 95–96
timber/wood, 121–22
Todd, John H., 46
trade, 21
Transylvania Land Company, 13, 153n6
Traveller's Rest: establishment and heyday of, 15–19; foreclosure, 134; Grigsbys' settling at, 47–52; land claims pertaining to, 13–14; leasing of during Civil War, 120–26; refurbishment of, 53–54; Virginia Shelby's management of, 30–32; Alfred Shelby's will and, 29–30; Susan's description of, 19; Susan's estate ownership, 56, 73, 74, 109–10; Susan's return to during Civil War, 126–31
True American (journal), 61

Underwood, Johanna Louisa (Josie), 112–13
Union army: confiscations and, 118, 121–22, 123–24; seizure of enslaved labor, 124
upper-class white women: hiring of white domestics, 3–4; as middle-class women in postbellum period, 136–44. *See also* plantation mistresses
Upper South: enslavers' conflicted antislavery views, 94–95; popularity of colonization, 25
urbanization, 60
US South: childbearing risks in, 50; compatibility of slavery with modernization and, 1–2; enslavers' conflicted antislavery views, 94–95; female agency and, 6–7, 27, 64; immigrants in labor market, 65; postponement of marriage in, 40, 44; urbanization and, 60; women's property rights in, 29

Vance, Letitia H., 46, 119
Vance, Morgan Brown, 112
violence: interracial sex/rape and culture of, 93–94; labor conflicts and, 66–67
Voorhies, Mary, 119
Voorhies, William, 43, 119

Wallace, Letitia P., 37, 42, 74, 88–89
Wallace, Susan (Sue). *See* Alexander, Susan (Sue) Wallace
Wallace, William, 37
Ward, James L., 133
Washington, George, 13, 14, 153n4
Watlington, Patricia, 17
Wells, W. W., 100
Wheeler, Joseph, 118, 123
white domestics: Black versus white labor in Grigsby household, 78–83; Jane Drummond, 89–92, 118–19, 128, 130, 131; Susan Grigsby's hiring of, 4–5, 68–69, 72, 78–83, 89–93; labor relations and, 80–81, 83, 93; popularity of, 3–4, 68–69; religion as hiring criteria, 82, 91
white women: childbearing and, 50, 163n50; in domestic service (*see* white domestics); education and, 38–40; female agency and, 6–7, 27, 64, 97; friendship with enslaved domestics, 95–96; hiring of white domestics, 3–4, 68–69; impact of Civil War on, 7, 114, 117–18; labor activism and, 67–68; labor market participation, 2–3, 63–68; plantation mistresses (*see* plantation mistresses); in postbellum period, 136–44; postponement of marriage, 40, 44; property rights of, 29; responses to slavery limited by male dominance, 95–97, 107–10
widows: as entrepreneurs, 64; estate management by, 29, 30–32
Wirt, Elizabeth Gamble, 39–40
women. *See* Black women; enslaved domestics; white domestics; white women
wood/timber, 121–22

Zaborney, John, 69